IN THE VALLEY
OF LOST SOULS

DIANA VAN EYK

BALBOA
PRESS

A DIVISION OF HAY HOUSE

Used with permission of the author from the song You Can Change the World written by Joe Mock, performed by Pied Pumkin www.piedpumkin.com

Balboa Press books may be ordered through booksellers or by contacting:

Balboa Press
A Division of Hay House
1663 Liberty Drive
Bloomington, IN 47403
www.balboapress.com
1 (877) 407-4847

Print information available on the last page.

ISBN: 978-1-5043-2751-0 (sc)
ISBN: 978-1-5043-2749-7 (hc)
ISBN: 978-1-5043-2750-3 (e)

Library of Congress Control Number: 2015901654

Balboa Press rev. date: 02/20/2015

ACKNOWLEDGEMENTS

I want to acknowledge Aldo van Eyk, Laurel Mercer, Suzelle Dube, Remi and Jordana Champagne, Rik Logtenburg and Wayne Sheridan for their enthusiastic support of my writing; Nicole Osbun and Andrew Carter and the staff of Balboa Books for their expert guidance; Bill Moore for persuading me to give fiction writing a try; Lonnie Shipe, Jason Yost, and my other IBOToolbox friends for their encouragement; Jess Grippo for her helpful online presence; Joe Percival and Jeannette Graf, and Jean and Derek Randall for our many philosophical discussions and great meals; Stan and Selina Vaneyk, Randy van Eyk and Mike Walmsley for their supportive presence; my parents, Betty and Jacob van Eyk; Michael Linton for the amazing Community Way model of local currency I've attempted to describe in this book, and Paul Hoepfner-Homme for introducing me to SPIN farming via my backyard. I also want to thank Joe Mock for permission to use the words to the song, 'You Can Change the World' written by him and performed by Pied Pumkin.

DEDICATION

Dedicated to Betty van Eyk, with love and gratitude.

CHAPTER 1

Nowhere to Go

Dagmar and Ross stood in the crisp evening air of autumn. Their Green Team meeting had just ended. The Green Team, Silverdale's main environmental group, was going through a reorganization. The group was taking its time, doing the best it could to engage its members in a process that would make it more effective and engaging.

Pipelines and tankers were the grist of the rumour mill at the meetings these days. There was talk of developing pipelines from the Alberta tar sands through their province, British Columbia, with the oil to be shipped on tankers to China.

A barrel of oil from the tar sands produced three times more greenhouse gas emissions than conventional oil. Tailing ponds holding the toxic residue from the tar sands spanned 176 square kilometres and could be seen from space. This operation had destroyed habitat for endangered wildlife and had polluted the drinking water of surrounding communities. In Canada, the tar sands represented the hope of the oil industry and the despair of environmentalists.

Everyone at the meeting hoped the pipelines wouldn't be approved, but with both federal and provincial governments favouring the oil and gas industries, most feared that the pipelines would go through despite the great environmental risks. The pipelines would go through some highly sensitive habitat, and the oil tankers would be travelling along the B.C. coast, through some of the most treacherous waters in the world. The risk of oil spills along the pristine coastline was enormous.

As Dagmar and Ross exhausted this topic of conversation, they realized that neither of them was in a hurry to go anywhere.

"So you don't have anywhere to go home to either, eh?" Ross asked Dagmar.

"No. I don't know what I'm going to do," she answered.

It was the end of the month, and she didn't have money for rent—for the fifth month in a row. In Ross's case, his long-time partner, Debbie, had just changed the locks of their home. Who would have guessed that Dagmar and Ross would find themselves middle-aged and homeless? Neither of them had any experience with this.

They each had a backpack. Dagmar's held her laptop, a few clothes and some personal effects. She had been able to do a bit of planning earlier, and her friend Phoebe was storing some of her things.

Ross had been surprised at the turn of events, so he had only his guitar in its case and his backpack with some music in it, since he'd been to a band practice before the meeting. He'd gone home after the practice to find that his house key no longer worked. Not knowing what else to do, he'd gone to the Green Team meeting as planned.

Dagmar was getting cold. "Would you like to come with me to my friend Phoebe's? I'm sure she'd put us up for the night."

"No, I don't want to impose. You go ahead. I'll be able to stay at a friend's," Ross said. "I had a feeling something like this might happen. I'll be fine."

"Do you want to meet somewhere tomorrow evening? Maybe we can check in with each other," she said. "Sometimes it's nice to have someone to talk to, to know you're not alone in the world."

"Couldn't hurt, I guess," Ross said.

"Say about seven or so here tomorrow night outside the Green Team building?" asked Dagmar.

"Yeah, that should work for me," Ross replied.

CHAPTER 2

Dagmar

Dagmar walked briskly to the food co-op that she knew would still be open for another hour or so. As she walked through the automatic doors, she welcomed the warm air against her cold face. It was busy as usual, and she was glad that she didn't run into anyone she knew. She didn't want to tell anyone about her embarrassing predicament.

She walked to the back of the store to the discount produce section and found some overripe bananas. Then she found some day-old, sliced brown bread and some peanut butter that was on sale. At least she'd have peanut-butter-and-banana sandwiches.

She walked over to the cashier and pulled out a ten-dollar bill, then dug around for her change purse. The cashier smiled at her and told her what she owed. She was relieved to have just enough.

"Enjoy your evening," said the cashier as Dagmar loaded the groceries into her backpack.

"Thanks. You too," Dagmar replied, happy for this small normalizing encounter.

Back out in the cold she headed toward Phoebe's place. As she walked up the hill, she looked at the windows on the bottom left of the fourplex where her friend lived and noticed that the lights of Phoebe's unit were all off. She knew that Phoebe often went to bed early and got up early, and Dagmar didn't want to disturb her. She stopped walking and stood on the sidewalk. Now what?

She knew there was a greenhouse in the backyard with a fold-out reclining lawn chair in it. She didn't feel good about going in unannounced, but she promised herself she'd let Phoebe know the next time she saw her. There, between the raised boxes of lettuce, chard and other greens was the lawn chair, folded and leaning against the wall. And draped over the chair was a blanket. Dagmar closed the greenhouse door, unfolded the chair and put her backpack on the ground. She lay down, covered herself with the blanket and fell into a deep sleep.

CHAPTER 3

Ross

Ross walked the few blocks to Nimby's, a nearby chain restaurant. He sat down in a booth, put his guitar in the seat across from him and ordered a beer and macaroni and cheese.

There were only a few other patrons in the restaurant. He could see the writing on the wall. Just like the photography shop where he used to sell frames, cameras and professional photography packages, Nimby's was being left behind. Ross had lost his job at the photography shop a few months ago, and things had gone downhill for him ever since. His relationship, his self-esteem—all of it just seemed to be on a downward spiral.

He was in a sour mood. Now what? Where would he go?

An old Beatles song was playing in the background. The words "He's a real nowhere man" blared through the restaurant, and he tried hard not to take them personally.

The waitress in her teal uniform brought him his beer and gave him a smile. Suddenly, he felt as if he was in a time warp, as if time had rushed ahead and left him outdated: sitting at Nimby's in a padded seat in the teal-and-brass interior, listening to music that was decades old, his occupation becoming obsolete. Actually, he assured himself, it was photography that was becoming obsolete, not his occupation. He was in sales. He could sell, and that was a transferrable skill. Too bad no one seemed to be buying much these days.

The food tasted okay, if unexciting, and he ate it quickly. He thought he'd give his friend Cole a call and see if he could put him up for the night.

When Ross paid his bill, leaving a tip he couldn't afford, he asked the waitress if he could make a local call. She dialled the number for him and handed him the receiver. The phone rang and rang, but there was no answer. Finally, it went to voice mail, and Ross said, "Hey, Cole, it's Ross. I'll call again." He didn't feel like giving Cole the details of his situation over voice mail or, he realized, in person either.

Ross went out into the night. Now what was he going to do? The air was crisp and fresh as he walked down the quiet streets, heading away from town. He walked toward his old home to see if he could get in. A wave of anger rolled over him. He and Debbie were going through a rough patch, but he'd been blindsided by this turn of events.

He reached his old yard and opened the back gate. The lights were out. He tried the back door and couldn't get in. He knew the windows were all secure, since he'd made sure of that when he'd lived there.

He went around to the front and knocked on the front door. There was no answer. No spare key under the mat either. Debbie either wasn't answering or wasn't home.

Impulsively, he kicked the step, hurting his toe in the process. He limped back to the alley and, suddenly exhausted, saw the neighbour's overturned canoe covered with a tarp in the backyard. He crawled under the tarp, pulled his guitar in and fell asleep on the ground using his backpack as a pillow.

CHAPTER 4

Looking for Options

Dagmar woke with a start. It took her a couple of seconds to figure out where she was. When she remembered, she got up quickly. The sun was just starting to rise. She guessed it was around 7:00 a.m., and she knew no one who lived in the fourplex would be in the backyard until the afternoon. This time of year, there wasn't much to do in the garden or greenhouse.

Feeling stiff, she got up and refolded the lawn chair and draped the blanket over it, just the way she'd found it. Then she left the greenhouse, closed the door behind her and walked to the alley behind it.

Phoebe drank only tea, and right now Dagmar needed a cup of coffee. Earlier she'd bought a coffee card at one of the local cafés, so she would be able to use it to get a coffee, sit in the shop and check her email. She quickly walked downtown, and as soon as she entered the bustling shop, she made her way to the washroom. She looked in the mirror, combed her greying brown hair and put on some makeup. An improvement, but her reflection still showed bags under her eyes. She straightened her hat and scarf. Many in Silverdale dressed casually, and she knew she probably wouldn't stand out. She felt like a criminal avoiding detection.

Once she'd ordered her coffee, she found a table at the back of the café and took out her laptop. She had a sip and welcomed the rush of caffeine through her body. There was lots of spam in her email and nothing important, but her social media had exploded with news about the federal government's approval of pipelines and tankers in her province.

It was a blow. Much of British Columbia was made up of pristine wilderness that provided habitat to many endangered species of animals and plants. Large amounts of this habitat would be destroyed with the installation of a pipeline, further endangering these species. Enormous oil tankers trying to navigate the treacherous waters between the many coastal islands was a disaster waiting to happen. She knew the Green Team organizers would be calling each other, working out strategies. Dagmar picked the most-informative posts and shared them with her online tribe.

Coffee finished, she put her laptop into her backpack and left the café. The day was clear, and she wanted to find a place to sit and think. She headed down the hill toward the lakeside and strolled along its edge until she found a quiet bank. Dagmar was hungry, so she took out the loaf of bread, the peanut butter and a banana. She had a few utensils in one of the pockets of her backpack and found a knife to cut the banana and spread the peanut butter.

Eating her peanut-butter-and-banana sandwich, looking over the lake at the mountains on the other side, she racked her brain for a strategy. She had a couple hundred dollars in the credit union, but her employment insurance had run out, and she still had no work prospects. *What to do?* She drew a blank. She looked out at the sailboats on the lake and saw an eagle overhead.

Silverdale had a high unemployment rate, but so did everywhere else in the country. Should she move? This was her home. This small, beautiful community was where she wanted to live. Phoebe might be able to give her some work, but Phoebe was just getting by herself. Dagmar was thankful for the bit work Phoebe had provided—data entry, help with the wording of her website and so on—but suspected that Phoebe couldn't really afford it and had mostly wanted to help Dagmar out.

Dagmar meditated on the bank for a long time. She was in a state of overwhelm and wanted to relax into a comfortable inner place where she might be able to find a way out of her predicament. Until she'd lost her job and even when she had been collecting employment insurance and doing odd jobs, she'd had an excellent credit rating, paid her bills on time and been a responsible citizen. But it all had evaporated in the past year or so. She didn't have a frame of reference for her current reality. It had been hard on her physically. She'd lost weight from the stress of not being able to pay her bills, avoiding her landlord and eating the least expensive food she could find. She'd learned wildcrafting and knew how to prepare dandelion greens, lamb's quarters and other things people considered weeds.

She made herself breathe deeply and tried to relax. After sitting for a long while trying to regain her composure, she headed to the library. In the small downtown core, people were going about their business as usual. There were more empty storefronts lately, although many had been empty for years. Buskers and panhandlers dotted the streets about every half block. Dagmar looked at the people walking, people of all ages, and wondered how they were managing. She probably looked just like one of them.

When she got to the library, she got out her laptop and set it up at one of the tables. After she'd checked her email and social media, she checked out the online job board for her region, and, as usual, there was nothing under the office/administration section. *Come on; be positive*, she told herself. Really? How many others were telling themselves the same thing? She looked out the window and saw a maple tree blowing in a strong wind, gold and oranges leaves flying off. She felt like one of those leaves. *Be positive.*

Dagmar put her laptop away and looked through the books about creative employment and how to reinvent oneself. Become a coach? Not likely. Blog for a living? She'd tried blogging but couldn't figure out how to make money that way. In her mid-fifties, how employable was she?

She left the library and walked up the hill to a park where she had another sandwich and looked at the view of the lake below and the mountains in the distance. The afternoon sun was warm, and that lifted her spirits. She watched some children on the merry-go-round at the playground and wondered what the future would hold for them. She thought of her son, Doug, who was working, going to university, doing well. What would she tell him?

Before she knew it, it was getting close to the time to meet Ross. She looked forward to having someone to talk to who was in a situation similar to hers.

CHAPTER 5

Reconnecting

"Hey, Ross," Dagmar called out as she saw him walking up to the Green Team building, his white hair blazing in the sunlight.

"Hi, Dagmar," said Ross. He was limping and looked tired.

"How are you?" she asked.

"Been better. You?"

"Lost. Cold. I don't know what to do. Other than that, I'm fine." Dagmar smiled. "Did you hurt your foot?"

"Stubbed my toe; that's all."

"Did you hear that the pipeline was approved?"

"No way!" he exclaimed.

They were both grim and silent. Then Dagmar said, "It was bound to happen, but it still stings. How was your day?"

Ross looked into her eyes intensely but said only, "It almost looks like Debbie moved. I've been running around in circles all day."

"Would you like a peanut-butter-and-banana sandwich?" she asked.

"Sure," Ross said absently.

Dagmar sat down on the stairs outside the Green Team building, took off her backpack and made them each a sandwich. Ross devoured his, and when she offered him another, he accepted it eagerly.

After they'd eaten their sandwiches, they walked aimlessly down a winding alley between some old houses, some of them boarded up. They chatted about the pipeline, work possibilities and reinventing themselves, and the banter cheered them both up a little. The sun was setting, and it was getting darker and nippier by the moment.

Finally, they stopped behind an old house that was tall and weatherworn and had boarded-up windows. It was beside an empty lot that, judging from the trail going through it, was a frequently used shortcut to the street. Not wanting to walk anymore, Ross leaned against the house, took his guitar out of its case and started playing a gentle melody. The music was comforting to them both.

Suddenly, a door creaked, and they turned around. A young woman peeked out from the old house's basement door and asked them to come in.

Dagmar and Ross looked up the staircase inside and could see a dim light at the top. As they followed the woman up the steps and headed into the centre of the house, the light became a bit brighter. A kerosene lamp burned on top of a kitchen table. There were chairs around the table, but the rundown room was furnished sparsely. Blankets covered the windows, so from the outside the light couldn't be seen and the house looked unoccupied.

There was another woman and a man who both looked to be in their early thirties. The other woman was holding a baby.

CHAPTER 6

Hidden Home

W here had Dagmar seen these people before? Maybe the outdoor markets? Or some of the second-hand stores when she'd still had the money to visit them? Maybe she'd seen them at public events or demonstrations.

The woman who'd invited them in introduced herself as Lydia. "Welcome. Would you like a cup of chamomile tea?" she asked, walking toward a big teapot sitting on an electric stove.

"Yes, please!" Dagmar said, and Ross nodded in agreement. Lydia poured tea into large, mismatched cups. It warmed their hands while comforting and calming them.

Lydia laughed. "We try not to draw attention to this house—that's partly why I invited you in so quickly. Here. Have a seat," she said, leading them into the living room and gesturing toward a sofa. Dagmar and Ross sat down and sipped their tea, appreciating this unexpected warmth, comfort and kindness. Lydia was thin and wiry. Her brown hair was pulled back in a ponytail, and youthful exuberance bubbled from her.

"Partly?" asked Dagmar. "Why else?"

"Well," Lydia said, "when you live the way we do, you pay attention to what's going on around you. You both go to Green Team meetings—I've been to a couple—so I know we're on the same page in some ways. What a drag about the pipeline being approved, eh?"

"Sure is! That's where I've seen you before!" said Dagmar. "You all look familiar to me."

The man walked closer to them, pushing his red curls away from his eyes. "Hi, I'm Tam," he said, "and this is Cammie and our baby, Bella."

Cammie, with her round face and straight, dark hair, smiled and said hi. She turned her sleepy baby toward them so they could see the girl's perfect face. Bella had pink cheeks and dark, fuzzy hair and was contentedly snuggled into her mother.

"How long have you been living this way?" Dagmar asked, intrigued by this living situation.

"We've lived in this house for the past six months," Cammie replied, "but we've been squatting in abandoned houses for the past two years or so. There's so little work in Silverdale, and it makes no sense to have boarded-up houses while there are people who can't afford rent. So this way of living just kind of evolved for us."

Tam added, "We put our skills to use for ourselves and others in the community. Right now our economy isn't working very well, so we're doing our best to roll with the times, fill some of the gaps and live the best way we can."

Ross looked a little perplexed. "So you, like, just decided to live like this out of the blue?"

"No, not at all!" Lydia guffawed. "We tried to make it in the world, but we just couldn't make ends meet. Times are tough! I was the one who took the first economic nosedive. Eventually, as our money dried up and we ran out of options, we decided to pool our resources and live together. We've been friends for years, so that helps."

Tam said, "It's our way of making the best of a hard situation. We know that most people are struggling right now, so we do what we can to get by and to help others in the community—and build relationships based on trust, caring and helping while we're at it. I guess you could say we're trying to be the change we want to see."

Cammie came closer to them. "How are you doing? We overheard you in the alley saying that you didn't have anywhere to go. Are you hungry?"

"Actually, I could use something to eat," said Dagmar. She was quite hungry—and tired of peanut-butter-and-banana sandwiches.

Ross nodded in agreement.

"Here, let me warm you up some soup," said Lydia, reaching into the fridge and taking out a jar. "This is left over from tonight's supper." She emptied the contents of the jar into a pot and put it on one of the burners on the stove.

"Would you like to sleep here? We have an extra bed," Cammie said.

Dagmar noted that Cammie had said *a* bed. She felt awkward but realized she wasn't in a position to be picky. Tears welled up in her eyes. "I'm so grateful to you. I don't know what we'd be doing right now if you hadn't taken us in like this. Thanks so much for your kindness and hospitality."

Cammie laid a gentle hand on Dagmar's arm. "We've all been in the same boat and know what it's like. Do either of you need a toothbrush?"

Ross replied, "I could use one."

After they'd finished their soup, Lydia gestured to them. "Come down here, and I'll show you your bed and where you can brush your teeth. We're pretty frugal with our water, so only use what you need, okay?"

The group exchanged good nights, and Ross and Dagmar followed Lydia to a small bathroom and then to an alcove with a double bed with thick blankets and a few flat pillows.

Brushing his teeth before bed felt great to Ross. Something about this simple act made him feel hopeful and human again.

Teeth brushed and bathroom used, they crawled into bed. Dagmar had changed into a nightgown she'd brought, and Ross was wearing his T-shirt and boxers.

"Look," Ross said, pointing to a high window. Before they fell asleep, they saw the new moon in a clear sky. They slept deeply.

CHAPTER 7

A New Day

Ross and Dagmar woke up to the sound of unrestrained, hysterical laughter. They lay there for a moment, feeling some discomfort at finding themselves in each other's arms. They didn't socialize outside their Green Team meetings, so both felt awkward. They disentangled themselves without comment.

They could smell coffee and fried onions.

"I'm hungry," Dagmar said as she wandered toward the smells and sounds coming from the kitchen.

Lydia, Cammie and Tam were watching a cartoon projected from a laptop onto a screen and howling with laughter. Tam had tears streaming down his face, and Lydia was holding her belly as she convulsed with laughter. Cammie, laughing so hard she was snorting, was cuddling baby Bella, who was enjoying all the merriment.

Lydia looked over at Dagmar, took a couple of seconds to compose herself and said, "Help yourselves to breakfast. The dishes are in the cupboard to the right of the stove, and the cutlery's in the drawer below. All the food is vegan and organic by the way."

Overtaken by curiosity, Dagmar took a better look at what they were watching. A cartoon of a thin man dressed in a light purple, skin-tight suit and cape was crawling along the ground, examining something. Tracks? Droppings?

Her hunger got the better of her, and she walked toward the stove. What a spread: tofu scramble, steamed greens, oatmeal with raisins, a jar of canned pears, coffee and a pot of tea. She opened the teapot and gave it a sniff: spearmint.

She sat down on a chair and looked over the group of laughing young people. As she ate her breakfast, she became aware of the fact that she was still in her long flannelette nightgown. It didn't seem to matter to them or to her. The homey, relaxed atmosphere made it feel natural.

Ross came in dressed, his hair combed. "Good morning," he said.

"Good morning to you!" Dagmar replied. "Hungry? The food's wonderful! The dishes and cutlery are over there," she said, indicating with her fork. "It's vegan and organic."

Ross raised his eyebrows and walked over to the stove. "Not exactly bacon and eggs, but it's better than nothing," he muttered, helping himself to a bowl of oatmeal and some canned pears. He sat beside Dagmar and whispered, "What are they laughing about?"

"Some kind of a cartoon," she whispered back. "I'm grateful to be eating breakfast, and you should be too."

They heard another roar of laughter from the other part of the room.

They ate in silence. Dagmar finished first, found a cup and poured herself some coffee. "Want a cup of coffee or spearmint tea?" she asked Ross.

"I could go for a cup of tea."

She sat down beside him, handing him the tea.

"Do you have any plans for today?" he asked her.

"Well," Dagmar said, "I want to get in touch with my friend Phoebe— she'll be worried sick about me. From there, I have no idea. How about you?"

"Hmm," said Ross, taking a sip of his tea. "I need to investigate what's going on with Debbie. I want to see if we can patch things up."

"It looks like they've got Wi-Fi here, so I'll see if it's all right with them if I check my emails," Dagmar said.

Dagmar walked over to Lydia and asked about checking email.

"Sure," Lydia said. "The password is 'healing.'"

Dagmar, perplexed, said, "I'm curious: How are you able to have Wi-Fi in an abandoned house?"

"It's actually our next-door neighbour's. He's allowed us to share his signal, and we pay half the monthly cost," said Lydia. "He's an older gentleman, and we befriended him. One of his kids sent him a laptop so he'd be able to Skype with his grandkids, and he was overwhelmed with the technology. We helped him to set everything up and showed him how to use Skype, and he was happy to share his signal in return. He's reclusive and self-sufficient and minds his own business. We trust him to keep our situation to himself."

"Hey, can I use your laptop to check my email?" Ross asked Dagmar.

"Okay," Dagmar said. "I'll get my laptop, and you can check yours while I get dressed."

She went to the sleeping nook and noticed the bed was made and their backpacks and Ross's guitar were neatly lined up. This bit of order felt comforting. She brought her laptop to the kitchen, logged in and handed it to Ross.

As she was getting dressed and combing her hair, she heard Ross exclaim. When she came out, he said, "Debbie's rented our place out and hasn't left a forwarding address. She's got all my stuff."

Dagmar wondered how a relationship could deteriorate so badly.

"What are you going to do?" she asked.

"I don't know," said Ross.

CHAPTER 8

Letting Go

Ross looked up through a high window. He watched as golden autumn leaves drifted off the branches, letting go gracefully and effortlessly. If only he could let go so easily.

He'd thought he was living the dream. He'd thought Debbie was his soul mate, that he'd found the love of his life. How could it all have gone so wrong? When did he go from being someone she'd looked up to, to someone she saw as a useless old man?

Lydia, who was sitting beside him and watching his face, touched his arm, interrupting his musings. She said in a compassionate tone, "I don't know what brought you here, but I can see that you're processing a lot of stuff. You too, Dagmar." Dagmar was sitting on his other side.

Lydia continued, "Since you're both here, I want you to know that you're welcome to stay awhile as you sort things out. Just contribute what you can, pitch in when you see a need and keep this house hidden. Otherwise we'll all get thrown out. We're squatting, so we're not supposed to be here. We don't use the way you first came in. There's a side door you can't see from the street, and it's beside an empty lot that people cut through regularly. We use that door and make sure no one sees us coming and going. I'll show you."

She led them down a dark hallway that brought them to a steep flight of steps. They heard someone running up the steps two at a time. A handsome, smiling man appeared, slightly out of breath. "Leroy!" exclaimed Lydia and jumped into his arms. They gave each other a big hug and a long kiss. "Welcome back! How was Vancouver?"

"Big and fun and chaotic." He grinned. "Glad to be home." He kissed her again on the cheek.

Lydia introduced Dagmar and Ross and said, "They found their way here last night."

"Pleased to meet you both." Leroy beamed at them. He took off his backpack and gave them each a big hug. Dagmar hugged him warmly in return, but Ross received the hug gingerly, feeling uncomfortable. They all continued strolling down the hallway.

"There's one more thing I want to show you," Lydia said, leading them into a narrow hallway. She opened a door at the end of it and lit a candle in a glass candleholder that was just inside. It illuminated a small room with cushions on the floor. At the far end of the room was an altar with sacred objects arranged on a shimmering lavender-and-fuchsia-coloured cloth. There were candles, feathers, icons, flowers and pictures—all sorts of different things.

"This is our meditation room, and we encourage people to spend time here, especially when they've just arrived," Lydia said. "Feel free to add something that's special or sacred to you."

Leroy added, "When we've reached the point where we've had to let go of our homes, the process that got us here has usually been pretty stressful. It's a time when we need to regroup, and the more centred we are, the better equipped we are to cope with whatever comes next."

"We want to help each other to heal," Lydia said with conviction. "It's all that makes sense to us with the world the way it is—economically, socially, environmentally. We ask that you take care of yourselves and help others to do the same whenever you can."

Dagmar could feel herself getting teary. "I had no idea I'd find people who make so much sense to me in an abandoned house." She hugged Lydia and Leroy and then gave Ross a big hug too. "I'm so moved by all your help and your vision."

"Thanks," Ross said in a voice that was cool and stiff. "If I find time to meditate between trying to get my stuff back, I'll know where to go."

Leroy looked at them both. "I know movies and TV shows encourage us to look out for number one, but look at where that's gotten us. Our society is crumbling. We're all struggling to get by, and more of us are falling through the cracks all the time. Meanwhile we're reaching environmental tipping points, and who knows what kind of natural disaster will hit next? All we really have are our relationships and the trust and goodwill we create together. The more we can count on each other, the better off we'll all be. We're all we've got." There was a solemnity about Leroy with his lanky, large-boned body and his straight, brown hair.

Dagmar nodded in agreement. This had been dawning on her intuitively for the past few years. It was as though these people were mirroring her deepest thoughts. "Lydia, I hope you'll let us clean up the kitchen," she said. "Ross, will you give me a hand?"

"All right," he answered.

Lydia snuffed out the candle.

CHAPTER 9

Meditations

T he dishes were stacked beside the sink, and dish soap was in the cupboard underneath, right where you'd expect it. This chore gave Dagmar and Ross a chance to find their way around the kitchen and get grounded.

There were plenty of cups, bowls and plates and lots of cutlery, all mismatched. There were also jars of beans, rice, lentils, other dried goods and home preserves of all kinds. And there were jars of sprouts on the countertop.

"Wow! They're set up, aren't they?" Ross said as he dried and put away some cups. "Not what I'd expect in a squat."

"That's for sure," Dagmar said as she scrubbed the last pot and put it in the drying rack. "They seem to have this thing down to a fine art—even the way they've treated us. They seem to know just what we need."

As she wiped down the counters, she asked, "Feel like meditating?"

"Do you really think it's worth it? It's a nice room and all, but I've never really been much good at meditating."

"It can't hurt to give it a try, can it? It'll just quiet our minds," Dagmar coaxed. "And it's better with a meditation buddy."

"I guess it can't hurt." Ross hung up the dishtowel.

They walked to the meditation room together; each found a pillow and sat down. Dagmar reached over and lit a pale yellow candle. It felt special to be in this peaceful, intimate space, with candlelight and the beautiful altar before them.

"Have you meditated before?" Dagmar asked.

"No, not really. It's something I've always meant to do but never seemed to get around to. How about you?"

"Not very often," said Dagmar. She found a beautiful earth-toned shawl stitched with intricate beadwork on a cushion. She unfolded it and pulled it around her. "Although I really enjoy it when I do. I can't think of a better time than now. How are you doing?" she asked, examining him closely.

"I don't even know." Ross shook his head. "I'm still getting my bearings. How about you?"

"Feeling relieved to be here," Dagmar answered.

"Do you trust them?"

"Actually, I do," Dagmar said. "Do you?"

"I'm not sure. It was kind of them to take us in, but I keep wondering, what's the catch?"

"I don't think there is one. Keep the place private, pitch in when we can, take care of ourselves and each other."

She crossed her legs and closed her eyes. Ross did as well, leaning on a cushion against the wall.

He looked over at her, sitting with her eyes closed. He could see the strain in her face, but she was quite beautiful regardless. Some of that beauty came from knowing her—her helpfulness and caring nature. They'd be getting to know each other better having landed in this crazy situation. He closed his eyes and breathed slowly and deliberately, chasing out the uncomfortable thoughts, the fears about the future, the emotional pain, the pipelines. Just breathing in and out slowly. And there was Dagmar, wrapped in a colourful shawl like a gift—for him?

Dagmar remembered the first time she'd seen Ross. He had been speaking at a gathering about a composting project. Her first impression had been of someone who was a little shady. As she'd gotten to know him through the Green Team meetings, she'd begun to like him better. She found him helpful but hard to know, as if he wasn't exactly the person he presented himself as. Well, they'd be getting to know each other better now. She was with her breath, feeling peaceful, thankful for the unexpected grace that had bestowed itself on her, on both of them. She tried not to think of the pipelines.

They sat together in the candlelight, their slow breathing in synch. They heard a church bell somewhere in the distance announcing the day: Sunday. It broke the silence, and they opened their eyes.

"Hey, Ross," Dagmar said quietly, "we're each other's continuity between where we were and where we are now." She touched his arm. "This is important. Let's treat each other with care, okay?"

"What are you getting at exactly?" Ross wasn't sure where she was going with this train of thought and fidgeted with the corner of his cushion.

"I mean we've just met these people. We have nowhere else to go, and we know each other at least. Let's—I don't know—realize we're on a strange kind of journey together and try to give each other moral support. Does that make more sense?"

"You scratch my back; I'll scratch yours—that kind of thing?"

"Sort of," said Dagmar. "You know, the whole focus of this place seems to be on healing. Let's just try to be the most healing presence to each other we can be. Let's treat our shared journey as the special thing it is."

Ross thought about that. She had a point: Why not look out for each other, since they were both in this together? "Okay, agreed," he said.

"Thank you." Dagmar gave him a gentle hug. She picked up the candle and blew it out.

CHAPTER 10

The Labyrinth

Ross and Dagmar took the staircase Lydia had shown them and, when the coast was clear, stepped into the empty lot. Ross wanted to see what he could do to get some of his stuff back, and Dagmar wanted to talk to her friend Phoebe.

Even though it had been only one night, it felt like a long time since they'd been outside. The day was crisp, sparkling and windblown, the leaves on the trees shivering in yellow, green and burgundy against the cold, blue sky.

Somehow, the experience in the abandoned house had altered the world for both of them. Everything looked bigger and brighter and, oddly enough, full of possibilities.

"Have you ever been to the labyrinth?" Dagmar asked on an impulse as they strolled in that direction. "It's just a couple of blocks from here."

"No, never. What's it all about?" he asked.

"It's a kind of walking meditation. I do it whenever I feel troubled or in need of guidance."

"A labyrinth. Is that like a maze or something?" Ross asked.

Dagmar laughed. "Something like that, but you can't get lost in it, and there are no walls. It's a large, flat circle on the ground made of bricks. There's a path that goes back and forth around a circle and eventually ends at the centre. You follow the path and then meditate in the centre for a minute or two, then follow the path back out."

A few minutes later they were in the park and saw the labyrinth, its carefully arranged grey and red bricks looking beautiful under golden tree branches that shimmered in the sunshine. The sight felt like an invitation.

They followed the path, slowly and deliberately. Dagmar got to the centre first, bowed to each direction and then clapped her hands three times. The clapping sounded almost metallic. Ross followed her example. When Dagmar reached the end of her walk, she turned around and bowed to the labyrinth. Ross did the same.

"What's with the strange sound when you clap your hands in the centre?" Ross asked.

"No one knows," Dagmar said, "but there are sacred objects buried underneath. Maybe that has something to do with it."

They stood silently in contemplation for a moment and then agreed to meet back at the house later. Dagmar gave Ross a hug, and they walked away in opposite directions. Dagmar headed toward Phoebe's place, which was up the hill, and Ross went in the other direction, toward his old house to see if he could get any information.

CHAPTER 11

A Visit With a Friend

P hoebe was having a quiet morning at home. The fourplex she lived in was the best of all worlds for her. She had private space and a sense of community with friends who lived in the other three units. They shared birthdays and yard work and generally helped each other out.

There was one main door into the fourplex, and there were two units on the bottom and two upstairs. Phoebe's unit was at the bottom, and there was a bench and an umbrella stand outside her door. Inside, her few well-placed and colourful possessions popped against pale walls. Plants lined the windows, and the furniture was comfortable and inviting.

She sat at her desk with a cup of tea reviewing some drapery and upholstery samples for her latest client. The patterns in shades of orange, red and lavender felt vibrant and optimistic.

Phoebe loved her job. As an interior designer with a focus on creating environmentally friendly spaces, she'd developed a good reputation and earned many friends—grateful clients and colleagues, including architects, contractors, landscape designers and permaculture specialists. Her vulnerability invited trust and was part of her mystique. She had the gift of helping people discover the interiors they yearned for, the sensitivity to feel her clients' needs deeply and to translate those needs into physical form.

Her work also satisfied her fascination for green home products. This included everything from paints without off-gassing, environmentally friendly flooring, antiques, organic bedding and shower curtains and green drapery fabrics right down to environmentally friendly toilet paper. These shifts in making things greener and cleaner one home at a time gave her some hope for a healthier world.

Her thoughts were interrupted by the sound of the doorbell.

"Dagmar!" Phoebe exclaimed. "I've been so worried about you! Come on in!"

Phoebe had watched helplessly as Dagmar's government job had been cut a few years earlier. Then her employment insurance had run out. Dagmar had tried various things and had a few temporary jobs, but none of them brought in enough money. The past few months Phoebe had seen less of Dagmar and suspected that things were extremely difficult for her, but she didn't know what she could do to help. Dagmar was proud and didn't like to take from others. About a week earlier, Dagmar had asked Phoebe if she'd mind keeping a few boxes of her stuff, and that had worried Phoebe. It was great to see Dagmar here.

They gave each other a big hug.

Phoebe had always had straight, white blonde hair, so as she'd aged, her hair colour hadn't changed. Now in her mid-fifties, she enjoyed good health. She was delicate—it was almost hard to believe that she was of this world.

"Cup of tea?" Phoebe asked. "I've got a pot of that nice orange vanilla. Can I pour you a cup?"

"That would be lovely," Dagmar said. "I hope I've come at an okay time." They sat down at the antique kitchen table with their cups of tea.

"This is the perfect time for a little break." She was about to turn off her laptop, then said, "My Facebook friend Alice just posted that university is free, even for foreigners, in Germany, Finland, France, Sweden, Norway, Slovenia and Brazil. Isn't that amazing?"

"It sure is. Just think of all that debt students can be free of."

Phoebe looked closely at her friend. "So ... how's life?"

"Well," Dagmar said, sipping her tea, "pretty crazy, but I think things are going to be all right."

"That's awfully cryptic," laughed Phoebe.

"I'm sorry. It's just been such a struggle these past few months." Her eyes welled up with tears. "I've been avoiding talking about it. Anyway, push finally came to shove, and I'm out of the apartment I was renting. And, Phoebe, I must tell you: I slept in your greenhouse last night," Dagmar confessed, embarrassed but happy to get this off her chest.

"I wish you would have come in," said Phoebe.

"I know," Dagmar replied, "but I didn't want to wake you up, and I felt uncomfortable telling you how desperate I was feeling. I'm sorry."

Dagmar told Phoebe about how the people in the abandoned house had taken in her and Ross, without revealing the house's location. "I feel so good about those people. I'm inspired and intrigued and, well, honoured to be part of whatever they're up to."

"Wow, that's fascinating!" said Phoebe. "What about Ross? What's going on with him?" She'd met him a couple of times and never quite trusted him. He seemed more concerned with the impression he was making than actually communicating meaningfully. He struck her as someone who cared less about people than what he could get out of them.

"He and his partner split up, and she's changed the locks on the house where they were living."

"Uh-oh," Phoebe replied. "Please, Dagmar, don't run to his rescue." Phoebe knew Dagmar's tendencies well.

"I know." Dagmar nodded in agreement. "I've had the same conversation with myself. I'll be careful."

Phoebe reached over and put her hand on Dagmar's. "Thank you," she said.

They chatted about things in general, including the recent news about the pipelines, revelling in each other's company.

"Say, are you hungry?" Phoebe asked. "I was just about to put on some soup, and have some crackers with guacamole. Will you have some with me?" She always had lots of healthy, delicious food around.

"That would be great!" Dagmar said. "How can I help?"

"Everything's pretty well ready to go—I just have to heat up the soup." Phoebe walked to the fridge. "Just relax, and I'll get it."

"You're a peach!" said Dagmar. Soon they were eating a hardy lunch together. Afterwards, Dagmar gathered up the dishes and washed them.

"Dagmar, I hope you'll take this the right way," Phoebe said, "but please feel free to take a bath if you like. I know how they relax you. Also, I just went through my winter clothes and was going to take some to the second-hand store. Why don't you see if there's anything you like before I take them away?" They wore the same size, were both small and slender.

Dagmar gave Phoebe a hug. "You're such a wonderful friend! I don't know how to thank you. I'd love to take a look at the clothes and then take you up on your offer of a bath."

Dagmar found a few items of clothing she liked and got the bath running.

"Oh, and one more thing," Phoebe said. "Could you use some cherry tomatoes and a few squash? I'm absolutely overrun and don't want them to go bad. Apples too. We've had a bumper crop this year."

"I'd love to bring them to the house," Dagmar said. "I feel the same way toward these people as I do toward you: I don't know how to repay them."

Phoebe laughed. She knew Dagmar would find a way. She always did.

"Try out the new shampoo and tell me what you think, okay? I just love it! And there are organic Epsom salts with baking soda in the blue container by the tub." Phoebe wanted her friend to feel indulged after the unimaginable stress she must have been through recently.

A short while later—Phoebe wished Dagmar had taken a little longer to relax—Dagmar, wearing beige pants and a peach sweater, emerged with her hair washed.

"Phoebe, I love you," she said and gave her friend a hug.

"I love you too, Dagmar," said Phoebe. She kissed Dagmar on the cheek. "Remember, I have a spare room if you ever need it, okay?"

"Okay, I'll keep that in mind," Dagmar said, looking down. Phoebe couldn't help but notice the tears in her friend's eyes, even though Dagmar tried to hide them.

"Anyway, see you soon! Thanks so, so much!" said Dagmar.

Phoebe opened the door for Dagmar and watched her walk away loaded down with produce and clothing.

CHAPTER 12

The First Supper

When Dagmar came back, she found Ross playing a tune on his guitar. She guessed the time was about three in the afternoon.

"Hey, Ross. How's it going?" she asked.

"Great!" he said in a way that she didn't find completely convincing.

"No, really." She touched his arm and looked at him. He just looked away. She let it go. She could see that he was well armoured emotionally. Did he even know what was going on for him?

"You're looking good," he said. "How was your morning?"

"I went to Phoebe's, and she spoiled me." Dagmar laughed.

"How's Phoebe these days?" he asked.

"Pretty good. Working on an interior she's enjoying, loving life as always." Dagmar sighed. Thoughts of her friend warmed her heart. "She gave me this produce from her garden, a bumper crop this year. Would you like an apple or some cherry tomatoes?"

"Don't mind if I do," Ross said, accepting the apple she offered him.

"Do you think I should put these squash in the oven? The gang might appreciate coming home to some warm food," Dagmar wondered aloud. "I bet they'd love to come home to a feast!"

"Would you like some help?" asked Ross.

"Sure, I'd love some help!"

They spent the next couple of hours in the kitchen cooking rice and currying lentils, baking squash, stir-frying vegetables and making an apple crumble. Around five or so, they heard the group climbing the stairs, talking and laughing.

"Smells *good* in here!" Leroy announced as he put a big box of pears down on one of the counters.

Tam said, "It was my turn to make supper, and I'm beat! Bella kept me up half the night, and I've been picking greens all day." He put down a box of chard, parsley, dill and some other greens beside Leroy's box. He bowed his head to Dagmar and then to Ross. "Thank you from the bottom of my heart!" Then he added, "I'll quickly throw together a salad with these fresh greens!"

Next came Cammie, baby Bella balanced on her left hip, and a bag of purple plums hanging from her right shoulder. "Big canning day tomorrow," she said. "Ross and Dagmar, thanks so much for preparing all this food!"

Lydia clamoured in carrying two wooden chairs. "I'm starved!" she said. "Am I in the right place at the right time?" She smiled at their two new guests.

Everyone helped themselves and sat down to a hardy meal. Afterwards, Lydia put on the kettle and made a big pot of spearmint tea, which they drank while eating their apple crumble.

As they were finishing up, Ross looked around the table. "So you just wound up living like this over time?"

Tam piped up, "Yup, probably much the same way you just did." They all laughed.

"Seriously?" Ross asked, forking up the last few crumbs of his apple crumble. "How do you deal with the stigma of squatting? How do others react to your situation?"

"We keep it to ourselves, but it's hard to make new friends, since we can't really invite them home," Cammie said. "It's by no means ideal, but it's the best we can do right now. And we contribute a lot to the lives of people in our community, so I think people are willing to turn a blind eye."

Lydia said, "Silverdale is our home, but we've got student loans to pay, and there's no work." She took a sip of her tea. "We tried our best, but we couldn't afford rent, loan payments, groceries, bills …"

Cammie said, "We've done all kinds of things together to try to make ends meet. We buy bulk wholesale food, have community garden plots and harvest abandoned fruit trees and have done this for years. We know about all the programs in town that offer free stuff and things that help save money, just like a lot of other people in this town."

"Even with that, we still couldn't cut it, so we live in this abandoned house and do our best to make it livable," Tam said.

"It became a challenge to live well and at the same time do what we could to address the unfulfilled needs of people all around us," said Leroy, helping himself to a second portion of apple crumble.

"As an example," Cammie said, bouncing Bella, "I got these plums from an elderly woman who isn't able to pick them from her tree anymore. I pick some for her, and she lets me have some, and I give some to the food bank. I also keep her company and help her around the house. A lot of older people get home support, but they need so much more, and the service is being cut all the time. It means a lot to her that I check in and see how she's doing when I'm in the neighbourhood."

"These greens are from our community greenhouse garden," said Tam. "We grow food for ourselves and for the food bank."

"If there's one thing we can all agree on, it's that we need to heal: as individuals, as a society and as a planet. We don't know what's going to happen or how, but we're just doing what makes sense to us, doing our best to heal and to help others do the same," Lydia said, and the rest of them nodded in agreement.

Dagmar said, "I'm honoured to be in the company of such pioneers. Thanks for including us."

Again the pipelines came up in conversation.

"I don't think the people in this province will let it happen," said Cammie. "Sure, the oil companies have been big donors to the politicians, but the people who live here are a different matter. We love this land and won't let it be destroyed."

"We'll get the dishes," Leroy told Dagmar and Ross. "Why don't you just sit back and relax? You have a lot of healing to do, just like the rest of us, but especially after having made such a radical departure from your regular lives."

That night as he fell asleep, Ross dreamt of luxury cruises and young women, of tropical islands and lavish homes. He'd lived this way before, and he would live this way again. Then he wondered, was this his dream, or was it the only dream he'd ever been encouraged to entertain? It felt distant and a little hollow. In the meantime, he had food in his belly, a roof over his head and Dagmar to keep him company and keep him warm at night.

Something about this situation was exhilarating to Dagmar. It felt like an adventure. But she still had reservations about Ross. Oh well. He was pleasant enough.

CHAPTER 13

Life in the Margins

Dagmar felt that if her life was a page, then her move to the abandoned house had her living in the margins: outside of society but oddly connected. She still visited Phoebe, and she and Ross still went to Green Team meetings and were meditating regularly each morning. She and Ross were becoming important threads in the fabric of their community—helping out when they could, observing what was going on with the people around them and getting closer to the people who had taken them in.

She'd discovered that Tam was the one who kept them in electricity, heat and hot water. He was very good at electrical, mechanical and creative jury-rigging. He'd designed a hot-water system through the use of black hoses on the roof fed by rainwater. The motion of the water powered a generator, which gave them electricity and heat before becoming their drinking water and then finally watering the garden in the back. He had lots of other tricks to keep the warmth and electricity flowing too.

Lydia and Leroy pooled their creativity to provide everything from food to furniture to clothing to online services in order to make money. They knew how to find, make, improvise and collaborate and loved developing new and better ways of doing things. Through the Internet they were connected to friends who also lived in squats, and they all would exchange tips and tricks.

Cammie had studied traditional Chinese medicine and was a natural healer. Knowing what people needed was almost second nature to her. Part Chinese herself, she was calm, grounded and gentle. She also had an extensive knowledge of permaculture, wildcrafting and food preparation.

What impressed Dagmar was the group's good nature. They were dedicated to healing: themselves, each other, society and the planet. When Dagmar had been their age, there had been a lot of blame and anger in the activist crowd she'd run with, along with infighting, immaturity and poor listening skills. Not so with these people. Their belief was that the people who were doing the most damage were the ones who needed healing the most. This group was keenly aware of the way the oil and gas industries threatened the earth's life-support systems. To them, risking the lives of their children and grandchildren for the sake of profits was a kind of sickness.

Cammie once had told Dagmar a story about an Auschwitz survivor she'd seen on TV. The woman had said she felt more sorry for the guards than anyone else because they'd lost their humanity. That's how Cammie and her friends felt toward the people who were causing all the damage to society and the environment. They felt that these people had had their humanity systematically removed. How to restore people's humanity was their challenge.

They'd concluded that whatever the outcome of the social, economic and environmental problems that were making people's lives so difficult, the ground had to be prepared for a better future, whatever that future turned out to be. They were improvising; they were doing what was needed in their communities and building relationships. They had lively discussions over dinner and in the course of the day about philosophical and practical issues but were always open to possibilities and dedicated to finding new ways of helping each other, their community, the planet and all of life.

There was an element of the sacred in what they were doing, a kind of faith in a better future—a willingness to learn, help and support each other and an openness to guidance from wherever it presented itself.

CHAPTER 14

A New Gig

One night after Dagmar and Ross had been there about a month, Leroy started singing "The Lion Sleeps Tonight" while doing the dishes, and everyone joined in with different harmonies. Afterwards, they realized they'd sounded pretty good, so they started singing regularly while cleaning up after meals.

Before long, they took their music to the street. Downtown Silverdale had a treed plaza at its core surrounded by small shops, where entertainers would sing, dance or perform for the enjoyment of passersby. The household sang songs that were happy and inspiring, songs about love and change. Ross accompanied them on guitar, and the rest of them did a simple choreography, with Lydia and Leroy doing a few featured performances. It was lots of fun and a bit of extra money too. They had a collection of percussive instruments: a tambourine, a shaker and a small drum they'd sometimes use to keep the beat.

Baby Bella loved being passed around the group and bounced to the music. She was developing more personality by the day and enjoying all the attention this living arrangement provided her with. She loved music and thrived on being steeped in it this way.

People stopped to listen, leave money and comment on the group's great energy. Nothing like music to uplift the spirits! Sometimes bystanders sang and danced along.

After one of their performances, a middle-aged woman stayed around until the rest of the crowd left. She approached the group and said, "Hi, my name's Maude. I'm wondering if you'd be interested in a Sunday-morning gig."

"Where would you like us to play?" Ross asked, since he had experience arranging musical performances.

"I own a little place called the Love Bite. Have you heard of it? The payment would be whatever you get when you pass around the hat and a free lunch for each of you," said Maude. "Do you have enough material for two hours, say 10:00 a.m. till noon?"

They glanced around at each other with looks of approval. Why not?

"Okay, we'll be there 15 minutes early so we can set up and do a sound check," said Ross.

"Great! See you then," she said and waved goodbye before briskly walking away.

"Wow! The Love Bite!" Dagmar exclaimed. "That's everyone's favourite restaurant!" They gave each other high fives.

The following Sunday they showed up at the agreed-upon time. They had mastered a collection of songs about love, hope and healing from different eras. Their music really resonated with the patrons of the café! There was a comment sheet, and people said, "You reminded me that love is what we're all about," and "This is one of the most spiritual Sunday mornings I've had in a long time. Thank you!" and "Keep spreading the joy! We need it now more than ever!"

A place after their own hearts, the restaurant had a menu that included fairly traded, organic coffee, a variety of herbal teas and an excellent selection of vegan fare. They ate happily, enjoying the fortuitous flow of events.

CHAPTER 15

Inner Changes

Ross and Dagmar were both being transformed by their new way of life. It was an abrupt change to go from living in society with its rules and things people are required to do to living in the margins. In the margins, things were done because they made sense. No one had to pretend or fill out forms or perform a meaningless task.

Dagmar and Ross noticed that the people in the house were watching them closely. It wasn't as though the others were suspicious of them but as though they were monitoring them to see how they were doing. They'd all been through this before. What were they expecting?

One day, Dagmar handed Ross a cup of tea, and he dropped it. "Damn it, Dagmar! Make sure I have the cup before you let it go. Now there's a big mess!" he shouted.

"We can clean it up. It's no big deal," she said. "Here's a rag. It's just the tabletop, and the cup didn't break. How about you clean it up, and I'll pour you another cup of tea?"

She tossed him the rag and walked over to the kettle and poured him another cup.

"You know we have to be frugal with the water!" Ross said.

"Ross, it's just a small amount. Is something bothering you? You've been upset all morning."

"What makes you think I'm upset? I'm just fine!" Ross shouted.

"Then why are you shouting?"

Ross sighed. "Okay, I guess I am upset. Did you ever meet my daughter, Lillian?"

"Yeah, once or twice. Why?" Dagmar sat down beside him.

"Well, she's coming to town; that's why. She sent me an email this morning." Ross started pacing. "I don't want her to see me living this way! She's used to me living in a nice house with nice furniture. I don't want her to know that I have to sneak in and out of a rundown, abandoned, old house."

"You're embarrassed about your daughter discovering the way you're living," Dagmar affirmed.

"Yeah, exactly," said Ross, calming down a bit. He took a sip of his tea.

"When is she coming?" Dagmar asked.

"In a month or so. She's getting a break from school and wants to come home for the holiday."

"And she doesn't know how you're living?"

"Not really. I've glossed over a few details," said Ross.

"Such as?"

"Well, I've told her that I'm sharing a house with some very nice people, but she doesn't know it's a squat." Ross sighed.

"If there's anything I can do to help with this situation, just let me know," said Dagmar, putting her hand on his and looking into his eyes. "I know there's such a stigma around squatting. I understand how hard it must be. My son, Doug, was skeptical at first too. Meeting everyone might really help. I think that would go a long way toward easing Lillian's mind."

"Dagmar," Ross said quietly that night as they lay in bed, "help me."

"What do you need?" He looked agitated.

"I'm feeling so much anger, and I don't even know why." He took a deep breath. "Why have I been jumping through these hoops? Why have I been chasing—I don't know—things that don't mean anything? Why have I been wasting my life putting on a show for other people who are putting on a show? I don't even know how to be real. My mind's so full of ... of little stories I tell myself to keep me from feeling. Who am I anyway?" He looked over at Dagmar, who was giving him her full attention. "Does that even make sense?"

Dagmar stroked his arm. "It does to me," she said. "You're very courageous for saying it."

"Thanks," he said. "I still feel rage, but it's subsiding a little. I want you to know that I'm glad you're the one I'm going through this with. This experience is actually very sane; the journey inside is what's strange. How are you doing?"

"I'm feeling like, like I'm suspended," she answered slowly, "like I'm flowing through time in slow motion. Why is it so strange to do what makes sense? It's like I have to adjust to a reality where we figure out what we need to do and then do it, from a reality where we jump through all kinds of hoops, as you say, just because they're there and everyone else is doing it. I feel like a part of me that's had the circulation cut off is tingling, like the blood's starting to circulate again, and I don't know what to do. Like something tentative is coming alive."

"I know what you mean," Ross said with conviction. "Do you remember that conversation we had the first night we meditated together? You were wearing a shawl and were all wrapped up like a gift. You were trying to communicate that we needed to treat each other with care. Dagmar, you've been a gift to me, but in a way I didn't understand at the time. Thanks for being here with me." He put his arms around her and stroked her hair. "It's great coming back to life in your company."

She lay there contentedly, feeling safe in his arms. She'd gotten used to his particular scent and felt comforted. "Thanks, Ross," she said quietly. "I'm loving this moment, and I'm glad you're the one I'm sharing it with." Then hesitantly she asked, "Is there something underneath the rage? Is there something deeper?"

Ross closed his eyes, tuning in to what was going on inside him. "Yes," he said finally, his voice faltering. "Grief." He held her tight, her head nuzzled against his chest. "Grief," he repeated quietly, with certainty. He was glad that she couldn't see the tears streaming down his face.

Before falling asleep, they lay motionless looking up through the high window at a star shimmering in the sky.

CHAPTER 16

The Lucky Ones

One morning, Ross found himself alone in the kitchen with Leroy. Everyone else had left, and Ross had a bit of a cold, so was staying home and taking it easy.

As Ross put on the kettle to make some wild ginger tea, Leroy pulled out his laptop. "Another trip to Vancouver coming up," he said to Ross. "My mom's taken a turn for the worse, and I want to be there with her."

"What's wrong with your mom?" Ross asked.

"Lung cancer, last stages," Leroy said matter-of-factly.

"Sorry to hear that. My mom died of cancer too. Not pretty, I know." Ross poured hot water into the teapot. "Want some ginger tea?"

"Sure, thanks," Leroy said as he typed on his laptop.

"How're you getting to Vancouver?"

"Ride share. It's an online program where people share rides. I put in a bit of money for gas and take a turn driving: kind of an organized carpooling system. Everyone wins."

"Neat! I'll have to keep it in mind if I need to go anywhere," Ross said, sipping his tea.

"Yeah, it's a great system!"

"You guys make being homeless seem so easy. I had no idea there were so many supports and systems in place," Ross said.

"We're the lucky ones," Leroy said. "Even though we're technically homeless, people assume that we're not and extend all kinds of help and trust our way. Lots of people aren't so lucky. Here, we're all friends; we're educated, white for the most part. If we were of a different race or had addiction issues or were all on our own, things wouldn't be so easy."

"I'd never really thought of that," Ross said.

"Yeah, you see a lot of people who are much more desperate than we are. Even though we're squatting, we really are among the lucky ones. It has its hardships, but it's important to be aware of our privileged position and to help those who have so much less," Leroy said. "Just being aware of our position is an important step."

"Anyway, got to run," Leroy said, taking a last swallow of tea. "Hope you're feeling better soon."

"Thanks," Ross said. "Safe travels, and I hope you have a good visit with your mom."

As they gave each other a hug, a tear rolled down Ross's cheek. What was happening to him? Lately he felt like an emotional ball of mush, and it was scary as hell.

"Thanks." Leroy smiled, then hoisted his backpack over his shoulder and ran down the stairs.

CHAPTER 17

The Love Bite

Phoebe and her friend Sophie, who lived across the hall, went to the Love Bite to hear Dagmar perform. They found a table and joined in with the other patrons who were singing along and clapping their hands.

The music fit the ambience of the Love Bite well. Wafting from the kitchen was the enticing aroma of onions and garlic. The space was filled with mismatched wooden tables and chairs painted in lavender, peach and cream. The furniture contrasted in a way that was clean and sweet with the walls, which were made of brick and stone. There were wicker baskets containing pots of herbs clustered in the café's corners and clay pots of live herbs that could be cut off and added to the meal on each table. People often bought pots of the high-quality, organic, non-GMO herbs to bring home with them. Local painters displayed their works on the walls. The Love Bite was a prized area to exhibit since the owner was very particular about what she displayed.

"Is your love enough, yeah—your love enough, yeah—is your love enough—or can you love some more?" Dagmar belted out with four young people as they passed a happy baby around among them and Ross played guitar and sang along.

They looked so normal, as if they could be anyone's kids, neighbours, co-workers or employees. Phoebe and Sophie never would have guessed that these people were squatting in an abandoned house. How exactly would they expect people living this way to look? Whatever stereotypes they were unknowingly harbouring about squatters were quickly being dashed. If these bright young faces couldn't make a go of things, what did that say about their economy?

The group started a new, beautiful tune: "Bless the kind heart that gives without asking. For anything you've done to help anyone, I want to thank you." This one was slower, and everyone swayed to the heartfelt sound.

After a few more songs, the group took a break. Phoebe and Sophie waved at Dagmar, who came over.

"Your music is so heartwarming!" Phoebe said as she hugged her friend.

"It's lovely!" Sophie agreed.

Dagmar blushed. "They're such an inspiration! You wouldn't believe the amount of goodwill and wisdom contained in those young bodies. We weren't like that when we were their age, were we?"

They all laughed.

"We should take some credit for having raised this generation." Phoebe smiled, thinking of their kids.

The friends chatted for a while; then Dagmar said, "It looks like we're back up. I'll introduce you to them after this set."

The next set was a little livelier. They sang, "Come on believe—believe! There's something up above. Yes there's something. What's that something? That something is love." It was Sunday after all. Tambourines and shakers brought the energy up. Excitement permeated the air.

For the next song, there was no guitar; they sang a cappella: "We are the dance of the moon and sun. We are the power that's in everyone. We are the turning of the tide. We are the hope that is deep inside."

Amid the clapping and swaying, the energy in the room was electric. They sang, "We are the flow and we are the ebb. We are the weavers; we are the web."

Lydia and Leroy danced in a free flow. The patrons of the restaurant sang along; many got up and danced. They sang a few more lively tunes and then wound down slowly, ending with a piece that was beautiful and peaceful: "Love is the opening door. Love is what we came here for. No one could offer you more. Do you know what I mean? Have your eyes really seen?"

CHAPTER 18

Around the Table

Amid much cheering and clapping, the group took a bow before walking over to the table reserved for them. Dagmar pulled a small table over so that Phoebe and Sophie could join the group. She then introduced them to her housemates.

"Your baby's beautiful!" Phoebe said, watching Bella bounce on Cammie's lap.

Bella was grabbing at Cammie's blouse, so Cammie pulled her close, undid the top buttons of her blouse and let her nurse. "Lunchtime for Bella too," she laughed. "It's really nice to meet you, Phoebe. Thanks for coming out to listen to us."

"It's the nicest Sunday morning I've had in a long time. Your music's so special. We need to hear more music about love and healing."

"Thanks!"

Cammie adjusted Bella on her lap, looked over the menu and placed her order of chickpea-and-kale soup with the dreadlocked server, who was brisk and happy and wore colourful clothing. Soon there was a plate of warm bread in front of her.

"Isn't this a great place?" Cammie asked Phoebe as she took a bite of the bread.

"Yes, it's one of my favourite cafés in town. I love knowing that I can eat as well here as I do at home." They laughed. A few seconds later the waiter placed a steaming bowl of thick soup in front of Cammie. She dipped a piece of bread into the soup and took a bite. "Delicious!" she announced.

Cammie asked Phoebe, "Would you do me a favour and cut a little bit of the cilantro and parsley into my soup? It's awkward with Bella nursing."

"A pleasure," Phoebe said, trimming the plants as she spoke. There was a small pair of scissors on each table for that purpose.

Phoebe had worked on the interior of this café with Maude, its owner, and knew that Maude would be pleased that Cammie felt comfortable nursing here. Maude was a force in the community who supported social and environmental progress in any way she could. The interior of the Love Bite was a model of eco-friendly paint, flooring and fabrics; the ingredients she used were all vegan, organic, non-GMO and locally sourced whenever possible. All leftover food was donated to the local food bank. There was virtually no staff turnover, since everyone was paid well, had excellent benefits and enjoyed being part of a happy, collaborative team.

Just then Lydia leaned over and whispered in Cammie's ear. Cammie raised her eyebrows, and her face broke into a smile. She leaned over to Phoebe and whispered, "Leroy just got the hat that was being passed around. We made over $120!"

"Hey, that's great!" Phoebe said. "You're a hit!"

Ross said, "That's more than what my band makes in a night!" The whole table laughed.

Dagmar introduced Lydia to Sophie. "You sure can dance!" Sophie said.

Lydia giggled. "Dancing's always been a fun part of my relationship with Leroy, so it's a chance for us to cut loose and enjoy ourselves."

"The fun comes through loud and clear!" Sophie replied. "There's such a great flow to your performance, and your dancing adds so much."

"I'm glad you enjoyed it! What about you? How do you spend your time?" Lydia asked Sophie.

"I make my living as a home-care worker and have a pretty quiet life. I like gardening, reading, hiking, eating good food, spending time with the grandkids … Life seems to get quieter as we age, at least for me."

"That's very worthwhile work you do, helping people to stay in their homes," Lydia said.

"I find it meaningful, even though it has some pretty stressful moments. I wish we had more time for the people we care for." Sophie heaved a sigh.

Lydia put her hand on Sophie's arm. "Thanks for what you do. Everyone who has parents and grandparents who need care in their homes is grateful. You make a big difference in people's lives."

Sophie smiled at Lydia and said, "Thanks."

CHAPTER 19

Up the Hill

"Hey, Dad, do you want to go and have some lunch?" Jared asked, tapping his fingers impatiently.

Sophie was writing her notes after finishing her visit with Lou, a client whose dementia was becoming steadily worse. Lou's son, Jared, had just put out a cigarette in an ashtray outside and was about to take his father out for lunch. They were going to Nimby's, Lou's favourite spot when he was able to remember.

Jared had just finished cleaning out the pool in the backyard—a little late in the year, but at least it was done. He and his siblings took turns staying with their father for a few weeks at a time. Although Lou's home was a mansion, he only ever used a few rooms on the main floor. His children used the second floor when they stayed with him.

When he'd been younger, Lou had ruled the house with an iron fist, and his children had borne the brunt of his tyranny. All were alcoholics, had stress-related disorders of one kind or another and were in the midst of various legal battles: ex-spouses and business partners for the most part. They were a tightly knit family in their own dysfunctional way.

Jared lived in Edmonton, Alberta, across the Rocky Mountains from Silverdale. He'd settled there when he was in his twenties, at that time wanting a large mountain range at the least between him and his family. Now in his fifties, he owned a house in Edmonton and ran a jewellery shop with two business partners. He liked working in the shop, since it attracted people when they were happy, getting jewellery for themselves or others. He wished his business partners could be as happy as their clientele.

Sophie said goodbye to Lou and Jared with a smile. Jared returned her smile nervously and walked with her toward the front door. Just then his girlfriend, Maya, came down the stairs, and he asked her if she wanted to go to lunch.

"Nimby's with your dad? I guess I'll come along," Maya sighed. She noticed Sophie, and the two exchanged pleasantries.

As Sophie headed out, she told Maya, "Nice to see you. Maybe see you next time." Maya didn't answer.

A moment later, Jared answered a knock on the door to find a man with red, curly hair in a plaid shirt who introduced himself as Tam. The man said, "I noticed that you have some apple trees in the backyard that need to be picked. I'd like to offer to pick them, give some to you, some to the food bank and keep some for myself."

Jared looked him over. He seemed honest enough, but who could tell? The arrangement made sense, and it would give him one less thing to do.

"Okay," he said tentatively. "I have a stepladder around the side. You're welcome to use it." He hesitated for a moment. "We're just on our way out, but you can pick them while we're gone if you like." Jared gave him a nervous smile. He hoped this wouldn't backfire somehow.

"Okay, I'll get right at it. Thanks for the use of your ladder!"

Nimby's had a salad bar and a standard family menu. The few customers were a mixture of seniors alone or in pairs, seniors with younger family members and men in business suits sitting by themselves. One of the servers approached their table and asked if they'd like to start with coffee.

"Do you have any chamomile tea?" asked Maya.

"Yes, I can get you a cup," the server said smiling. "Coffee for the rest of you?"

Jared and Lou nodded.

The meal felt strained to Jared. Lou had his usual grilled cheese, and Jared had a bowl of soup. Maya quietly sipped her tea. Jared paid and left the server a substantial tip, then guided his dad out of the restaurant.

When they returned, Jared helped his dad settle down for his nap that would last until suppertime. Then he wandered into the backyard, where he saw Tam coming down the ladder to three bags of apples lined up in a row.

"Hello," Tam greeted him. "Here's your bag of apples. Thanks again for letting me pick them."

"You're welcome," Jared said, lighting a cigarette. "It's really good of you to help out this way." He was still feeling distrustful, still wondering if he should have let this stranger into his yard.

"It's a pleasure," Tam smiled. "Would you like me to put the ladder back?"

"Sure, just over there in the shed. It hangs on the wall." Jared took a puff of his cigarette and indicated some large hooks protruding from the wall.

Tam hung up the ladder.

33

"You must be cold after all that picking. Would you like a cup of coffee or something?" Jared offered.

"A cup of tea might be nice," Tam said.

"Sure, I can get you a cup of tea. My girlfriend just bought a new blend from the health-food store." Jared rolled his eyes as he remembered some of the things she'd bought. He thought of her a little disdainfully as his granola princess and knew other members of his family saw her in the same way or worse.

"Sounds like just what I need!" Tam said.

CHAPTER 20

Broke-Down Palace

J ared put out his cigarette, and he and Tam walked through the back door into the kitchen where Maya was cooking quinoa and chopping up fresh vegetables.

"Maya, this is Tam. He just picked the apples from the tree in the backyard," said Jared.

Maya gave him a smile. "Hi!" she said. "Pleased to meet you. Are you hungry by any chance? I've just made a veggie stir-fry."

"Sure, I could use some lunch. It smells great!" Tam said.

"Maya, you could have had lunch at Nimby's, but you just had tea," Jared said mockingly.

"That stuff's not food. It's full of GMOs. I wouldn't touch it with a 10-foot pole!" Maya exclaimed. "Do you want to eat some real food too?" she asked Jared.

"I guess I'll have a little bit," he said. His stomach felt kind of queasy. He put out three place mats and took some fine china out of the cupboard and sterling silver out of a drawer and set the table. All were quite worn.

"Just bring your plates up and help yourselves," said Maya. "There's plenty." Then she opened the oven and took out some bread she'd been warming up. "Freshly made this morning, and here's some pesto you can spread on it."

"I really appreciate the trouble you've gone to. Thanks for this unexpected meal!" Tam said.

"I bet you're someone who eats healthy food too!" she said conspiratorially.

"Yes, I do, as a matter of fact. The way I see it, it's an investment in our health and the health of our planet. Besides," Tam chuckled, "it just plain tastes good."

Jared looked at them, feeling outnumbered.

"Is this your house?" Tam asked Jared.

The house contained a lot of expensive paintings and ornaments, but the wallpaper looked as if it was at least 30 years old. Everything looked faded.

"No, it's my dad's," Jared said. "He has dementia, and my brother and sisters and I take turns staying with him. He's been deteriorating, but the home-care workers come by daily, give him his meds and keep us posted on his condition."

"That's good of you and the rest of your family to care for him," Tam said.

"It's hard," Jared confessed. "None of us live in town, and we all have our own lives, so we spend a lot of time scheduling and planning. We've been doing this for the past two years."

"Wow!" said Tam. "And you've managed to maintain your relationships with each other under all that strain?"

Jared and Maya gave each other a meaningful look. "Well, for the most part," Jared laughed. "We've all felt the strain; that's for sure."

"You know how it is with some families," said Maya, barely concealing her antipathy.

Jared laughed nervously.

"Anyway, I should get going and deliver these apples," Tam said, finishing up his meal. "Maya, thanks so much! That's just what I needed. Nice to meet you both! I'll see you around the neighbourhood, I'm sure."

"Nice to meet you too," Jared said. "Thanks again for picking those apples."

"My pleasure," Tam replied.

"So glad you enjoyed the meal." Maya smiled. "It's nice to have an ally in the food department!"

CHAPTER 21

News From Vancouver

Tam ambled toward home, intending to drop off one of the bags of apples before dropping off the other at the food bank.

There was snow on the ground now. In order to conceal footprints going to the house, he'd rigged up a fence post that could be drawn down like a drawbridge over a small bush in the empty lot. That way their footprints blended in with those of others who cut through the lot along this path, and never led to the house. The bush cushioned the post and hid the rope.

He left the bag of apples for the food bank just inside the door so he could grab it on his way back out. He ran up the stairs and took their apples to the kitchen, where he found Cammie. She had tears in her eyes.

"Hey, what's up?" he asked her, brushing away a tear.

"Leroy's mother passed away," she said and gave him a hug. He held her and shared her sadness. Although they'd known it was coming, it was still hard to hear. They'd both met her and had enjoyed her good humour and generous nature.

After a moment, he asked, "Does Lydia know?"

"She's on her way there now, so she can be with Leroy."

"Is Bella napping?" Tam asked.

"Yup, I just put her down."

"I could use a nap myself," said Tam, realizing he was tired after picking apples in the cold. "I think I'll lie down too. Feel like joining me?"

"Sure, a nap would do me good." Cammie smiled.

They climbed into bed, careful not to wake Bella. Making love suddenly felt like what they needed to do, and they tenderly shared that physical intimacy and release before falling into a deep sleep.

CHAPTER 22

The Green Team

Dagmar and Ross were at a daylong Green Team meeting. Large banners were displayed outside the building and along the inside walls: "Our children's children's children are counting on us" and "Stop the pipelines" and "There's no planet B."

The team had been through a lot of growing pains over the years. It had survived different leadership and personality issues but not without cost. Despite these challenges, they had accomplished some important community initiatives. Among their achievements were the creation of outdoor summer farmers' markets, a radio program and newspaper column that raised awareness of environmental issues and the establishment of a community garden. During the past few meetings there had been a lot of breakout groups, questionnaires and trust-building exercises.

Then there were the pipelines. A number of Aboriginal groups had filed lawsuits as soon as they'd heard the news since most had not signed treaties with the government and there were major legal issues around putting pipelines through unceded First Nations territories.

Some people at the meeting wanted to find alternatives to being end users of oil, natural gas, coal or any other fuel that was going to cause environmental degradation. How could they collectively make their homes environmentally benign in a way that was affordable and duplicable? They wanted to be able to share the solutions they found with other communities. Being end users of dirty technology was becoming hard to ignore.

A breakout group discussed starting a sister-city program with a similarly sized city in China, which is where the oil from the planned pipelines was destined. If their town and a similar town in China could support each other in utilizing alternative energy, they would decrease the demand for the dirty stuff and reduce greenhouse gas emissions. In the process, they would build relationships and share solutions.

The local food co-op provided lunch. Organic and locally grown foods were laid out on buffet tables, and all participants helped themselves. The array was amazing: everything from baked goods to fresh greens to potato and yam dishes to a variety of soups. There were large pots of tea made from locally grown herbs.

Besides the regular environmental crowd there were a lot of ragged-looking people. News of events with free, high-quality food spread quickly through the network of street people.

Dagmar and Ross stepped outside where big snowflakes were swirling down. The effect of the falling snow was hypnotic.

"I love the idea of a sister city in China," said Dagmar.

"First things first," Ross retorted. "We've got pipelines to stop. No sense diluting the issue. If we spread ourselves too thin, nothing will get accomplished."

"We can't just say no to oil without offering an alternative. How can we complain about it when we use it?"

"That oil is for export to China," said Ross. "It has nothing to do with us."

"You don't think it's hypocritical to condemn the pipelines when oil is used widely in B.C.? Even by environmentalists?"

"Just because we're environmentalists doesn't mean we're rich," Ross said. "It costs a lot of money to go green."

"Then maybe we should figure out how to make it affordable for everyone."

They walked back into the building ready for the afternoon's activities. Dagmar and Ross's conversation reflected the two schools of thought that dominated the meeting. By the end of it, the group decided that the immediate short-term goal would be to work with other groups to stop the pipelines and that in the long term they would investigate ways of getting off dirty fuels, including a sister-city initiative with China.

CHAPTER 23

Musings

As Ross and Dagmar crunched through the snow on their way back from the Green Team meeting, they discussed what had happened. Both felt that their views had been affirmed: the pipeline issue was urgent, but finding ways to help people switch to non-polluting energy sources for their homes and transportation was also important.

Something blue and sparkling against the white ground caught Dagmar's eye. She walked over to it and found a beautiful marble that looked like the planet earth. Its blue of the oceans was transparent and the green of the continents more opaque.

"Look what I found!" Dagmar exclaimed. "Isn't it gorgeous?" She handed the marble to Ross, who examined it.

"What a find!" he said. "I've never seen a marble like that before." He gave it back to her, and she held it in her hand.

"How fitting—right after our Green Team meeting," laughed Dagmar. "Puts things into perspective, doesn't it? Our one precious jewel of a home. Will enough of us make changes in time to preserve it for future generations?" Her voice trailed off.

"Getting through all the politics, personalities, priorities—it's such a maze, isn't it?" Ross mused. "How do we get through it all and do what we need to do?"

"If we could only put things into perspective! The choices we make now—large and small—will have a profound effect on everyone in the future. Whether life will continue on this beautiful little marble depends on us," Dagmar said solemnly, holding up her newly found treasure.

"Dagmar, you and I are literally living on the edge, but so is everyone alive today in some way or other. Our kids and theirs are counting on all of us to do the right thing. If we're alive, we have a responsibility to turn things around."

"It's such an uphill battle, isn't it? I mean, what can we do that's really effective? Honestly, I've been trying to figure that out my entire adult life. Nothing ever feels like it's enough."

"I guess we just have to keep plugging away and keep our eyes open for opportunities," Ross sighed.

"There are so many of us doing what we can, but we're not aware of each other," Dagmar said. "The fact that there are people all over the world working on the same things brings me comfort sometimes." She looked at her marble again and said decisively, "I'm going to put this on the altar."

"Hey, do you feel like walking the labyrinth?" Ross asked on a whim. "We're about a block away, and I could stand to clear my head."

"Great idea!"

CHAPTER 24

For the Altar

S omeone had carefully swept away the snow from the stones of the labyrinth. Silently, Ross and Dagmar walked to the centre, Ross first, then Dagmar. They each clapped their hands three times and bowed to the four directions when they got to the centre before walking back.

As they strolled toward their home, a perfect white feather floated gently down on a soft breeze. Ross reached out, and it landed in the palm of his hand. All the membranes were intact, and there was a wisp of down at the bottom. He showed it to Dagmar.

"It's so delicate," she said, "so bright, clean and perfect."

"I think we need to put our newly found treasures on the altar and meditate when we get home," Ross said.

"We've been given the signs; that's for sure." Dagmar laughed.

In the meditation room, there was a spot on the front, left-hand side of the altar that was just right for Dagmar's marble. She placed it there. Ross put his feather just behind it, so the feather appeared to enclose and protect it. As they sat in their usual spots, Dagmar wrapped in the shawl and seated on a pillow and Ross next to her, they contemplated their offerings.

Dagmar thought about what this small sphere she'd found represented. Humanity shared this jewel in space, and it was their one and only home, the place that housed the intricate, exquisite glory of nature and everything that humans had evolved from. Its future was in the hands of the people living now: she and everyone else wielded the power to preserve this planet, whose value was beyond comprehension. They could make the changes that would allow future generations to enjoy this earth, or they could continue on in a way that would destroy it.

She pictured her little marble floating in space—this miraculous, life-giving home of everyone and everything she knew. She marvelled at its endless dance with the sun and moon bringing night and day, the seasons and the tides. She took a breath and chose her words carefully as she said her silent prayer. She realized that between the ancestors that came before her and future generations, her breath put her in a special place of power. She acknowledged her sacred duty to both. *May we see the importance of our actions. May we honour our glorious home. May we see the miracles that make up our lives and commit to their continuation. May we heal enough to protect our earth, each other and all of life.*

Ross breathed deeply and contemplated his feather and the air that had enabled its flight—pure, white and delicate. He meditated, *May my thoughts mirror this state; may I see things in a pure, clean light. May I protect the earth, just as my feather appears to on the altar. May I imagine, create and enable things from this sacred place, and may I be attuned to this place. May I be soft and kind while doing whatever it takes to protect this beautiful planet. May we all live in peace and harmony while finding new ways of being together, ways that nurture all of life, honour the gifts of nature and help us to co-exist happily and respectfully.*

He brought his attention to the room he was sitting in. What could he do right here, right now, to be in alignment with the message his beautiful white muse had brought him? What could he do to live his life in a way that was congruent with this inspired vision? He thought about Dagmar and the abandoned house and how his life had been changing. *May it change in a good way, in a way that will help me see more clearly and be a better person.*

Ross and Dagmar sat in contemplation for about 20 minutes. As if on cue, they opened their eyes at the same time. Dagmar stood up and found a small bell in the front and centre of the altar. She picked it up and rang it. Its sound was pure and true. They gazed into each other's eyes and smiled warmly.

CHAPTER 25

Love Beyond the Grave

Leroy and Lydia stayed at the home Leroy's mother, Amelda, had shared with her partner, Dan. They spent time with friends and relatives, helping out and giving and receiving emotional support.

Dan was a lost soul without Mel, as she was called, and was having a hard time just being in his own skin. Lydia and Leroy made sure he ate properly and did their best to console him. Their presence seemed to help. Some things were beyond words to express, and grief surely was one of them.

Mel was buried the day after she died. In the spring a headstone would be set, and a cherry tree would be planted. A family friend had given a small, intimate service. All of it passed in the blink of an eye for Dan, Leroy and Lydia.

When it had become evident that she wasn't going to win her battle with cancer, Mel had made all the arrangements for her burial and had chosen to have a green burial. It involved no embalming and an inexpensive, non-polluting coffin. It had taken quite a bit of looking to find a funeral home that wasn't owned by a large corporation that was focused on upselling, but with the help of friends she'd found what she'd needed.

She'd also arranged to have a grief counsellor for her son and her partner. Her will was straightforward, and she asked that those she left behind support each other in every way they could. Her love for them shone through, even after her death.

Mel had touched the lives of many. It struck Leroy that when all was said and done, life was really about caring relationships. The time people had together was finite, and then they were gone. Relationships and the contributions people made gave life meaning.

Leroy ached for his mother and knew how much it would mean to her to have him and Dan care for each other. She'd been a kind, supportive mother and partner. She'd listened well, and others had known they could count on her. She left a big hole in everyone's life, and they'd have to try to weave around that hole for one another.

"Dan," said Leroy, "we're torn between leaving to give you space and staying to give you emotional support." Leroy put his hand on Dan's shoulder. "Would you like us to stay awhile longer?"

Dan closed his eyes and put his hand over Leroy's. "I'm not ready to be all alone yet. If it wouldn't put you and Lydia out, I'd really appreciate it if you'd keep me company for a week or two."

Leroy and Lydia decided to stay with Dan as long as he needed them. A good friend of Dan's was planning to visit him just after Christmas, and they felt that would do him good.

CHAPTER 26

Diminished Voices

The next Sunday morning, there were just five from the house at the Love Bite, since Leroy and Lydia were staying with Dan. The small group sang, but their songs all came out sounding sad. A few minutes into the first set, Cammie explained to the patrons of the restaurant that Leroy had just lost his mother, and her explanation made the sadness of their music more meaningful. Everyone felt the sacredness of their own personal losses. Everyone who had ever loved had known loss in some form or another. It was the price people paid for having open hearts: sometimes they were broken. There was a sense of communion and solemnity with the quiet of the music.

The group was surprised to have brought in more money than usual when the hat was passed around. Perhaps it was because their sadness had given the crowd permission to feel emotions that were often suppressed.

Tam noticed that Jared and Maya were sitting at a table near the back. Tam leaned over to Dagmar and said, "See that couple at the far table? From their body language, what would you say is going on?"

"Hmm. It looks like she's backing away, disinterested. And it looks like he's trying to please her," she said.

"That's what it looks like to me too. I have a feeling that being here is a concession to her," said Tam.

Over lunch, Ross asked Cammie and Tam if they'd met Leroy's mother. They both nodded.

Cammie said, "Just a couple of times, but she was wonderful: a great listener, years ahead of her time. She was a pioneer in the environmental movement and instilled a strong sense of responsibility for the environment and for community in Leroy. I think she influenced a lot of his friends too."

"And she was light-hearted and fun at the same time," Tam said. "She loved a good joke and always encouraged Leroy's creative endeavours."

"Did she know how he's been living?" asked Dagmar. "You know, squatting?"

"She did," Tam replied. "And she had the wisdom to know that he's doing well, even though it's a desperate situation in many ways. She listened to his explanation and believed her eyes and ears. She could see that he was happy and healthy, and that was her main concern."

"Sounds like she was a truly amazing woman," said Dagmar. "A lot of parents wouldn't be that open-minded. Even some of our children wouldn't be that open-minded. I feel very lucky to have a son who sees things the same way." Dagmar paused and then asked, "How do your parents feel about the way you live?"

Tam laughed. "My parents aren't exactly in a position to judge—they're too busy managing their own disastrous lives. They're so self-absorbed that the way I live is really a non-issue to them." Cammie reached over and put her hand on his knee. Tam put his hand on Cammie's and said, "I remind myself that they're doing the best they can with what they've got. They both endured incredible hardships in their childhoods, and it damaged them deeply. I know that by comparison I had a much easier time than they did. I didn't have to endure extreme poverty, violence or the same degree of humiliation."

Dagmar looked closely at Tam, really taking him in for the first time. Under those curly, red locks was a face mature beyond its physical age. He had the dignity common to ordinary folk. Compassionate and well intended, she realized he'd always demonstrated a down-to-earth, respectful and inclusive moral code. She was happy that he had the stability and caring that Cammie and Bella provided.

Dagmar looked over at Ross, who was also looking deeply at Tam. What was the expression on his face? Smugness? Contempt?

Cammie spoke up. "My parents had a mixed reaction. On the one hand, they can see that Bella is happy and healthy, and they value their relationship with us as a family. So they try hard to accept our unusual lifestyle, but I can tell that they don't quite understand why we live the way we live." She paused. "They're back east and paid for us to fly out when Bella was born. They wanted us to stay with them, but we chose to stay here. This is our home, and it's where we want to live and raise Bella. And they understand why we love it here. I like to think our situation's only temporary. Hopefully we'll have a place to live one day where we won't have to hide. For now, we have a roof over our head, food in our bellies and good people to share our lives with."

CHAPTER 27

Here but Not Here

I t was odd for Leroy to be in a room that his mother had put so much love into now that she'd passed on. She still embraced them in so many ways. This room was a prime example. Mel had always loved rummaging through second-hand stores, finding old furniture and fixing it up. The rooms she'd decorated were unique, whimsical and put together with comfort in mind. This bedroom was cozy and dark. The bed was a sturdy antique, the bamboo sheets were soft and silky and the richly coloured paisley comforter was warm and heavy. The colours in the room were shades of maroon, burgundy and dark brown with touches of pale blue and light golden yellow here and there. Amelda would have put it all together light-heartedly—almost effortlessly— giving it most of her attention for a week or two, before moving on to whatever new project inspired her.

In her last days, she'd urged Leroy to enjoy himself while he was in the city—get in touch with friends, do some shopping, eat at some nice restaurants. She'd given him some money and told him to have fun. She'd realized she wouldn't be around much longer and wanted to help him get through what she'd known would be a difficult time for him. They'd been very close, and she'd known how much he would miss her.

Leroy had been struggling with his grief, helping with the arrangements for her memorial and doing what he could to help Dan, while trying to take his mother's advice and enjoy the city.

As Leroy woke up, pale sunlight peaked between the heavy draperies. His mother's death still wasn't real to him, and it took him a few seconds to remember. He'd just dreamt about her. He felt Lydia snuggling against him in the warm, comfortable bed. He pulled her close and kissed her forehead.

"Good morning," she said sleepily. "How'd you sleep, hun?"

"Well and deeply," Leroy said. "I just dreamt about Mom. She was asking me what Simon and Lester are up to these days. How'd you sleep, sweetie?"

"Really well," Lydia said. "Your mom sure knows—knew—how to put together a restful bedroom. Have you seen Simon and Lester lately?"

"Not since I got to Vancouver. Simon left a message on Mom's answering machine, but I haven't gotten back to him yet."

"Sounds like your mom wants you to get in touch with them. Maybe you should give them a call after breakfast."

CHAPTER 28

Old Friends

Leroy called Lester and Simon and set up a dinner for the three of them and Lydia that evening. Then after a hardy breakfast and some coffee with Dan, Leroy and Lydia decided to take Amelda's advice and have a fun day in the city. They'd be out of Dan's way while he had a friend over who could help him get through the legal obligations arising from Mel's death.

Vancouver was overcast, but it wasn't raining. Leroy and Lydia spent the morning looking around some second-hand shops and picked up a few clothing items for themselves and some small gifts for their housemates, before having lunch at a Middle Eastern restaurant. In the afternoon they checked out an art gallery, brought some flowers to Amelda's grave and spent some time there. Later they sat on a park bench overlooking the ocean listening to the waves. On their way to Simon and Lester's they stopped at a liquor store and picked up a bottle of wine.

They were greeted at the door by two smiling men and the smell of onions cooking and something sweet and dessert-y. After hugs all around, they walked into the kitchen and sat at the big table with turquoise Arborite and rounded chrome edging. The house was decorated with furnishings from the 1940s that Simon and Lester had gotten second-hand. The effect of the many rounded corners and the creamy white walls with rich yellow accents was welcoming, cheerful and homey.

Leroy pulled out the bottle of wine. "The local wines are getting better all the time, aren't they?" Lester grinned. "A perfect way to support the local economy! I love getting local, organic wine that even tastes good," he laughed as he got out four wineglasses. The quality of the local wines had improved greatly over the years.

"Leroy, I'm so sorry about your mom," Lester said earnestly. "She was wonderful, and we'll miss her terribly." Lester put his hand on Leroy's arm. "I'm so glad to have known her. Is there a date set for the memorial?"

"Yeah, the day after tomorrow," Leroy said sadly. "It still feels so unreal, but I've been going through the motions and getting things arranged."

Lester sighed. Sometimes there just weren't words to express the depth of one's feelings.

Simon opened the bottle of wine and poured some into each of their glasses. "A toast to Amelda! Thanks, Mel, for all the joy you brought into this world."

They clinked their glasses and took sips, savouring the sentiment and the taste of the wine.

CHAPTER 29
Wined and Dined

Lester brought out a salad made with greens from a local greenhouse and put some on each of their plates. He then brought out a simple dressing he'd made from peanut butter, tamari, minced garlic, hot sauce and water.

Leroy realized how long it had been since he'd had a leisurely dinner with old friends. It was like falling into welcoming arms.

"The latest version of your cartoon had everyone in the house in stitches," Leroy said between mouthfuls of salad. Lester and Simon created an online cartoon starring a superhero who peacefully solved problems, commiserated with others and convened with the elements, among other things.

"I don't think Dagmar and Ross watched it. Wasn't it their first morning with us?" Lydia asked.

"Oh? You have some new people staying with you?" asked Simon.

"Yeah," said Lydia, "a couple of middle-aged people. They're working out pretty well. Dagmar is taking to this way of life like a fish to water, but

Ross? I don't know. It seems like quite an adjustment for him. They're both very helpful and good-natured, though, and fit right in."

"And we're all singing together with Ross playing guitar. We even have a paying gig at the Love Bite on Sunday mornings! It's a lot of fun and a bit of money too," Leroy said. "This salad and dressing are great, by the way." Lydia nodded in agreement with her mouth full.

"That's great about the gig at the Love Bite!" said Simon. He then added, "I love getting fresh greens from the greenhouse, and I've been on this peanut-butter-dressing kick lately. I'm glad our reluctant hero's latest episode had you all laughing. We appreciate the feedback."

"Ready for the main course?" asked Lester. "We have sweet potatoes, refried beans and steamed veggies." He put platters of food with large serving spoons on the table. Everyone helped themselves as Simon topped up the wineglasses.

Lester and Simon were both techies who created and hosted websites among other things. Their peaceful-superhero cartoon was their first, and they were having a great time with it. Whenever they created a new episode, they sent it to a few of their friends online.

Leroy asked, "Will you have another episode coming out soon?"

"We should have something up in a few weeks," Lester said. "Oh, and make sure you leave room for dessert. I have a chocolate-banana-coconut-cream pie, and I promise you're gonna want some!"

"You guys, I'm in heaven!" Lydia leaned back in her chair contentedly. "It's so great spending time with you again. And your cooking is amazing!"

Leroy said, "It's great to be able to just relax and have an evening of wining and dining and catching up. It's been so stressful lately, and I really appreciate this."

"It's our pleasure," said Lester. "Honestly, it's hard to know how to be there for you right now, so getting to feed you and relieve some of the stress feels great for us too. Would you like to spend the night? You can stay in the spare bedroom. It'll save you the walk home."

Leroy and Lydia looked at each other. Leroy finally said, "I think I'd rather go back and see how Dan's doing. I've got so much pent-up energy the walk will do me good."

"I agree," Lydia said. "Dan's having a pretty tough time right now."

Soon they were digging into pie, drinking tea and feeling full and cared for. After fond goodbyes, Lydia and Leroy both enjoyed the cool night air on their walk back.

CHAPTER 30

The Food Bank

A few days after he'd picked the apples, Tam brought a bag to the local food bank.

"Hey, Tam. How are you doing?" Mary asked. Her grey hair was in a tight bun, and her sleeves were rolled up as she washed vegetables in the sink. "What have you got there?"

"Some winter apples," he said as he took off his boots, which he left beside the door. "I'm pretty good. How 'bout you?"

"Can't complain," Mary said. "More hungry people than ever—trying to stretch the food as far as we can. Thanks for those apples. Every bit helps. We've got a few businesses collecting on our behalf, so that's making a difference. And our website lets people know what we need here, so that's helping too. And the greens from the greenhouse are really appreciated. It all adds up." She put her right hand on her lower back, applying pressure to a spot that was obviously painful.

Tam shook his head. "It shouldn't be like this. Mary, thanks for all you do. Are you getting much help these days?"

"Oh, yeah," she said. Tam knew she was the one the food bank counted on to get things done, but others helped out too.

Tam peeked into a large adjoining room where people were seated at tables, chairs and sofas, chatting and playing cards—the regular crowd but with a few new faces. There was a small group of women talking and laughing. Tam waved at them, and they waved back. In the corner was a young, pale woman with stringy, blonde hair and worn-out clothing talking with a middle-aged man. Tam didn't get a good feeling about him but couldn't say why. Everything about him was nondescript, as if he just wanted to blend in and not be noticed.

Tam closed the door and stepped back into the kitchen. "Anyway, Mary, see you again," he said, putting his boots back on.

"Thanks, Tam," Mary said as she wiped her hands on her apron and started chopping onions. "Good to see you."

CHAPTER 31

Lillian

R oss and Dagmar were walking home from a Green Team meeting that had focused on how they could most effectively collaborate with other environmental groups to stop the proposed pipelines. They walked along silently for a while and then started talking about Christmas. They each had a bit of money from their music gig and were going to get their children gifts, although nothing lavish.

Dagmar had told her son, Doug, about her new living situation, and she knew he'd be grateful for whatever he received from her. They had a loving, trusting relationship, and although her new situation was unusual, she was able to reassure him that she was doing all right and that her new situation was actually quite beneficial in some ways, despite the stigma associated with squatting.

Ross went quiet, then blurted out, "Lillian's going to be here tomorrow, and I still haven't told her about how I'm living ..."

"So what are you going to do?" Dagmar asked.

"I don't know how I'm going to tell her."

"At least she'll get to see for herself and meet everyone," said Dagmar, "but I get that it's going to be hard for you to tell her."

"I'm looking forward to seeing her, but I'm afraid of what she'll think," he said. "I've arranged to borrow my friend Cole's car to pick her up at the airport tomorrow. And she can stay in Leroy and Lydia's room while they're away."

"You'll have time on the drive back from the airport to let her know. I'm sure the right words will come to you and that she'll understand."

CHAPTER 32

A Short Visit

" D ad!" exclaimed Lillian as she ran toward Ross at the airport terminal. She threw her arms around him.

"Hey, honey, great to see you!" he said. They walked over to the luggage carousel and retrieved Lillian's two suitcases.

"Sorry it's such a short visit, but I promised Mom I'd spend time with her over the holidays too. So I'll be off to Vancouver in a couple of days."

"How's your mom these days?" asked Ross.

"Oh, she's fine, same as ever really," said Lillian. Then looking at Ross closely, she said, "Dad, you're looking really good."

"Thanks. I've been eating well and getting lots of exercise."

They walked to Cole's car, and Ross put her luggage in the trunk.

"Is this your car?" asked Lillian.

"No, it's Cole's. I borrowed it," Ross said. "Lillian, I haven't told you everything about my new living situation."

"Oh?"

"Yeah, I'm sharing a house with some very nice people, but the truth is it's a squat," said Ross, feeling relief at finally telling her.

"A squat. Like an abandoned house that you have to sneak in and out of?"

"Yes. It sounds much worse than it is. When Debbie and I parted ways, I didn't have anywhere to go, and these people took me in. Both Dagmar and me, that is. Do you remember her?"

"I think so," said Lillian. "Don't you know her from the Green Team?"

"That's right," said Ross. "We've become good friends. I'm looking forward to you meeting everyone. You'll be staying in Lydia and Leroy's room, since they're away in Vancouver. You'd like them too, I'm sure."

"Dad, that must have been really hard for you to tell me," said Lillian, leaning her head against his shoulder. "Thanks for opening up. I'm sorry you had to hold that for so long."

"It was hard," Ross said. "Thanks for not being disgusted. I've been dreading having to tell you. The thing is, life's actually pretty good. I think you'll see what I mean when you meet everybody."

"Squatting and other creative ways of living are more common than you'd think," said Lillian. "It's taking a lot of ingenuity for people to get by these days. I notice it on campus—people sharing houses, squatting, you name it."

"You're comfortable and doing well at school?" asked Ross.

"Yes, everything's going well."

Ross pulled up in front of Cole's house and unpacked Lillian's suitcases.

"We'll have to walk a couple of blocks to where I live. We enter from an empty lot beside the house." They walked to the house, and Ross pulled down the makeshift drawbridge when the coast was clear.

When they opened the door, the smell of dinner wafted in to greet them. They went upstairs and into the kitchen, where Dagmar was stirring vegetables at the stove.

"Hello, Lillian! How are you?" Dagmar smiled. "I'm so glad you're able to join us for a while."

"Thanks," Lillian replied.

Tam and Cammie, who was carrying Bella, came out of the living room. "Hello, you must be Lillian!" said Tam. He introduced himself and his family. "So nice to meet you!"

Ross could see that Lillian felt welcome. He led her to Leroy and Lydia's room and put her suitcases there.

"Dad, they seem like lovely people," said Lillian. "It's crappy that you have to live in a squat, but I'm really glad these people are in your life."

"I'm so glad you feel that way, honey," said Ross. "I didn't know how you'd react."

"You usually live in nicer houses, but these seem like some of the nicest people you've lived with."

Ross and Lillian spent their two days together eating well, walking around town and exchanging small gifts. When Ross drove his daughter to the airport, he felt lighter—his secret revealed, his heart unburdened.

"Daddy, thanks for a really great visit. I feel so much closer to you than before I came," she said. She kissed him on the cheek and went to catch her flight.

CHAPTER 33

'Tis the Season

Lydia and Leroy got back between Christmas and New Year's, since they stayed with Dan over Christmas. It was hard without Mel, and they kept it low-key.

They had done their best to be there for him, preparing his favourite foods and listening to his tales of life with Mel. And the grief counsellor, an older man named Jerry with a short beard and kind eyes, helped them all.

Dan's friend Jim had arrived on Boxing Day, so Lydia and Leroy left a couple of days later. They could see that Jim's presence was doing Dan a lot of good. Jim was a jovial yet sensitive man, and Dan appreciated both traits, especially at this time. Jim was going to be there on business for a few months so would be staying with Dan. He was a film director working on a movie set in Vancouver. Leroy and Lydia both felt that Dan would be okay between Jim's friendship and his grief counsellor's occasional visits.

That evening, their ride share dropped them off at a corner near the abandoned house, and Lydia and Leroy trudged through the snow in the darkness toward it, weighed down with heavy backpacks and a couple of bags.

As Lydia walked over the jury-rigged drawbridge and opened the door to their home, she had mixed feelings. After the simple comforts of living the way many still did, returning to the drudgery, secrecy and darkness of this place was difficult. On the other hand, it was a return to her everyday life and the people in it, where she belonged and felt understood.

They were greeted with gifts of food, warm socks and things that only people who lived with them would know they appreciated. For Lydia it was a top in her favourite shade of indigo. For Leroy it was a bowler hat.

"Solstice and Christmas weren't the same without you," said Cammie. "Welcome home!" She walked over to Leroy and gave him a hug. "Leroy, I'm so sorry about your mom." She then turned and hugged Lydia.

"Me too," said Tam, hugging Leroy then Lydia. Dagmar and Ross welcomed them back, expressing their condolences and hugging them both.

"Thanks," Leroy said, hanging his head. "It still doesn't seem real."

"Thanks for the great welcome home," said Lydia. "Oh, and Simon and Lester say hi."

"How are they doing?" Cammie asked. Looking at Dagmar and Ross, she explained, "They're friends of ours in Vancouver."

"Still having a great time with their cartoon," Lydia answered. "Another one should be out in the next couple of weeks. They had us over for dinner and were in fine form."

"What's new here?" Leroy asked.

"Not much," Tam said. "We've still been singing at the Love Bite on Sunday mornings, and we've all missed you."

"And my daughter, Lillian, stayed in your room for a few days," Ross said. "Thanks after the fact."

"Good timing! I'm glad that worked out for your daughter," said Leroy.

Lydia looked at Bella, who was sitting on a cushion on the floor playing with some spoons. "Amazing how quickly you're growing! We've only been gone a couple of weeks, and you're looking so grown up. Hi, Bella!" Cammie picked Bella up and handed her to Lydia. Lydia bounced her for a while and then handed her to Leroy.

"We've got a few things for you too," Leroy said. He brought out some chocolate-banana-coconut-cream tarts that Simon and Lester had sent along. They gave each of their friends some simple treasures they'd found at second-hand stores—sweaters, percussion instruments, baby booties, this and that. "A little taste of the city for you," Leroy said. "We missed winter solstice and Christmas, but we're still in time to ring in the New Year with you. The way things are happening in the world, who knows what it'll bring."

He meant to sound inspiring, but his words came out sounding ominous.

CHAPTER 34

January

C old, snow and darkness enveloped them in a kind of dogged drudgery that was their lives in the abandoned house. Root vegetables, grains, spongy winter apples and what they'd canned were their staple foods, along with greens from the greenhouse and the sunflower and alfalfa sprouts they'd grown.

Cammie made sure she always had soup on the stove, this comfort food being especially good for those who were grieving as Leroy obviously was. These days he looked diminished: his eyes looked dead, and his movements seemed mechanical.

January was a reality check for them and drove home the limitations of their living situation. Because they had to keep the home a secret, they couldn't have anyone over. Revealing the fact that one lived in a squat was a boundary that couldn't be crossed except with close friends and family. The cold, lack of light and the stigma of living in a squat were getting them down.

Leroy was on autopilot, still grieving the death of his mother, and Lydia felt emotionally exhausted. Leroy was emotionally absent, caught up in his own pain, and the contrast between their living situation and her recent taste of normal life in Vancouver weighed her down.

One night Ross stumbled into the bedroom, waking Dagmar up. "Bloody hell!" he exclaimed.

"What's going on?" asked Dagmar, still not quite awake.

"Oh, I just tripped on my shoe," said Ross in an irritated voice. He took off his clothes and crawled into bed.

"You woke me up, and you reek of beer." Dagmar got out of bed. "I'm going to sleep in the meditation room."

"Well, aren't you the princess," said Ross sarcastically.

"Not really. I just want to get some sleep without the smell of beer," she said, leaving the room.

The next morning, when Dagmar came in to get her clothes, Ross apologized.

"Okay, apology accepted," she said, "but next time you come home drunk, would you mind sleeping on the chesterfield or in the meditation room or something? I didn't appreciate being woken up and having to leave the room."

"Sometimes me and the boys just get carried away," Ross said. "My head hurts."

"Well, what did you expect?"

"A little sympathy perhaps?"

"Come on! You wake me up in the middle of the night and want sympathy? Nice try," said Dagmar as she gathered up her clothes.

Tam and Cammie just plugged away at keeping things going. Of all of the housemates, they seemed the most content to carry on, watch Bella grow and maintain their home.

Would spring ever come? Would this dreariness ever end?

CHAPTER 35

George

G eorge lounged beside the pool sipping a glass of red wine and reading a book about traditional Chinese medicine.

After some world travelling—India, Canada, China, Mexico—it was pleasant to be at his mother's estate in the south of France. He'd been back for a week and was becoming a little bored.

George was a tall, stalky man with thick, dark hair. He looked more like a farm boy than someone from a family of old money. Often, he felt more like a farm boy too. In his early forties, he hadn't decided what he wanted to do, hadn't really done anything of consequence. George felt as if he lived inside a riddle that he needed to solve. Maybe he needed to frame the question, but it felt so elusive. What was missing from his life? It obviously had nothing to do with money and everything to do with meaning. Why was he here? What was his purpose in life?

George was intrigued by ancient ways of viewing the world. Traditional Chinese medicine was one of the oldest healing systems and had been in continual practice for thousands of years. He thought ancient ways of seeing the world might give him a clue as to what was missing from his life.

Claudia, the young woman who was sitting beside him, interrupted his thoughts. "Have you ever thought about buying a sports team? I'm considering buying a football team and would love your advice."

George looked at her blankly and said, "Sorry, but I've never given it any thought," and went back to reading his book.

His mother had invited Claudia over. Sure, he'd love to meet someone. But his mother's thinly veiled attempts to set him up with the nice girls she'd met at the club were annoying. They were nice, certainly, but he couldn't care less about the latest sports team they were buying or something equally uninteresting.

His cellphone rang; it was his friend Rodney, who lived in a little town called Silverdale in Canada. Now that was an inspiring place! Always something happening there.

"Hey, Rodney. How are you?" George said into his phone.

"Pretty good. How and where are you?" Rodney asked.

"Oh, I'm in the south of France, visiting my mom." George sighed.

"I was hoping you might have the travel bug," said Rodney. "I'm going on a bike tour in a few months, and I don't want Beaner to be lonely while I'm away." Beaner was Rodney's cat.

"Are you inviting me to Silverdale?" asked George, feeling excited at the thought.

"Yes," said Rodney. "When you were here last, you talked about how much you loved Silverdale, so here's your excuse to return."

"I'll keep your invitation in mind and get back to you."

"Hey, I'm counting on you! Get back to me soon, okay?"

"Will do," said George. "Thanks for thinking of me."

"Only the best for Beaner!" said Rodney. "Bye for now."

Silverdale. He'd been there two years earlier on one of his trips and had found the place fascinating. Not only did he remember lots of great food and a strong community with all kinds of innovative ideas but beautiful wilderness areas too. Tempting.

CHAPTER 36

The Velveteen Rabbit

"Dagmar," said Ross one night as they curled up in bed, "what's going on with us?"

"Good question. What do you want to be going on with us?"

"I'd like to be closer. We're sleeping together in this bed every night, but you don't seem to want things to get physical. I mean, why not?" Ross blurted out. "Do you find me unattractive? Is there something you don't like about me?"

Dagmar was quiet for a moment and then let out a deep sigh. "Ross, I guess my problem is an issue of trust. You're so secretive, even with your own daughter." She put her hand on his arm. "Honesty and trust are a really big deal to me, and I need that in any relationship, especially in an intimate relationship." Then she added, "Just so you know, I find you attractive, but I have to be honest with you about my reservations."

He lay there silently and then asked, "What do you want me to tell you?"

"I don't know, just whatever's happening in your life, how you feel about it, who you are as a person. The only secret I have is that I'm living in this abandoned house, and my friends and family know that, just not its location. I hardly know anything about you. I don't know what you value or what you want in a relationship."

"Then lets talk about that. What do you want to know exactly?" Ross asked.

"You. I need to know you, see if we have similar values, if we're on the same page. If you find it hard to be open and honest with your daughter, how can I assume you would be with me?"

Ross thought about that and then said, "It's not that I want to hide things from her; it's just that I don't want her to worry. I do it to protect her. And I want her to look up to me, so I try to show her only the better things about myself."

"What do you think that's teaching her about trust and honesty? And authenticity for that matter?"

"I don't know. It's not like I'm lying to her. I'm just selective about what I tell her and leave things out that she might find troubling," he answered, sounding defensive. "Besides, I did tell her about living in a squat."

"You had no other choice," said Dagmar. "You haven't even told me what happened between you and Debbie. I don't know what kinds of issues come up for you in relationships. It's good to at least be aware of these things, so we can try not to repeat them."

He held her closer to him, and she laughed a little awkwardly. "Ross," she said in a quiet but intense voice, "tell me who you are. Tell me what you value deep down, okay?"

"Dagmar, I don't even know right now. I know that what I once believed is changing since I've lived here with you and these people, and I'm not even sure what I believed before. I went along with a lot of things ..." His voice trailed off. "Even with Debbie, I felt out of touch with my deeper values." He lay still for a moment. "I care about environmental issues and the planet I'll be leaving for my daughter. That's why I go to the Green Team meetings." He stopped and adjusted his position. "When I look back on it, life didn't make a lot of sense, and I wasn't really true to myself." He stroked her hair gently. "Sometimes I think I compromise too much and lose a part of myself when I get into a relationship."

"I know what you mean," Dagmar said. "I think I do that sometimes too. Thanks for telling me that much."

"That happens to you too, eh?" Ross said.

"Yeah, I think it happens to a lot of people. Do you think you'd do that if you got involved with me?" she asked. "Would you be able to be true to yourself and true to me too?" She wrapped a lock of his hair around her finger. "I'd need you to be honest with me and faithful to me. For me those things come naturally, and you could trust me to be those things with you. Is that something you'd want too?"

He kissed her forehead. "Dagmar, will you let me try? We're living on the edge. Together. Let's be a team, you and me. Let's be there for each other on this crazy precipice we've found ourselves on."

"Can I help you to open up and be honest with me? I want to know you, and I want you to know me too." Then she said with feeling, "Ross, we need to be able to trust each other. Do you trust me?"

Ross thought about it for a moment. "Yes, I do trust you. You're one of the most trustworthy people I've ever known."

"What about you? Can I trust you?" she asked. "I need to be able to trust someone I'm involved with."

"Dagmar, I have so much love for you. I don't want anyone else," Ross said. He added with a little laugh, "These feelings just kind of snuck up on me. I never would have guessed that I'd feel this way toward you. You're not the usual kind of woman I get mixed up with. Usually the women I go out with are much younger than me, and they're—I don't know—not like you. But you're different in a good way, a way that I've just been discovering lately. Since we've lived here, you've become my anchor, and life seems simpler and better somehow here with you."

"Thanks, Ross. I'm honoured." She then confessed, "I have a lot of love for you too. It's hard for me to admit it and to allow myself to be vulnerable. I guess we've all been hurt before."

"Dagmar, let's make a pact to be true to each other and ourselves. I know we'll change and grow, but we can do it together," Ross said, inspired. "We could do so much to support each other."

"This can be a starting place for us if we want it to be, don't you think?" Dagmar asked. "We can heal and grow together and help to create the kind of life we really want. We go to the Green Team meetings for the same reasons, don't we?"

"Yes, I've always wanted to help our planet, and I know you have too. Maybe we're meant to start over. Here. Together. We both have to make so many changes. Being true to ourselves, each other and to our healing and growth could be so amazing." Ross stroked her hair gently.

"Tell me what you dream of," Dagmar whispered.

"Well," Ross said slowly, heaving a sigh, "these days, I dream of being real. And that's not easy when so much of my life has been focused on selling, presenting an image, you know? Do you know the story of the Velveteen Rabbit?"

"I think I read that story when I was a kid. Isn't that where a stuffed rabbit becomes real because of the love of the child he belongs to?"

"Yes," Ross said. "I feel like the Velveteen Rabbit coming to life because of your love. Being with you, I've realized that's what I want, and now I have to figure out how. Help me, Dagmar, and tell me how I can help you."

"Just be here for me, and be who you are," Dagmar said. "The times when I love you the most are when you're just being you." She paused and then added, "You do it more often than you might think." She smiled at him and kissed him lightly on the cheek.

Looking up through the window, they watched as two ravens flew overhead. They kissed each other tenderly on the lips, then passionately. Their words had conjured up a magic that was still and sensual, and they surrendered to its spell. Through the window above them the stars shimmered in a deep blue sky, full of enchantment and possibilities.

CHAPTER 37

An Offer

The Sunday gig at the Love Bite was always a high point in the week. The household sang together, Leroy and Lydia danced, and the patrons cheered them on.

Tam noticed that Jared had become a regular on Sunday mornings but that Maya was no longer with him. One Sunday Jared approached Tam during a break and said a little awkwardly, "Hello, Tam. I've been enjoying your music."

"Thanks," Tam said, smiling good-naturedly. "How are you? I've noticed you here the past few Sundays. We really appreciate the support."

"I feel so much better eating the food here than the stuff at Nimby's, and it's great to listen to you and your friends," Jared said, fidgeting with a fork on the table, "Although, I must confess, I'm a little out of my element. It's not the kind of environment I'm used to." He continued, "There've been a few changes in my life. Dad's been committed to a facility for people with dementia. And Maya and I have parted ways. She enjoyed your performance and this place too. It's more her style, but I think I'm starting to appreciate it."

He hesitated for a moment. "And there's a lot of uncertainty about what to do with the house. My family all have different ideas about what to do with it."

"I'm sorry to hear about your dad and about you and Maya," said Tam. "Are you still staying at your dad's sometimes?"

"For now, at least while Dad gets used to being in his new setting and until my brother, Ray, gets back from Britain," Jared said. "He's away on business but lives not too far from Silverdale and should be back in a few weeks, so he'll be able to make sure everything's okay with Dad. I need to get back to my own home and take care of things there." Then he heaved a sigh. "I wish I knew a good house-sitter! That would simplify things a lot."

"You're looking for a house-sitter!" Tam exclaimed, feeling a tingle of excitement. "When would they need to start?"

"In about two or three weeks, once my brother gets back."

"What kinds of responsibilities would they have?" Tam asked, trying to sound casual.

"Basically, we'd just want the place kept clean and tidy, the yard maintained, the mail collected and a presence in the house. Members of my family and I would stay there now and then, but we all have rooms we use on the second floor, so the house-sitter would have the run of the main floor," Jared said. "It's a large house—four bedrooms on the main floor, five on the second floor and two on the third floor. There are also two studies, six bathrooms, a sewing room and a full rec room in the basement."

"And what qualities would you be looking for in a house-sitter?" Tam asked. "Would you be open to a family of people house-sitting?"

"As long as they were trustworthy and responsible, I think so." Jared nodded thoughtfully.

Tam hesitated for a moment and then said carefully, "You know, it might be an ideal situation for my family and me. They're the people you see singing here, and we're a very decent bunch."

Jared smiled. "I've been watching you and wishing I could find people as wholesome as you all seem. Why don't we both think about it and then discuss it again next Sunday?"

"All right," Tam said. "I'll run the idea by the others and see how they feel about it. Any idea how long the arrangement would last?"

"Not really," Jared said. "It would depend on how long it takes to sort things out with my family. We aren't all on the same page, to put it mildly. Frankly, it could be years."

Tam's skin prickled with excitement. "Okay, we'll see you here next Sunday then, eh?" he said, smiling at Jared.

"You bet!" Jared smiled back.

CHAPTER 38

Developments

"Seriously, we might get to house-sit a mansion!" Tam said to the group in the abandoned house over breakfast. "Jared's going to talk to his family about it, and I said I'd talk to the rest of you to see if you're interested. What do you think?" Tam could barely contain his excitement.

"Sounds great to me," said Ross, who was all smiles this morning.

Lydia sighed. "I've got to admit, having to be so sneaky about where we live and our rustic situation has been wearing thin for me, especially after being in the city and enjoying some of the comforts of a normal life." She took a sip of her tea. "I'm ready for a change."

Tam continued, "Jared's brother and sisters would stay at the house sometimes, so we'd have to contend with them. And they'll eventually want to sell the house. So it wouldn't be forever but could be for a number of years."

Cammie said, "I think it would be nice for Bella as she gets older. I'd like her to be able to have friends over." Then she added, "Heck, I'd like for us to be able to have friends over."

"What would become of this house?" Dagmar asked. "Do you know anyone else who could benefit from having this place?"

"As a matter of fact, when I was at the food bank the other day, I noticed that some of the regulars have become pretty good friends with each other. We could probably pass it along to them," Tam said.

"It can't hurt to investigate," Lydia said. She added with a grin, "The thought of living in a mansion suits me just fine!"

"So are we all agreed that we like the idea and will investigate further then?" asked Tam, looking around the room. Everyone looked around at each other as they nodded their heads in agreement. "Okay, we're agreed," he announced. "All right, since we're all here, something else that's been on my mind is what we should call ourselves, our musical group that is. Anyone have any ideas?" He looked around again.

Leroy said, "Well, since we began with the song 'The Lion Sleeps Tonight,' what about something like the Sleeping Lion?"

"Hmm. The Sleeping Lion ..." Cammie said. "I hear where you're coming from, but there aren't any lions where we are. What about the Sleeping Dragon? I know, I know—there aren't any dragons either, but I like dragons. Every culture has its own version of a dragon, yet it's mythological. I've always thought that was neat."

"The Sleeping Dragon ..." Dagmar repeated. "Doesn't that phrase have a meaning? I think it's a civil disobedience technique where people handcuff themselves to things and then put the chains of the handcuffs through PVC pipe to make it difficult to cut through them."

"Really?" asked Lydia. "I like it."

"Me too!" said Leroy. "Both peaceful and powerful. What do the rest of you think?"

There were more nods of agreement around the table.

"We've got a name, and we might just be moving into a mansion—wow!" exclaimed Cammie, bouncing a smiling baby Bella on her lap.

"Okay, one last thing," Dagmar said. "My friend Jon has a SPIN farming operation, and he's moving to another province so is looking for someone to take it over. First of all, does everyone know what a SPIN farm is?"

"Jon's moving?" asked Leroy. "What a loss to the community!"

Lydia, nodding in agreement, added, "And he's put so much into that SPIN farm over the years."

Ross said, "I've never heard of a SPIN farm." Cammie and Tam also looked perplexed.

Dagmar explained to them that small plot intensive (SPIN) farming was when someone grew food in other people's yards to sell at markets and to restaurants. In return for the use of their yards, the property owners received a weekly bag of produce harvested from all the yards that were part of the operation.

"Anyway, I figure with all of us pitching in, it should be pretty manageable—especially if we move into a mansion and don't have to sneak in and out anymore." Dagmar looked around the room at their faces. "What do you think? Should I set up a meeting with Jon? He's super helpful, and even when he moves, I'm sure we can email any questions we might have. He's even had the yards certified organic by the local certification body."

"There's a local certification body?" asked Ross. "How does that work?"

"As I understand it, it's a bunch of organic farmers, so they inspect and certify a yard when it meets their standards, which, I might add, are very high." Dagmar's eyes twinkled. "You know how picky people in this valley are about the food they eat and grow."

They all laughed, since they knew exactly what she was talking about.

"How about if I invite Jon over if and when we find out about the house-sit?" she asked. Still laughing, the group agreed.

Lydia smiled and shook her head. "What a morning!" she said. "Suddenly life's becoming a lot more interesting!"

CHAPTER 39

Next Steps

The Sleeping Dragon's next Sunday gig at the Love Bite was inspired! The new name and possible new home had the group exuding enthusiasm. Even Leroy, despite his emotional slump over his mother's recent death, was perked up by his friends' energy. The New Year seemed to be bringing new opportunities.

The place was packed with an exuberant crowd. Among them was Jared sitting with a dignified older man. After the group's lively and fun-filled gig, Jared approached Tam and invited him back to his table.

"Tam, I'd like you to meet my brother, Ray," said Jared, pulling up a chair for Tam. "Ray, this is Tam."

"Pleased to meet you," said Tam, extending his hand. Ray stood up, smiled and gave Tam a hearty handshake before they all sat down.

"A pleasure to meet you," Ray said. "Jared has said a lot of good things about you and mentioned that you and your family might be interested in house-sitting Dad's place. These are your family?" he asked, indicating the group with his head. "Your music's wonderful, by the way." Ray gave an appreciative smile.

"Yes, we live and work together," Tam said. "The dark-haired woman is my wife, Cammie, and that's our daughter, Bella. The others are our close friends. They aren't directly related but feel like extended family. Great people, all."

"Do you have references?" Ray asked.

"I could get you some," Tam said.

"And what do you do for a living?" Ray asked.

"We do a number of different things," Tam said. "I am a tradesman and am skilled in carpentry, electrical, plumbing—pretty much anything that needs to be fixed, and I'm also trained in permaculture so can take care of yards and gardens. My wife practises Chinese medicine."

"Chinese medicine, really?" Ray said. "How interesting. Is it effective?"

"Yes, very," Tam said. "It's an ancient form of medicine that can help with all kinds of ailments. Lydia and Leroy, the couple who were dancing, are skilled with computers: website design, that sort of thing. To tell you the truth, that realm is a bit of a mystery to me, but they're both quite advanced. They're also very creative and restore furniture and clothing and resell it." Tam paused and went on, "Ross and Dagmar, the older couple, have a variety of skills. Ross, who plays the guitar, is in sales among other things. Dagmar has managerial and administrative skills." Then he added, "And we all do community work of various kinds and are considering an extensive urban gardening venture."

"A multi-talented lot, I must say," Ray said. "We're in a bit of a pickle right now and need to have a presence in Dad's place within about two weeks. Would that work for you?"

"It's a bit tight, but I think we'd be able to manage it," Tam said.

Ray continued, "I'd like to arrange a time for you to come over and take a look at the place. Would Wednesday after supper work, say around six or so?"

Jared added, "I'll be going back home on Thursday, so it would be nice for both of us to be there, show you around and meet the rest of your family."

"I'll check with the others, but I think Wednesday at six should work. Can I get your phone number just in case anything comes up?" Tam asked.

"Certainly," Ray replied and handed him his card, which bore the name of a financial company in blue and gold lettering. "This is my direct line."

"A pleasure to meet you, Ray, and I'll get those reference letters to you before we meet." Tam stood up and again shook Ray's hand. He held out his hand to Jared and said, "Jared, it's great to see you again. I look forward to seeing you both on Wednesday at six."

Jared shook Tam's hand warmly and smiled. "See you then, Tam."

CHAPTER 40

Meeting at the Mansion

The group peered into the empty lot to make sure no one was coming before Tam lowered the drawbridge. They walked quickly in the dimming evening light and headed up the hill toward the mansion that belonged to Jared and Ray's dad.

Cammie had Bella pressed against her in a Snugli, and they were all dressed in their most presentable clothes. They felt upbeat and giddy as they strolled in the crisp evening air. It was clear and cold out, and the sky was a deep shade of cobalt blue with a few stars beginning to appear.

"This is it!" Tam announced as they reached the front of the property. A circular driveway led to the front porch. The mansion loomed before them. The porch light was on, and light seeped through the draperies of the windows on the left.

"Wow!" exclaimed Dagmar. "This place is massive!" She and Ross were holding hands, and he gave her hand a squeeze.

"Our new home, maybe," said Ross. "Incredible."

"Maybe?" Lydia tittered. "It feels like home already!"

They climbed the porch stairs, and Tam rang the doorbell: bing bong. Its tone was rich and elegant.

Ray answered. "Hello! Thanks for coming," he said, smiling warmly at them. "Come in."

He helped them take off their coats and hats and hung them up in the spacious front hall entrance.

He then waved them into a large, lavish living room. "Please, make yourselves comfortable," he said as he directed them toward three deep sofas arranged in a semicircle. Jared was seated on one of them. Tam sat down beside Jared, patting him on the back and saying, "Hello, Jared. How are you this evening?"

Jared smiled at him. "I'm well! So glad you could make it! Can I offer you something to drink? A glass of wine?" he asked the group, who all nodded gratefully.

He left the room and came back with a bottle of red wine and a corkscrew, which he handed to Ray. He then reached into a china cabinet and brought out eight sparkling crystal wineglasses. Ray removed the cork and poured the wine. When everyone had a glass, Tam introduced his household to Jared and Ray.

"Cheers!" said Jared, and they all clinked their glasses. The wine was exquisite.

"Dad's taken a turn for the worse and has to remain institutionalized," Ray sighed, getting right to the point. "Leaving the house empty just isn't an option. It needs to be maintained, and no one in our family is in a position to stay here on a continual basis. If you could take care of the property, it would save us a world of trouble. Is that something you'd be in a position to do?"

Tam said, "We've discussed this, and from what you've said, we believe it could work for us. Have you had a chance to review the reference letters I dropped off yesterday?"

"Yes, thank you," said Ray.

Cammie caught Ray's eye and said, "Baby Bella is almost crawling, and I have concerns about damaging some of the beautiful vases and ornaments around the house. Would we be able to put some of them in storage to keep them out of harm's way?" she asked as she stroked her sleeping baby's head.

"Jared and I can do that," Ray said, giving her a genial smile. "As a matter of fact, we have a high chair in storage that you're welcome to use that might also help to make this place more suitable for a baby. Can we give you a tour?" he asked. The group nodded their assent.

Ray and Jared led the way. "Here's the kitchen," Ray announced, leading them into a sprawling kitchen with cupboards and counter space galore and a large wooden table in one corner. "We'll have everything cleaned out for you by the time you move in."

Jared said, "Maya bought all kinds of weird foods that we have no idea what to do with." He laughed. "So we'll throw it all out, and you can start fresh." As he opened one of the cabinet drawers, they saw jars of rice, chickpeas, lentils and lots of other dried goods.

"Oh, don't throw it out!" Tam said. "No need to waste good food. We'll be happy to use it."

"Really?" asked Jared.

"Yes, we can clean out the cupboards. You have enough on your plates. We'll be happy to sort through it and bring what we don't want to the food bank. They're always looking for donations," Cammie said.

"All right," said Ray.

Lydia said, "We always have lots of good food ready to eat, so I hope you and the rest of your family will feel free to join us for a meal any time you're here. This is your home, and we'd always want you to feel welcome."

"Thanks. We have a kitchenette upstairs where we cook, but we appreciate the offer." Jared smiled, leading them out of the kitchen and down a long corridor.

He showed them four large, elegant bedrooms, each with a queen-size bed, walk-in closets and two chests of drawers. One of the bedrooms had a high window, positioned similarly to the one Dagmar and Ross were used to looking through from their bedroom in the abandoned house. Pointing at the window, Dagmar whispered in his ear, "I hope we can have this room." He smiled back at her.

One of the bedrooms had a massage table next to the window. "Will that massage table be staying?" asked Cammie.

"No reason for it not to," Ray said. "This is my dad's bedroom. As his health declined, we hired a massage therapist to try to keep him comfortable, and we bought this table so he could have massages in his own home."

"Would I be able to use it?" Cammie asked.

"I don't see why not," Jared said, and Ray concurred with a nod.

There were two bathrooms, and each had a shower and a claw-foot bathtub, and a laundry room adjoined one of them. Besides the large living room, there was a smaller study with a TV. There was also a small room with a beautiful stained glass window with a stylized picture of a dragon on it. In front of the window was an ornately carved table that looked Indian. Tam and the rest of the group all had the same thought: the perfect meditation room!

Back in the living room, they thanked Ray and Jared for the tour.

"One more thing," Ray said. "You're welcome to use Dad's car, and there's a pickup truck in the back that you're also welcome to use."

"We're really moved by your generosity," said Tam. "Thanks so much! We'll do our very best to keep this place well maintained." Then he asked, "What do you usually do with the yard?"

Jared said, "We have a few simple flower beds in the front and just a lawn and trees. In the back there's a pool, a vegetable garden and the apple tree that you're familiar with, Tam. You're welcome to use the pool when it gets warmer."

Ray said, "Dad owns this house outright, and the bills are automatically paid through his account, so you needn't worry about costs. Just take good care of the place, and we'll be happy. Once you've moved in, make yourselves at home, and use whatever you need. I've written up a contract to that effect and have a copy you can take home and review. Any questions, just give me a call." He handed Tam an agreement on the same letterhead as the business card he'd given him. "Otherwise, we'll see you bright and early on the first of the month. In the meantime, we'll get the main floor childproofed."

Leroy asked, "So there are three storeys to the house?"

"Yes, and a full basement," Ray answered.

"What's on the third floor?" Leroy asked.

"We mostly just use it for storage—old furniture, that sort of thing," said Ray.

"Thanks again for your hospitality, Ray and Jared," Tam said. "We look forward to moving in and taking good care of your dad's house."

"Lovely to meet all of you." Ray smiled. "And thank you for helping us out. You have no idea how grateful we are that you're willing to take this on. It's a weight off our shoulders."

CHAPTER 41

Elation

Walking home, the group could barely contain themselves. Still giddy with the wine, they started giggling.

"Tam, when you said 'mansion,' you really meant it!" said Ross. "The place is huge!"

Dagmar snuggled closer to him as they walked arm in arm. She exclaimed, "Can you believe where we'll be living?"

Lydia and Leroy broke into a little dance routine as they ambled down the street. "I'm walkin' on sunshine, oh-oh!" Lydia sang.

Tam said, "Yeah, the place is massive!" Then, turning to Cammie, he asked, "Will you come to the food bank with me tomorrow? I'd like for us to offer our current house to a few of the regulars. Is that okay with everyone?"

"Sure," Ross replied. "May as well let others who need somewhere to live have it." They all indicated their consent.

"I'll be glad to come with you tomorrow," Cammie said. "It's great that you've got some people in mind. It would be a shame not to let someone else stay where we are now."

"I shudder to think of how some people are living these days," said Tam, slowly shaking his head.

"So do I," Cammie said in a sombre voice.

"Since our new place is furnished, we can just leave everything there for whoever moves in," said Lydia, "and we can just bring our personal belongings, the sewing machine, our tools and some of our food to the new place and leave a bunch for them, eh?"

"Sounds reasonable to me," Dagmar said. "Although, what if it doesn't work out?"

"I say we hope for the best and take our chances!" said Ross.

"We sure lucked out with Maya and the food she bought!" Tam added.

"Who's Maya again?" Dagmar asked.

"Jared's old girlfriend. Remember the couple I pointed out at the Love Bite? The woman who seemed to be distancing herself from Jared? She eats the way we do," Tam said, "so that's why she had the kitchen stocked with organic food."

The sky was dark and starry, and they could see their home in the streetlight. Careful to make sure no one was coming, they walked into the empty lot and entered the abandoned house. After the excitement of the evening, they went to bed almost immediately, and all slept soundly.

CHAPTER 42

Passing It On

T he next two weeks had the household packing their personal belongings, some of their food and the objects they'd each placed upon the altar.

Cammie and Tam, with Bella bundled up in a Snugli against him, walked to the food bank intending to talk with a group of women about moving into the house they'd be vacating.

When they got there, they waved hello to Mary, who quickly returned the wave and then turned her attention back to the pots on the stove that were hissing and bubbling. Tam looked around the room that adjoined the kitchen and saw the regulars chatting, sipping on cups of coffee and tea and playing cards together. The couple he'd seen the last time he'd been there were again sitting at the back of the room. The young woman with the blonde, stringy hair was talking quietly and intensely and looked as though she was on the verge of tears, while the older man she was with looked disinterested. Tam thought about going over to see if everything was all right but then decided not to, since it really wasn't any of his business. He scanned the room and spotted the women he was looking for.

Glenda, Rose and Jay had become fast friends and each other's support system while living on the streets. They helped out at the food bank and used the services there. Their friendship set a happy tone to their surroundings. Glenda had an Afro, thick-lensed glasses and an infectious laugh, and the three of them were finding creative ways of getting by together.

Cammie asked if they could join them, and the women warmly invited them to sit down.

"Hey, what's up?" Glenda asked, smiling broadly at Bella, who returned the big smile.

"Well, we have something that might interest the three of you," Tam said quietly. "We're moving out of our squat. It's nicely set up, and we thought we'd like to pass it along to you if you don't have something better already."

"Oh, yeah?" Rose said, eyebrows raised and looking at her two companions. "I'd love to take a look." Her friends nodded eagerly in agreement. "When can we come by?"

"We could take a wander over right now, if that works for you," Cammie replied. "We're moving out in just a few days, so the sooner the better."

"Cool!" said Jay. "I'm up for a little stroll …"

When they reached the empty lot beside the house, Cammie said, "This time of day is pretty quiet, but we look around to make sure no one's watching us, just in case." They crunched along the path through the empty lot between dirty, melting mounds of snow. "There isn't much traffic through this empty lot, and it's well hidden by the trees."

They looked around and saw that the coast was clear. Tam lowered their makeshift drawbridge, and they all followed him into the house.

"This is great!" Jay exclaimed. "It's like a mansion compared to where we're staying right now!"

"Seriously?" Rose asked. "You're giving this up?"

"Yeah, we've got an indefinite house-sit, so we want to pass this place along to others who can use it," Cammie said and then smiled at them. "It may as well be you."

Glenda said, "Wow! This is amazing! We're sleeping in a hollow under a sidewalk these days. We have a mattress on the ground with a few blankets and a heavy curtain hung down to keep out the elements. To stay warm and cook, we have a handmade heater and stove, so it's like camping out every night."

"Sounds pretty rustic," Tam said. "I bet that gets old quick. Anyway, I'll show you how the electrical and hot water systems work."

"For real?" Rose asked. "Electrical and hot water? I'm pinching myself just listening to you say those words!"

Tam and Cammie showed them around.

Jay said, "Believe it or not, we're going to be doing exactly what you're doing—passing our little digs onto someone who's going to be happy to have shelter."

Cammie shook her head slowly. "It's all relative, isn't it?"

After the tour, Tam said, "So we'll be moving into our new place the first of the month. We'll be out that morning, so you're welcome to move in first thing in the afternoon."

The women were overjoyed to be moving up in the world. Heat and electricity—what a luxury!

CHAPTER 43
Final Details

It was the first of the month, and the household walked excitedly toward the mansion in the brisk morning air. When they arrived, Jared greeted them at the door. Jared gave Tam the keys to the house and vehicles and a sheet of paper with passwords for the voice mail, Internet and security system. In the background, they could hear Ray on the phone, saying heatedly, "Look, Tina, they'll be fine. I know you haven't met them yet, but we have, and we've checked their references. Really. They'll be fine."

Ray came into the room, looking embarrassed. "That was our sister Tina, and you'll get to meet her sometime soon. We should have kept her in the loop about you moving in, but she'll be fine after I've discussed it with her a little more."

"Do you think we'll need the security system, since there are so many of us?" Tam asked the brothers as he looked at the piece of paper.

Ray replied, "I'd appreciate it if you'd turn it on at night." He paused and then explained, "Places like this can be a target. There are a lot of valuable things in this house, and our insurance policy requires that we take that precaution. Will you do that please? The alarm isn't triggered easily, but when it is, it makes a lot of noise, and the police are contacted immediately. We have a separate outdoor entrance to the second floor and a second security system that our family will take care of."

"All right," Tam conceded. "I guess some things are different in a home this size."

They had all looked over the agreement, which was quite straightforward. It basically stated that they would maintain the property while they lived there and in return would have the bills paid through the owner's bank account. Each set of signatories would be required to give two months' notice if they wanted to terminate their arrangement. They had all signed.

They looked around the living room and saw that the breakable ornaments had been removed and that the sofas now had new washable plaid covers on them. There was also a high chair in the kitchen and plastic covers over all the electrical outlets.

"Cammie, I'm so grateful that you brought up your concerns about the place being suitable for a baby," said Ray, facing her. "Being proactive about these things can prevent a lot of grief."

"Thanks for paying such close attention to our needs," Cammie said. "This will make our lives much easier."

"Yes, thanks for doing such a thorough job of childproofing the place," said Tam. "We'll do our best to be as conscientious on our end."

"We want you to be happy and comfortable here. It means a lot to us to know that Dad's place will be well looked after," said Ray.

Tam and Cammie were able to bring their belongings, which included Cammie's Chinese medicines, in two trips. The rest of their household also had very little to move. They had all brought some of the food from the kitchen but had left a good amount for the new occupants of the abandoned house. Leroy carried Lydia's sewing machine that she used to create, alter and repair clothing for all of them. Dagmar and Ross didn't have much more than what they'd brought with them a few months earlier—their two backpacks and Ross's guitar in its case.

It was gratifying for the group to be able to leave the house well stocked and in good order for Glenda, Rose and Jay. When they had left the abandoned house that morning, it was clean and tidy and ready for its new occupants.

CHAPTER 44

Moving

It was the second-lightest move that Dagmar had ever experienced and Ross too. Their move into the abandoned house had been the lightest for both of them. Leaving the abandoned house, she felt gratitude and a bit of sadness. She remembered how amazing it had been to be invited in and to suddenly have a home. She knew she'd always feel nostalgia for that humble place.

As Ross and Dagmar carried their belongings to their bedroom, Dagmar said, "I feel a bit sad leaving the old house behind. I still can't believe how lucky we were to have stopped there. Your playing the guitar got us invited in."

"I'm really excited about our new digs, but I know what you mean." Ross smiled. "Look where this journey is taking us: now we'll be living in a mansion! There's some kind of mysterious alchemy happening. I don't understand it, but I'm grateful for it and am allowing myself to go with it."

"It really is some kind of magic, isn't it?" Dagmar said. "Even for the people we moved in with, things have gotten better: the music gig, the mansion—something very special is happening."

"What's next? I wonder," Ross said. "We live in a mansion; we have each other." Ross squeezed her hand. "We have a music gig and now maybe a SPIN farming business. How much better can it get?"

"I don't know," Dagmar laughed, "but I'm open to continued miracles!"

The others had been happy to give Ross and Dagmar the bedroom with the high window. As they looked up, a Steller's jay flew past.

"The bluebird of happiness!" exclaimed Dagmar. "I think it's a good sign," she said and kissed Ross on the cheek.

He looked deeply into her eyes and gave her a kiss on the lips. "I think it's a good sign too."

There were two huge walk-in closets and two chests of drawers in their bedroom. They chuckled at how much room there still was after they'd put their few belongings away. Ross put his guitar, in its case, in a corner of the bedroom. Dagmar placed her laptop on a small desk in a bay window at the side of the room.

Then they walked over to the small meditation room and put the marble and white feather on the altar. The others had already set it up, and it had the same beautiful lavender cloth and a few candles on it already.

"What a beautiful meditation room!" Dagmar exclaimed. "I just love this stained glass window. A dragon, like it's meant to be. Only this one's awake."

"Uncanny, isn't it?" said Ross. "This kind of synchronicity makes me feel like I'm doing something right."

"I know what you mean," Dagmar said. "I think we're on the right path, even if we don't understand where it leads."

CHAPTER 45

First Meal at the Mansion

After putting away their few belongings, the former residents of the abandoned house wandered around their new home. Sunlight streamed in through the windows and brought joy with it. They were used to being in semi-darkness in their old place, in order to keep their living there a secret. The sunshine warmed their hearts and showed them an interior that was massive and beautiful yet worn and faded. The plaid sofa covers Ray had recently bought were by far the newest and most colourful things in the mansion.

Cammie went into the kitchen and prepared a celebratory meal for them all. Smells of beans and quinoa permeated the air, helping to make their new place feel more like home. Leroy and Dagmar pitched in and made some of their specialty dishes.

Each of them had taken turns meditating in their new meditation room. It was a happy and contemplative time for all of them. Such a dramatic change in scenery had a profoundly positive effect on their moods.

That evening they sat down together at a large oak dining table under a sparkling crystal chandelier. They lit the candles on the table, creating an air of intimacy. The sunny morning had clouded over and turned into a full-blown storm. Outside, they could hear the wind howling, and it made them feel all the more cozy.

They began with corn chowder that Dagmar had made and then shared a lavish meal of beans, quinoa, homemade bread, guacamole and a wide array of vegetables. For dessert Leroy had made a trifle with coconut cream, rehydrated pineapples, figs and raisins and homemade plum liqueur he'd brewed earlier that year.

After they'd finished their desserts, Lydia exclaimed, "How did we ever get so lucky?"

They all burst into laughter, since they were all wondering the same thing, still half in a state of disbelief.

When the laughter died down, Dagmar, looking into the eyes of everyone around the table, asked, "Does anyone else feel like doing something ceremonial? This moment feels so magical, and I'd like to honour it somehow."

There was a longish pause, and then Lydia said, "Hey, why don't we do what the Quakers do? They sit silently and speak only when they're moved to."

Everyone agreed.

After a moment, Leroy spoke. "I just want to say how grateful I am to you all and especially to you, Lydia." He paused and squeezed Lydia's knee. "I'm dealing with a lot of feelings right now around the death of my mom." His eyes became teary, and his voice rose a little. "It's so great to share a home with people I can be myself with, who know what's happening for me and who accept me as I am right now." He paused again. "This beautiful interior feels like an outer reflection of the special dynamic we share." Each of them nodded in acknowledgement.

Cammie cleared her throat. "I'm aware that something very special is happening, something beyond my comprehension. I'm grateful too and want to stay attuned to whatever this magic is. Maybe it's just the harmonious family we've created, even if by chance. Thanks to all of you for your part in this magic. Tam, Bella, I'm so happy to have you and so glad that we're sharing our lives with such wonderful people." She gave Bella a squeeze and put her free hand on Tam's arm.

After a few moments of silence, Ross spoke. "I left a Green Team meeting with nowhere to go and discovered that Dagmar didn't have anywhere to go either. I was unexpectedly turned away from a living situation that was deteriorating rapidly. Since then, I've felt like the Velveteen Rabbit, coming back to life through being loved. Thank you so much, Dagmar, for your love and for sharing this grand adventure with me. Thanks to every one of you for creating a space where we can be real. I'm finding out who I am underneath what I now realize was mostly just a sales pitch, and I'm so grateful." He squeezed Dagmar's hand. She smiled warmly at him.

The wind howled in the trees.

A moment later, Tam said quietly, "I just thought I'd wander a little further up the hill one day and offer to pick the apples I'd seen in this backyard. Just a whim, and look where it's taken us. I also wonder what's leading us, where these whims are coming from and how we can stay in tune with them. I'm so happy to have you all in my life. Cammie and Bella, thank you for sharing life so deeply with me. I cherish this special time with you and the rest of our household and will do my best to be worthy of all this."

The candles flickered, and the faint sound of wind chimes jangled somewhere far away.

Dagmar nodded her head. "I'm so touched that you took us into your home and welcomed and cared for us," she said. "You've softened me. I was so stressed before moving here, trying to make ends meet and failing. I'd never been in a situation like that before; I was someone who always paid my bills on time, that sort of thing. Anyway, none of it matters anymore." She added, "I've let you into my life, Ross, and am so enriched." She rested her head on Ross's shoulder for a moment, then continued, "The rest of you were strangers, and now you're my family. Things are upside down, but they're perfect, and I want to stay attuned to this new kind of perfect, whatever it is. Thanks for all your kindness, care and common sense and each of your unique, special loveliness. You're so very lovely, every one of you."

Lydia looked around the table and smiled. "I remember opening the door to the two of you that fateful night," she said, gazing over at Dagmar and Ross. "It's all I could think to do because I didn't want to draw attention to the house," she laughed. "Since then so much has changed. We have a musical group; we're living in a mansion ..." She turned to Leroy and stroked his shoulder. "Leroy, thanks for being that special someone in my life. I know how hard things are for you now and am grateful to be here with you through this. I'm also grateful for the support of our friends who are really more like our family." Lydia paused for a moment and then sighed. "I can't believe we've landed in this mansion. Honestly, after coming back from the city, I realized I was getting pretty tired of the darkness, dowdiness and secretiveness of our old place, and I am so excited about this new chapter that's begun in our lives together. I welcome our continued adventures with open arms." Lydia held out her arms and smiled again at everyone around the table.

As the candles flickered and the wind roared outside, they sat contentedly around the table. Bella looked around at everyone and made cooing sounds. They all laughed happily and thanked her for her contribution to the conversation.

As the rain hammered against the windows, Tam said in a solemn voice, "My thoughts are going out to those in our old house and to everyone in this town who is struggling to get by. My hope is that somehow they're all managing to stay warm and dry."

They all closed their eyes for a moment, sharing Tam's sentiment. The people he described could have been any of them but for the series of events that had brought them to this place.

Cammie, rocking Bella in her arms, stood up and said, "How about if we give the place a smudge after doing the dishes? I have some cedar and sage. It might be nice to bless it with all of our good feelings and intentions."

It felt like the right thing to do to all of them, so after they cleaned up, they walked together from room to room with the burning smudge, leaving fragrant smoke everywhere they went. Soon after, they took turns washing up in the bathrooms and went to bed, eager to experience their first night in their new bedrooms.

CHAPTER 46
New Home

Having so much space felt wonderful, but it took some getting used to after living in an abandoned house. After breakfast the next day, the group spent their first full day walking around and exploring their new home in a daze. This was the largest house any of them had ever lived in.

The wind had died down quite a bit, but it was overcast and looked cold outside, with small blowing snowflakes circling in the air.

They gathered in the kitchen and took stock of what they had in the cupboards. In one set of cupboards above the counter were jars containing grains, nuts, flours, dried fruit and legumes. Dagmar opened the fridge where they found miso, tamari and other organic condiments. In a lower cupboard beside the fridge were bags of potatoes, onions and garlic, all with stickers on them that said "certified organic."

In another set of cupboards above the countertop was every gadget under the sun: a bread maker, which Cammie had already made use of the previous day; a food processor; a juicer; a dehydrator; a popcorn popper and loads of other gadgetry. In the cupboard below the counter were high-quality stainless steel pots and cast-iron frying pans. They found a drawer full of candles of all colours, shapes and sizes with labels that indicated they were made from GMO-free soy. Below this drawer was a cupboard filled with washcloths and tea towels. Above the cutlery drawer was a cupboard full of matching antique plates and bowls and an assortment of cups, glasses and mugs. Under the double sink were a variety of different natural cleaners: dish soap, window cleaner, baking soda, vinegar and general cleaners.

"Thank you, Maya!" Tam said under his breath, baby Bella draped over his shoulder. Bella was looking around, wide-eyed, at her new surroundings. Tam continued, "She's very particular about what she consumes. All this organic food is what she would have insisted upon and probably the natural cleaners too. Are we ever lucky she spent time here!"

"Too bad they split up," Dagmar said. "It would be nice for Jared to have someone in his life. It seems she had quite an influence on him, since he's now a regular at the Love Bite. I think he's developed a taste for higher quality food."

"We just never know what kind of an influence we have on others, do we? I wonder if she's aware of the effect she's had on his life," Lydia said contemplatively.

They walked over to another drawer they hadn't noticed and found fresh fruit and some cookies from the Love Bite.

"Jared and Ray must have done some shopping and picked these things up for us," Ross said. "How thoughtful of them!"

"Do you feel like having tea and cookies and sitting in the living room?" Cammie asked, looking inquiringly at everyone. They all liked that idea, so they put the cookies on a plate, cut up some pear apples, made some tea and headed over to the living room, Dagmar lagging behind.

Suddenly Dagmar exclaimed from a large closet next to the kitchen, "Look at this!" They all came over. "I thought I might find a broom and a vacuum cleaner ..." She opened the closet door to reveal shelves holding large jars of every kind of dried food imaginable.

"Eureka!" said Ross. "Dagmar, you've hit the jackpot!"

"I hope we can return the favour somehow," said Leroy. "What would people with all this money need from us?"

"They seem awfully grateful that we're here," said Cammie. "If we take good care of this place and keep our eyes and ears open, I bet we can find ways to return the favour."

They wandered back into the living room for some tea and cookies and settled into the comfortable sofas.

"Well, here we are! And getting here has just flowed so easily, hasn't it?" Lydia laughed. It amazed them all that their transition into such an enormous space had seemed almost effortless.

"Since we're all here, would you like me to arrange a time to have Jon come over and talk to us about the SPIN farm?" Dagmar asked.

"Yeah, that would be great!" said Tam. "Why don't we invite him over for dinner sometime in the next couple of nights."

They all loved the thought of having Jon over for dinner and discussing the SPIN farming venture. Dagmar said she'd give him a call later in the day and invite him to dinner sometime that week.

The rest of the day drifted by lazily, each of them exploring and getting comfortable in their expansive new living space.

CHAPTER 47

Entertaining at the Mansion

Dagmar opened the door and invited Jon in. He handed her a box and said, "This is for dessert. I just baked it this afternoon." She looked inside at a beautiful chocolate cake decorated with nasturtiums. "I've been growing them indoors," he said with a smile.

She'd spent some time helping him with his SPIN farm operations, and they'd become good friends in the process. They gave each other a big hug.

"How did you manage to get into a place like this?" he asked her.

"It's a long story, but it's basically an indefinite house-sit." She smiled. "I know—we really lucked out. Come on in and meet the fam," she said, leading him into the dining room and carrying his cake.

"Hi, Jon!" said Leroy. "Great to see you! Come on in." Leroy walked over and gave Jon a hug.

"Hey, Leroy. I'm so sorry to hear about your mom," Jon said. "It's great to see you." He gave Leroy another hug.

"Thanks. I really appreciate that," said Leroy.

"Welcome to our not-so-humble abode!" laughed Lydia, giving Jon a hug.

He laughed too. "Thanks for having me. I'm glad it's not beneath you to have humble folk like me for dinner."

"It hasn't gone to our head—yet!" joked Lydia with a smile and a wink.

"Jon, this is Ross, and this is Cammie and Tam and baby Bella." They all smiled and said hello.

"Are you hungry?" Dagmar asked Jon. "Dinner's ready, and we can eat any time."

"As a matter of fact, yes, I am quite hungry," Jon said.

Dagmar brought the cake Jon made into the kitchen; then she and Ross set the table. The group put platters of food and a big pot of bean-and-barley soup in the centre of the table. There was an avocado and pomegranate salad with baby spinach and marinated figs, a mix of wild and brown rice with green onions, steamed green beans and tempeh with mushroom sauce. Tam lit candles in the centre and at either end of the table.

"Thanks for this incredible meal!" Jon exclaimed. "Now that all this lovely food's in front of me, I'm famished!"

"Dig in!" Dagmar smiled. "You're the first friend we've had over since moving in. It's so much fun being able to entertain here. Would you like some wine?"

"Yes, please," he said. They poured wine all round and clinked their glasses.

"To friends," said Leroy, "our true riches!"

They sipped their wine and dug into the food. When they were finished, Lydia and Leroy cleared the table and brought in Jon's cake and a tapioca pudding they'd made.

After they finished and the plates were all cleared away, they sipped on wine and relaxed.

Lydia said, "So I hear you're going to be leaving us, Jon."

"Yes," he replied. "I love it here, but my grandma back east is getting old. She has a big garden, so it's time for me to move in and give her a hand. I'll really miss living here, but I'm also looking forward to spending time with her and helping her out."

"And you're looking for someone to take over your SPIN farm operation?" asked Tam.

"Yes, and I'm hoping you're still interested," Jon said. "I've put a lot of time and energy into all aspects of the business. I have a website and spreadsheets to keep track of the planting. The plots I've been gardening have been certified organic by the local certifiers, and I've developed excellent relationships with the landowners where I farm." He paused for a moment. "To tell you the truth, it's hard to give up."

"It's funny we've never met before," Tam said. "I've studied permaculture and have quite a bit of experience. It's an honour to meet you and to take over your operation. I promise it will be in good hands."

"I have no doubt about that." Jon smiled. "And having this many people will make room for all kinds of possibilities."

"For the first year, we'll probably just want to do exactly what you've been doing, get to know the landowners and get a feel for the operation. Then we'll take it from there," Tam said. The rest of the group nodded in agreement.

"How long will you be in town?" Dagmar asked. "It would be great if we could have you introduce us and share some of what you've learned before you leave."

"I'd like to get going in the next three months or so, so that gives us a good amount of time," Jon said. "I sell some of my produce to a few of the local restaurants, so I'd like to introduce you to my contacts there too."

"We'd really appreciate that," Lydia said. "We know how well you treat people, and we promise to do our very best to continue the great service you provide. I know that would mean a lot to you."

"Thanks," Jon laughed. "You know me well!"

"As far as the money goes," Dagmar said, "we have some that we could give you now but were wondering if you'd mind getting payments on instalment. Even though we're living in a lavish place, we have very little money coming in at the moment. Would it work for you if we paid you in instalments when we start making money with the produce?"

"I think so," said Jon. "I like the idea of having money that I can count on coming to me in the future, and I won't have a lot of expenses when I'm at Grandma's. And I have some other online work in the meantime so am okay for money at the moment."

"We really appreciate just how helpful and accommodating you are," Leroy said, getting a little teary. "This means so much to us, and you can count on us to get the money to you as soon as we're able and to do our very best to maintain your high standards."

"To tell you the truth, I can't think of a better situation or a nicer group of people to leave my business to. I know you're all conscientious, and I believe that with all of you working together the business has a great chance of succeeding," Jon said. "When can I show you around? Tomorrow would work for me."

"No time like the present!" said Ross. "Would you like to come over for breakfast, and we can take it from there?"

Jon blushed. "You're too good to me!" He smiled. "Okay."

CHAPTER 48

SPIN Farming 101

Jon arrived back at the mansion early the next morning. Ross answered the door and invited him into the kitchen, which was filled with the enticing aroma of coffee, toast, cinnamon and something savoury. Everyone was helping themselves to toast, jam, coffee and tea, stir-fry and oatmeal with cinnamon, raisins and bananas. They sat down at the table to eat and invited Jon to join them.

"Thanks for the great breakfast!" Jon said as he served himself. "Do you usually eat like this first thing in the morning?"

They all nodded. It was the way they always began their day.

"I thought I'd take you around to the gardens and tell you about each of them. Right now I have 16," Jon said as he sat down at the table with a bowl of oatmeal. "I have electronic notes about each one that I'll email you, so don't worry about writing things down. It's just nice to see the gardens so you get a better idea of what you're dealing with."

Dagmar smiled at him from across the table. "You're making everything so easy for us, Jon," she said. "Much appreciated!"

After breakfast, they all put on their coats and boots. Cammie helped Tam put a happy baby Bella in a Snugli against his chest before they all went outside. The air was brisk, and the sun was shining weakly.

"We'll start at the top of the hill and end closer to the bottom," said Jon. "I try to grow a lot of the heavier crops like squash and corn closer to the bottom so I don't have as far to haul it. But I use a bike with a trailer, so this might not be an issue for you, since I understand you'll have the use of a pickup truck."

"That's right, so it'll be much easier for us," said Tam, "but we appreciate any tips you've discovered over the years."

"Where to begin!" laughed Jon. "The biggest mistake I made starting out was spending too much time trying to make things perfect, especially cleaning the greens. I have an amazing mentor in another town, and she really helps me out. I'll pass her contact information on to you, if you like."

"That would be great! The more connected we are with other SPIN farmers, the better. I'd love to learn what works for her and what doesn't," Tam said. "So how do you streamline washing the greens?"

"When you wash them, go through and pick out the leaves that are obviously brown or wilted, but limit the time you spend doing it. Also, there will be some veggies—carrots, potatoes, beets—that are irregularly shaped but are still good to eat. I've been reducing the price and selling them as veggies of interest."

"So that must also reduce waste, eh?" asked Lydia. "It's still perfectly good food but just looks a little odd."

"Exactly," Jon said. "I try to retrain my customers to understand quality in a different way. These veggies may not be beautiful but are so much healthier than what you get from supermarkets." As they walked up the hill, Jon continued, "We're conditioned to seek out food that looks perfect, even if it's ridden with pesticides, contains GMOs, comes from hundreds of miles away and involves terrible labour standards that harm workers. Pesticides and herbicides go into the soil, groundwater and air—and directly into our bodies. We're supposed to ignore that and only pay attention to price and appearance."

Ross said, "I've heard some people—my brother, for instance—say that organic produce is the very same as the stuff you buy in the grocery stores and that buying organic is just a big money-making scam."

Jon caught his breath as they hiked up the hill, then said, "It's a hard myth to dispel. The price is low because the government subsidizes large agribusinesses and transport companies, using our tax dollars because of international trade agreements. It can be a struggle to get people to understand that vegetables in the supermarkets cost less because of these subsidies. There's even a term for this practice, *dumping*, and it's done all over the world, often destroying local economies in the process. Local farmers are barely scraping by, even though they charge more than supermarkets do."

As Jon opened the gate to one of the yards, he said, "Fresh, organic vegetables are much more nutritious, even if they don't always look as nice. It's quite a re-education process, but more and more people are getting it. I know I'm preaching to the choir here, but over the years I've noticed that the choir's getting bigger."

"That's one of the things I love so much about this valley," said Cammie. "So many people here understand what you're saying. There's a pervasive outlook in our society that has us seeing some things and ignoring others. In a lot of places, your view of vegetables and farming is so far from the norm."

"I think that's changing pretty quickly," Jon said. "Lots of places around the world are becoming GMO-free and are insisting on higher-quality foods. The health and environmental consequences are becoming too hard to ignore. When bees and birds are dying because of the way we grow food, something's seriously wrong."

"It amazes me that some people still haven't heard of GMOs," said Leroy, shaking his head. Their whole household avoided genetically modified organisms (GMOs). This untested, pesticide-laden process that had been applied to an estimated 80 percent of processed foods struck them as toxic to people and the environment. Although unlabeled in Canada, there were apps people could use to find out whether or not the foods they were buying contained GMOs.

"Me too," Jon said, "but awareness of them and the risks they pose is increasing. Over the years I've seen lots of people learn about the benefits of eating organic and locally grown food." He held the gate open for the others and announced, "Anyway, here we are at the first house. I always access it through this gate in the alley." Pointing to a gravelly area by the lane, he added, "There's a spot where you can park your truck."

Jon took them around to all the gardens and let them know the nuances of each. A few of the landowners were in their yards, and he introduced his friends to them.

"Some of the landowners don't mind watering, and that helps a lot," said Jon. "I'll email my list of landowners and restaurant contacts and let them know I'm selling my business to you, and I'll make sure you've met them all by the time I leave." Turning to go home, he said, "Thanks again for the great breakfast!"

They thanked Jon for the tour and parted ways at the bottom of the hill. Jon went back to his place, and the housemates—soon-to-be SPIN farmers—returned to the mansion.

For lunch, the group prepared spaghetti with homemade garlic bread, putting the bread maker to good use. As they ate, they discussed the new SPIN farming opportunity and assigned the necessary tasks. Since Tam had a permaculture background, he would be in charge of the gardening duties, with everyone helping in the gardens as needed. Leroy and Lydia, being good with all things electronic, would handle the spreadsheets and the websites. Dagmar would do the blogging and take care of the banking. She would make sure everyone had read-only access to the online account so they could see what was going on with the finances, and they would all receive weekly allowances based on what the group could afford after expenses. Ross and Tam would set up the cold storage and cleaning area in the backyard. Ross, Lydia and Dagmar would be in charge of setting up the table at the market to make it eye-catching. Cammie agreed to liaise with the restaurants, taking their produce orders and finding out what kinds of fruits and vegetables they'd like for their menus. All of them would take turns selling at the Saturday market.

CHAPTER 49

Tina the Ballerina

As they finished lunch, the doorbell rang, and a woman laughed loudly outside. Dagmar got up from the table and opened the front door. She found a middle-aged woman with hair dyed reddish brown and wearing a fair amount of makeup with a younger, very toned, very tanned man. They were both holding their coats over their heads since it had started to rain.

"Hello," said Dagmar.

"Hi. I just thought I'd come by and introduce myself to our new house-sitters. My name is Tina—Tina the ballerina!" she said, attempting a pirouette in the front hall and almost falling over. "I'm Jared and Ray's sister, and this is my sweetie, Steve," she added, rubbing herself against him suggestively.

"Come on in, Tina, Steve," said Dagmar. As they entered, she noticed that they smelled of alcohol. "Here, I'll take your coats." She helped them get their damp coats off and hung them up. "The others are in the kitchen. I'll introduce you."

She led the way with Tina and Steve following her unsteadily.

"Jared and Ray's sister Tina came by to introduce herself and her friend Steve," Dagmar announced to her housemates.

They all stood up. Dagmar introduced each of them to Tina and Steve.

"And what was your name?" Tina asked, looking at Dagmar.

"Dagmar," she answered. "Would you like some spaghetti and garlic bread? We've just finished our lunch, but there's plenty."

Tina laughed shrilly. "Spaghetti! That sounds almost as good as pizza! Steve, do you feel like some spaghetti?"

"No, not really," said Steve, disinterested.

"Maybe another time," Tina said to the group. "Anyway, lovely to meet you all. Steve and I will be staying upstairs for the next little while. See you again!" Tina and Steve walked unsteadily toward the door.

Dagmar accompanied them and helped them with their coats. "Thanks for coming by and introducing yourselves," said Dagmar. "We'll see you again, I'm sure."

"Have a wonderful day!" Tina gave her an exaggerated smile. "Bye for now."

They looked at each other, all trying to wrap their heads around this latest development, not knowing what to say. The normally placid baby Bella had started crying, and Cammie bounced her. She then checked to see if Bella wanted to nurse and finally just held her tight, rocking her back and forth.

They made a pot of chamomile tea and carried on with their earlier conversation about SPIN farming. Bella eventually fell asleep in Cammie's arms, and Cammie held her sleeping baby against her as they spoke.

"So have we covered everything? Is everyone comfortable with their duties?" asked Ross distractedly.

"To tell you the truth, I feel discombobulated, as Mom would have said," Leroy said. He shook his head back and forth slowly and then sighed. "I wonder how long Tina and Steve will be here."

"People everywhere are in need of healing, sometimes where you'd least expect them," Cammie said.

"I wonder what the rest of the family's like …" Tam said.

Lydia piped up, "Back on the topic of our new business venture, I wonder how we can integrate the other things we were doing. For example, I like upcycling and selling what I've restored. Can we sell that stuff at the same booth as the produce?"

"Upcycling?" Ross asked. "What's that?"

Lydia laughed. "The word's a combination of *upscale* and *recycling*, so it's finding things that need repainting or repairing and turning them into unique and attractive new items. It's a lot of fun, and people appreciate that they're one of a kind."

"Neat!" Ross exclaimed.

"Yeah, and I wonder about the people we visit and help out. How can we make sure they're kept in the loop?" Lydia pondered.

"I wonder if Glenda and her friends at our old place are getting to know some of them. It might be nice for them to get to know their neighbours," said Tam. "I still want to stay in touch with the people we used to visit, since they've become friends, but Glenda and her crew might like to make new friends in the neighbourhood, and our time is going to be limited when we take on this SPIN farm. Realistically, we probably won't see them as much."

"Another thing that's coming up for me is scheduling in downtime. My feeling is that it would be great to continue with our gig at the Love Bite but make the rest of Sunday as leisurely as possible," said Dagmar. Then she added, "Lydia, I think selling upcycled items at the same booth would be great, and, Tam, I'm with you on seeing if people in our old place would like to get to know their neighbours."

Leroy agreed. "Scheduling downtime seems wise to me. With so much on our plates, it would be easy to overdo it." Then he smiled and added, "And aren't we all about healing? Getting time to recuperate is vital to staying well."

Ross said, "I feel like we have a pretty good plan for what's coming up. Even if we've missed something, with the number of us, we have quite a bit of wiggle room."

CHAPTER 50

Movie Night

After dinner that evening, Lydia opened her laptop and exclaimed, "Hey! Simon and Lester just sent their latest cartoon!"

"What?" asked Ross.

Leroy said, "Our friends Simon and Lester, who've been creating a cartoon, just sent their latest instalment!"

"Oh yeah, I remember now," Ross said. "Those friends of yours in Vancouver." He struck the side of his head with the heel of his palm.

"And we now have a big-screen TV we can hook this up to—it's movie night at the mansion!" proclaimed Lydia. They hooked the laptop up to the TV, made bowls of popcorn with olive oil, sea salt and nutritional yeast and settled into the comfy chairs in the TV room.

"Before we put on the show, I'd like to read the email from Simon and Lester to everyone," Lydia announced. "It says, 'This installation is a little different. We wanted to try something less plot-based and more philosophical. Let us know what you think, okay? We dedicate this work to Leroy. S&L.'"

There was a close-up of a serene face that slowly faded back to show a man in a lavender superhero outfit meditating. Soon some violin music began, then a woman's voice: "Earth moves in a mysterious way, her wonders to unfold." As the song about the wonders of nature continued, scenes in the cartoon matched the words to the song. Later, the vocalist sang, "I lose her face a thousand times in crowded streets of fear, but when I look at starry skies I see her shining clear." At that point, a dazzling photograph appeared of Leroy's mother, Amelda.

Leroy held Lydia close, his eyes teary. They all watched silently until the end. Simon and Lester had created a beautiful tribute to the natural world and to Leroy's mother, Mel. A sense of the sacred and mysterious enveloped the group. Ross felt his throat tighten. He couldn't help but think of his mother also. He put his arm around Dagmar and pulled her close. Popcorn gone, cartoon over, they all cleaned up and went to bed.

As Dagmar and Ross lay in the darkness in their comfortable bed, looking through the window at the sky, they saw a full moon.

"It feels like a full moon, doesn't it?" Ross asked.

"Yeah, with Tina the ballerina making an appearance and then that film tonight …" Dagmar said.

"That film made me think of my own mom," Ross said, heaving a sigh, "and I've never seen Bella cry as much as she did after Tina's visit."

Dagmar snuggled closer to Ross. "That cartoon must have been pretty emotional for you," she said, "and I bet seeing Tina and Steve was really different for Bella. I bet she's never been around that kind of energy before."

"I wonder what the rest of the family's like," Ross speculated, then went quiet.

The night cast its spell, and they tuned into the warmth and closeness of their bodies. Quietly, almost hypnotically, they made love before falling into a deep sleep.

CHAPTER 51

An Evening With Friends

S ophie, who was coming to dinner with Phoebe at Dagmar's invitation, was surprised when they walked up the circular driveway. "Are you sure this is the right place?" she asked.

"It's the address Dagmar gave me," Phoebe said. "Why?"

"I've been here before. I provided home care to—" She stopped, embarrassed that she'd almost let confidential information slip out. "Phoebe, forget what I just said, okay? My work is confidential, and I shouldn't have revealed that much. Let's just keep it between ourselves, and we won't mention it to any of them. Do you mind?"

"No, not at all," said Phoebe reassuringly. "I understand, and it won't go any further."

They rang the doorbell, and Dagmar answered the door.

"Hi! Come on in!" she welcomed them enthusiastically. "Sophie, I'm so glad you could make it too!"

"Does it ever smell good in here!" said Phoebe. She handed Dagmar a bouquet of yellow roses. "Congratulations on your new home!" she said, smiling.

Sophie handed her a basket with basil, parsley and thyme plants. "I got these from the Love Bite. Pretty soon you'll be growing your own, I know, but I thought you'd like some fresh herbs to add to your food before you can harvest them from the gardens you're caring for."

"Thank you, both of you!" said Dagmar appreciatively. "It's so wonderful to be able to have you over for dinner! Come on back to the dining room, and I'll get a vase for these beautiful roses."

In the dining room, Dagmar said, "I know you both met everyone briefly at the Love Bite, but I'll just introduce you again." She repeated the names of each of her housemates to her two friends.

"Dinner's almost ready, so have a seat and we'll feed you soon!" Lydia announced, placing a fresh loaf of homemade bread on a cutting board on the table.

Dagmar found a crystal vase, placed the roses in it and put it in the centre of the table. Then she lit two candles and put one at either end. She put the basket of herbs that Sophie had brought onto the table with a pair of scissors before sitting down beside Ross and across the table from her two friends.

Tam and Leroy brought out platters of curried red lentils, rice, salad and cauliflower with mushrooms from the kitchen, along with green beans, chutney for the lentils, dressing for the salad and a garlicky spread for the bread.

"Suddenly, I'm starving!" Phoebe announced. "Thank you for this wonderful meal."

"Me too," said Sophie. "Thanks so much! This looks and smells delicious!"

They ate happily, enjoying being in the company of friends. Although Dagmar's housemates didn't know these two women very well, they all seemed to like them, and the conversation flowed easily. Baby Bella, in her high chair between Tam and Cammie, happily sampled some of the vegetables that had been blended for her.

The housemates were interested in learning more about Phoebe's career as an interior designer with a focus on environmentally friendly materials.

"That sounds like a dream job!" said Lydia.

"In many ways, it is," Phoebe replied. "I love my job, but it has its challenges. It's hard to keep up with all the new environmentally friendly products coming out. Because it's an emerging field, I'm learning constantly, and sometimes there are surprises—not all of them pleasant. But living my values is so rewarding. I like to think I make the world a little greener one home at a time." Then she added, "It's nice to have colleagues who have similar values too. I often collaborate with architects and suppliers who all want to make the world a better place. I like that it inspires others too. My Facebook friend Alice loves to spread good news, and she shares green success stories widely."

"I know what you mean about shared values," Leroy said. "Conversely, it's weird when you wind up in a work situation where people have very different values."

Everyone laughed, and Dagmar said, "I'm sure we've all been there." Then she added, "It's wonderful to share a home with people who have similar values too. And I don't just mean the environmental side of things either. We seem to have similar values around the way we treat each other, and that's just as important. There's such a nice flow between the group of us, and I really appreciate how well we get along."

"That's so true," said Cammie. "There's a synergy that has brought us a lot of success—the gig at the Love Bite, moving into this mansion, and now the SPIN farm. I just know it's going to work out because we work together so well. We're just a really good fit."

Lydia looked at Sophie and said, "As I recall, you're a home-care worker; is that right?"

"Yes," said Sophie. "I love my job too. I help people stay in their homes, and that means a lot to them. It's pretty down-to-earth, but it feels good to help people when they need it most."

"That's such a valuable service to the community," Leroy said. "I know it really helps the family members who care for those whose health is declining. I remember what my mother and those closest to her went through before she passed away, and I don't know what we would have done without the help and support of home-care workers."

When they finished their dinner, Dagmar went into the kitchen and brought out a strawberry cake with vanilla-coconut cream for dessert. Ross brought out a pot of chamomile tea. They all enjoyed the cake, the tea and the peaceful, friendly ambience that permeated the room.

After dessert, Dagmar asked Phoebe and Sophie if they'd like a tour of the floor of the house they were occupying.

"Of course!" said Phoebe.

It was interesting to both of them. Although Sophie had been there before when caring for Lou, she'd spent most of her time in the kitchen and living room with him. She hadn't gotten to see the bedrooms, other than his, or the meditation room with the stained glass dragon window. This was a different perspective, and she enjoyed it. She wondered how Lou was doing but didn't want to ask.

"According to Jared, we may wind up house-sitting for a number of years. His dad, Lou, is now in an institution, but last I heard he was adjusting to his new circumstances quite well," Dagmar said.

"You are so lucky to be living in such a beautiful place!" said Sophie, happy to hear that Lou was doing all right.

"It still doesn't quite feel real," Dagmar said, "but we're settling in well. Living here is going to make running the SPIN farm doable, so we're all very grateful for that. The abandoned house was a roof over our heads, and we got by. But with having to sneak in and out, I don't think we would have been able to manage the business of a SPIN farm."

Phoebe and Sophie were both getting tired so went back to the kitchen, where the rest of the household was finishing the clean-up after dinner. They thanked everyone and said goodbye.

As they left, Sophie couldn't help but wonder how many of the other family members the group had met and how the interactions had gone. She'd seen the way the family interacted with each other when she cared for Lou, the owner of the mansion.

CHAPTER 52

Velvet

Tina woke up with a hangover. She reached into the drawer in her bedside table and took a couple of aspirins. She was back home again, in the little town of Amaranth, which was a four-hour drive to her dad's place in Silverdale. As far as she recalled, he seemed to be adjusting well to the facility he was in. And didn't she meet the people Jared had told her about who were house-sitting? Freeloaders, no doubt. Jared and Ray had a habit of being taken in by those types.

Where was Steve? She expected him to be in bed still. "Steve?" she called. No answer.

"Mom! We're out of cereal! There's nothing for breakfast!" her teenage daughter, Velvet, called.

"Can you go to school early and get something at the cafeteria?" Tina called back, lifting her head, which suddenly pounded. "I'll give you some money." Then she added, "Have you seen Steve?"

"Steve left about an hour ago," Velvet replied. "He was just walking out the door as I was coming downstairs." Velvet brought her mother's purse into the bedroom and put it on her bed.

"Is $10 enough?" Tina asked while rifling through her purse and finding her wallet. "Here's $20—that'll buy you breakfast and lunch."

"Thanks, Mom," Velvet said. "I better get going then. I have an exam to study for, so I'll try to find a quiet place in the cafeteria where I can eat and study." Velvet gave her a kiss on the cheek. "Have a good day, eh?" She knew her mom probably wouldn't, by the looks of her.

"Thanks. You too, Velvet." Tina sighed and stroked her daughter's long, black hair. "I love you." What had she done to deserve this smart, beautiful young woman in her life?

"I love you too, Mom. Bye."

CHAPTER 53

Rude Awakening

Tina got up slowly, holding her aching head. She put some water on to boil and ground some coffee—maybe that would ease her pain. Where had Steve gone? They were supposed to buy gym passes this afternoon and work out together.

She walked into the bathroom and looked in the mirror. Bad idea. She made a mental note to get a few more Botox injections when she went to her dentist later in the week. She wandered back into her bedroom and noticed a folded piece of paper on her antique dresser. Unfolding it, she recognized Steve's printing, slanted aggressively to the right. "Dear Tina, It's been a slice, but it's time for me to move on. Sorry if I've let you down. Thanks a mill! Your friend, Steve."

She fell to her bed. "I'm not ready for this," she said to herself. She'd been seeing Steve for about a month and had thought maybe this time things would be different. Steve was, well, warm. It had seemed as if he really cared for her. Tina looked around her room, which spun slightly in her vision. *"Time for me to move on"—what the hell did that mean? Move on to where? Why didn't he talk to me about it?*

She heard the kettle screeching in the kitchen and got up to make coffee. She sat down at the table with her cup of coffee and took a sip: strong, sweet and black. It was comforting, something she could always count on to lift her up.

The clock read 8:30, so she'd have to wait another hour to call her therapist, Ellen. She felt embarrassed that the only time she called Ellen was when she was between men, which was about every month or two. Here we go again!

She knew what Ellen would say: *What are the issues I'm not facing? What do I need to do for myself before I can be in a healthy relationship? What about the drinking?*

It was one thing to name the facts—the abuse while growing up, the pressures to hide it and maintain appearances, her rebellion against this—and another thing altogether to understand the effects they had had on her, never mind recovering from them. All she could do was keep on trying.

She and her siblings had made a pact to do what they could to make sure their own children didn't have to go through the same thing. All her siblings were alcoholics. All had been severely traumatized by childhood abuse, so parenting was a challenge for them. They took parenting courses, shared tips and insisted that everyone treat their children well.

The latest thing Tina had read was about not allowing anyone to put themselves down in front of their children, to avoid the tendency to model that way of regarding themselves. This had been a challenge, especially for Tina and her sister. It seemed to be helping both of them to silence their inner critics, who tended to dominate the dialogue inside their heads.

She had an hour to kill. She would have a shower and make herself presentable. Hopefully Ellen would be able to see her sometime this morning. She finished her coffee and went into the bathroom to have a shower.

CHAPTER 54

Sea Cruise

George sat on the deck of a yacht in the Mediterranean. It had been his mother's idea to go on a cruise. She was inside playing bridge, while George wandered around outside. He enjoyed the sound of the waves and the fresh air.

An elderly gentleman beside him had struck up a conversation and was rambling on about investment strategies.

"I believe in loyalty and have always done well by the Fortune 500 companies," he said.

"What about technologies for the future?" asked George. "What do you think of wind turbines, solar panels, that sort of thing?"

"I know for a fact that there are price wars in the solar-panel market. Wind turbines might be another matter, but I'll stick with the tried and true."

"Do you pay attention to what these companies actually do?" George asked.

"Not at all. As long as they're making money I'm a happy investor."

George looked out at the water and wondered why he felt so disconnected.

His cellphone rang. "Hello, Rodney," said George, "still want me to come to Silverdale?"

"Yeah, have you decided one way or the other?" asked Rodney.

"Yes, I'll be there! I think a trip to Silverdale is just what I need."

CHAPTER 55

Anticipation

Back at the mansion, things were happening! Spring had almost sprung and brought lots of activity with it. Dagmar had her birthday, so the household had a celebration. Ross found a velveteen rabbit at a second-hand store and gave it to her. She loved it and what it represented. Her housemates invited Phoebe and Sophie over and prepared a wonderful meal, complete with a birthday cake and candles. It was one of the nicest birthdays Dagmar had ever experienced. She didn't know if she'd ever felt so happy with her life.

Ross, with help and input from Tam, created a washing station for the produce and a cold-storage area. They'd also become familiar with the various sprinkler systems Jon had set up and the idiosyncrasies of each garden, its soil, what had been planted previously and what would grow well in each spot this season. Jon was a thorough and thoughtful mentor.

By now they all knew the landowners and the chefs they'd be dealing with at the local restaurants. They also got to know the people who ran the outdoor markets. And Maude, who owned the Love Bite, agreed to buy fresh vegetables from them for use in the restaurant.

Lydia found a collection of large wicker baskets that she was able to get for a good price from a shop that was closing down. They would be perfect for displaying the vegetables at the market.

Life in the mansion was great and busy for the household of friends. Baby Bella was just starting to crawl, and Cammie and Tam were happy to have a safe, clean place for her to explore.

The days were getting sunnier, but there was still ice on the puddles in the morning and piles of dirty snow here and there. It was a season of eager anticipation, and they all had visions of lush gardens in their heads.

CHAPTER 56

On the Couch

Ellen, Tina's therapist, was able to squeeze her in late that morning. Relaxing on the couch, Tina realized that this room had become a comfort zone and Ellen felt like a trusted friend, albeit a handsomely paid trusted friend.

Tina sighed heavily and looked at Ellen's earnest face. "Three guesses," Tina said, her head still throbbing.

"Problems with, um …" Ellen looked at her notes. "Steve?"

"He's gone!" said Tina dramatically, with tears in her eyes. "He just left this morning before I woke up." She paused, then continued, "He left a note saying 'It's been a slice, but it's time to move on.' What does that mean anyhow?"

"So he left before you woke up this morning and also left you a note," Ellen reflected back. "How are you feeling about this?"

They'd had this conversation so many times before. Tina wondered how Ellen had the patience for these visits.

"I feel abandoned," Tina said, her voice becoming high-pitched and tight. "I feel small and alone." Then she added, "I also feel trapped and angry that I keep repeating this situation and don't know what to do about it."

There was a pause, and then Ellen asked tenderly, "Tina, do you think there's anything you could do to make 'alone' into a more enjoyable place for you? I know it's really hard after you've had someone you thought you could count on. But I wonder if it would be useful to learn how to just be by yourself for a while and learn how to enjoy that."

"But I don't want to be alone!" she said in that high-pitched voice. "I want to have a man in my life, a man who really loves me."

Another pause. Then Ellen said, "Do you think it's possible for anyone to love someone who doesn't love themselves?"

"I love myself sometimes, just not all the time."

"Do you think you treat yourself like someone you love?"

"I don't know. I know I shouldn't drink so much, and I know I often don't have a lot of patience for trying to heal. It just seems impossible! How do I do it?" she asked, exasperated. "I mean, I've read all the self-help books, done affirmations, tried everything under the sun it seems. But then it all just feels like too much, and I don't know what else to do besides drink."

"Would you be willing to try something different?" asked Ellen. "Because after all this time, I've been thinking about what might work for you, and if I have your permission, I'd like to give it a try."

"What have I got to lose?" asked Tina desperately. "If you've got ideas, I'm willing to at least listen to them."

"I have another client who has similar issues," Ellen said. "She's about your age, and I think you might really hit it off. Part of the problem is that you just go back to your regular life and fall into the same patterns and traps. What if you agreed to be buddies and support each other in making positive changes? You'd have similar goals, so you could plan activities together that don't involve drinking, sort of be a mutual support system."

"Let me mull that over," said Tina.

"If you agree to this, the three of us could touch base once or twice a week, so you'd still have my support too."

"Well, okay," said Tina in a small voice, "I guess I'll give it a try."

"So do I have your permission to give your phone number to her if she agrees?" asked Ellen.

"Yes," said Tina, giving her a meek smile.

"I know it sounds a little scary, but I think it could really help both you and her." She smiled reassuringly at Tina. "Worth a try anyway, don't you think?" she said, standing up.

Tina took her cue and got off the couch. The pain in her head seemed to be receding a bit.

Ellen stroked her back as she walked Tina to the door and said, "Thanks for being courageous at a time I know is very hard for you."

"Thanks for seeing me on such short notice and for setting up this new situation," Tina said, facing Ellen. "It can't hurt to give it a try." She smiled weakly and then walked through the door out of Ellen's office.

"Bye, Tina. Take care of yourself, and thanks again for being brave." Ellen smiled warmly at Tina as she started closing the door. "Let me know how it goes and we can set something up for the three of us within the next week. Her name's Jess."

"Jess," Tina repeated. "Maybe we'll become friends. Might be nice."

CHAPTER 57

Jess

When Tina got home, she made herself a cup of chamomile tea and heated up some soup. Her daughter, Velvet, loved to cook and always had homemade soup in the fridge. This one was tomato barley. She could smell the basil Velvet has used liberally as the soup heated.

She lifted her head up and took in the aroma, the sound of the rain outside and the pumpkin colour of the walls in her kitchen. She felt comforted by them. Her headache was gone, and she felt better after her session with Ellen. Maybe things would be all right.

The phone rang. "Hi, is this Tina?" asked a woman.

"Yes," Tina answered.

"Hi, my name's Jess. Ellen gave me your phone number. Sounds like we've got a few things in common." She laughed.

Her laughter was endearing. Tina laughed too. "Hopefully some of the things we have in common are good." They both laughed some more. This was a good start.

"Jess, can you hang on for just a second?" Tina asked, noticing the pot of soup bubbling noisily on the stove. "I just have to turn off a burner."

"Sure," Jess said. "Is this a good time for you?"

"Yes, I'm just heating up some soup, but I'll leave the lid on, and it'll stay warm. I'm drinking a cup of tea anyway, so I'm not quite ready for it."

"Soup! That sounds healthy."

"Very," said Tina. "I'm lucky to have a teenage daughter who loves cooking healthy food. Thanks to her, there's always some in the fridge. This one's tomato barley."

"Lucky you!" Jess exclaimed. "I have lots of healthy food around too, since I love to cook. My son, Ronnie, enjoys it too. I vacillate between very healthy and let's say not very healthy."

"I know what you mean," said Tina, "especially the not-very-healthy part."

"Honestly, I'm getting too old for this not-so-healthy stuff," Jess sighed. "It's literally killing me."

Tina's body felt the truth of Jess's words. "Jess, at this moment, I'm so with you," Tina replied, meaning it.

"Hey, why don't we get together for a coffee or something this afternoon? How's your schedule?"

Tina thought for a moment. "That would work for me," she replied, looking forward to meeting her new friend.

"Do you know that new little place kitty-corner to the car wash? I can't remember what it's called, but it's small and painted an outrageous shade of light purple," Jess suggested. "It has delicious, healthy desserts."

"I've been by the place but have never been in there," said Tina enthusiastically. "I'd love to give it a try. Say two o'clock?"

"Sounds good!" said Jess. "I really look forward to meeting you in person!" then she added, "I'll be wearing a red hat."

Tina gulped down her soup and got ready for her coffee date. She was amazed at how quickly the day had changed. Suddenly, she was excited.

CHAPTER 58

The Phoenix

When Tina pulled into the parking lot, she was again dazzled by the beautiful lavender colour of the restaurant. The neon sign above the doorway read "The Phoenix" with a multi-coloured bird rising up with its wings outspread. Right! That was the name! The trim around the windows was painted a bright red-orange. The rain intensified the colours. If this was the beginning of the road to recovery, it looked like fun.

She ran the few steps to the door through the rain and looked inside. There were booths for two, booths for four or more and a few stools along the countertop. The decor was sleek and modern, and against the creamy white walls were hints of the same intense lavender and orange here and there, including the patterned fabric on the seating of the booths. There were large, abstract paintings on the walls that created a feeling of excitement and exuberance.

She looked around and saw a few people sitting in booths or at the counter. Then, there she was: Jess, the woman wearing a red hat over a head of red curls. She was tall and rounded and looked to be in her forties, like Tina. They smiled at each other as Tina walked toward her.

Jess stood up and said, "You must be Tina!" She started to hold out her hand but then took a step closer and gave Tina a hug.

Tina hugged her back. "So nice to meet you!" she said before sitting down.

A nicely dressed young man with black hair walked over to them and, smiling, handed them both menus. "Welcome to the Phoenix!" he said, nodding to them both. "Would you care for something to drink?"

"I'll have a latte to begin with," Tina said, smiling back.

"And I'll have a cappuccino," said Jess.

He nodded to them again and left them to make their selections.

"This almost feels like a blind date," laughed Jess. "I haven't just met for coffee with someone in a long time. What a fun thing to do!"

"I was just thinking that this might be a pretty fun road to recovery," Tina said. "Why don't we make a point of doing fun things together? This is a great way to start!"

"Good news: I hear that the desserts in this place are out of this world!" Jess said. "We're in the right place to recover your way; that's for sure!"

They both laughed, opening their menus. After scrutinizing the menus, they ordered crème caramel for Jess and chocolate mousse for Tina. It wasn't long before their desserts arrived.

As they spread their napkins on their laps, Jess said, "Why don't we try a spoonful of each other's?"

"Good idea!" said Tina, reaching over with her spoon and trying some of Jess's crème caramel. "The raspberry sauce on the side is such a nice touch."

"Mmm. Delicious!" said Jess as she tried some of Tina's chocolate mousse. "That orange rind complements the chocolate mousse nicely."

After a few more bits, Jess asked, "So who wants to go first? We barely know each other, so we should probably tell each other a little bit about ourselves, don't you think? I know we both see Ellen. She's a peach, isn't she?"

"She is," Tina confirmed, "and so far I like her idea. I don't mind starting. This morning the guy I was seeing disappeared. I woke up, and out of the blue he'd left me a note saying he was moving on or something like that." She paused. "I was hung over. I seem to go through men pretty quickly and don't understand why. Even though I want things in my life to change, I can't seem to get out of this pattern. Otherwise, I have a nice little house, a wonderful 16-year-old daughter named Velvet, and am a retired ballet dancer. How about you?"

"I've been sober for about a week. The last time I woke up with a hangover, I had this realization that I can't do this anymore. I'm too old for this and want to grow up now," Jess said. "How do people recover? My guess is that it has something to do with substituting behaviours that hurt us with behaviours that don't. Know what I mean?"

Tina nodded in agreement.

Jess continued, "I'm an investigative journalist, though I don't take on that many assignments these days. I've been watching people who seem like they're—you know—happy, not addicted, that kind of thing, and it seems like they have coping skills that I don't but that I want to develop. Have you ever noticed that?"

"Yes," Tina said. "For me it feels like things build up, and then I just have to drink. My whole family's like that. It's how we've learned to cope."

"Really? All alcoholics?" Jess asked.

"Wealthy, hardworking, neurotic: I think that describes everyone in my family to some degree or another."

"I have a son, Ronnie, who's 17, and he's so down-to-earth," Jess said. "I really hope the cycle ends with him. My parents were both alcoholics too, and it seems like a whole other way of living."

"Since you're an investigative journalist, maybe we can be detectives together. What do other people have and do that we don't, and how do we develop those things?" Tina proposed.

"I agree. Let's take notes and share what we learn."

"On another note, I have to go into Silverdale on the weekend. Is there anything you'd like me to pick up for you while I'm there?" Tina asked.

"Actually, I'm going to the city on the weekend too. Why don't we drive down together?"

"Sure. Do you have a place to stay?" asked Tina.

"I was just going to stay in a hotel."

"Why don't you stay with me at my dad's? He has dementia and is in a facility, and I have access to his place." Tina added, "Believe me; there's plenty of room. We have some freeloaders on the bottom floor, but they shouldn't give us any trouble."

"Freeloaders? What are they doing there?"

"Ostensibly taking care of the house. But my brothers barely know them. My brothers heard them singing in a restaurant or something. They sure know how to pick 'em!" Tina sighed.

"Okay! Sounds great! Freeloaders or no." She added, "Since I won't be paying for a hotel, let me get the bill today. It's the least I can do. When are you going down, and when do you need to come back?"

"My schedule's pretty open, but I thought I'd go down after Velvet gets home from school on Friday and then return on Sunday afternoon. Is it okay with you if Velvet comes along?"

"Sure, if you don't mind that Ronnie comes too," Jess said. "Is there room to put him up at your dad's place as well?"

"You bet," Tina replied, laughing. "There's lots of room at Dad's!"

"It's been a slice!" said Jess.

Tina winced. "Ouch! That's what Steve, my old boyfriend, wrote in the note he left this morning."

"Ew, sorry." Jess bit her lip. "At least coming from me you know it's meant in the best possible way. I'm really happy to know you, Tina, and am looking forward to our trip to the city. Here's my number. Call any time, okay?" She handed Tina a business card.

"You too, Jess," said Tina. "Call any time. I look forward to our trip too and to being detectives together in the world of wellness."

CHAPTER 59
Abandoned House Update

After looking through the dry goods in the closet hallway one day, Tam said to the rest of the household, "Can we donate some of this stuff to the food bank? There are lots of things we don't use much, and I'm sure they could use some of this stuff."

They all agreed, knowing that they'd be making money soon and that they had a lot more than they needed. Soon they were loading jars of dried chickpeas, lima beans, brown rice and seven-grain cereal into the truck. Tam and Cammie delivered them to the food bank and helped Mary put them away.

"I can't thank you enough!" said Mary. "This is really going to help."

"You're welcome," said Cammie. "Thanks for all you've done for us and for everyone else here who depends on this kitchen."

Looking into the adjoining room, Tam saw Glenda looking fresh-faced under her head of frizzy hair. He turned to Cammie and said, "Hey, let's go and see how things are going at the old place."

They walked over to Glenda's table, waving. She waved back and beckoned for them to join her.

"So how's life at the house?" asked Cammie.

"It's going well," Glenda said, "and we have a new addition!" She smiled.

"Really?"

"Yes, I don't know if either of you noticed a couple who came in now and again. She had blonde hair and looked pretty worn down; he was older and kind of nondescript."

"I know exactly the couple you mean!" said Tam.

"Anyway, Jay wound up having a long conversation with the woman, and she was pretty unhappy in that situation. It was emotionally abusive to say the least." Glenda paused. "It took a few conversations, but eventually she decided to leave him and come and join us. She's getting stronger every day. She, Elly, is recovering slowly, although she already looks like a new person. She's starting to thrive in the more nurturing environment we provide and is contributing lots too."

"What about him? Does he know where she is?" asked Cammie.

"No, and she's not coming here anymore, so she won't run into him," Glenda said. "He comes in here once in a while looking for her. He's discreet about it, but we can tell."

"I think that house is a very healing place," said Tam. "It helped us, and I hope it helps all of you. Is everything working out?"

"Yeah, just fine," Glenda said. "And we've been getting to know the neighbours too. Gardening season's coming, and we're going to give a lot of them a hand."

"So glad to hear it!" said Cammie. "We don't get by as much as we'd like to anymore. I hope you'll say hello from us."

"Will do," Glenda promised. "And you're all well?"

"Yeah, we're doing great! Bella's growing like crazy and starting to crawl. She's back at home with the others." Then Cammie added, "We should run—she'll be wanting to nurse soon. Anyway, great to see you, and hello to the rest of your household from us." She gave Glenda a hug.

"I will, and hi to yours from us," Glenda said, hugging them both.

They said goodbye to Mary and drove back to the mansion, which was feeling more like home all the time.

CHAPTER 60

Gaia

Velvet sat in her bedroom thinking about the essay that was due on Monday.

Being 16 in this crazy time, especially in the dysfunctional family she was born into, was challenging. She and many others her age were feeling the weight of the enormity of the problems the world was facing. Their future was in the balance right now. What could they do?

Coming from a wealthy, privileged family, she sometimes felt guilt about what her ancestors had done: sometimes but not often. As she and her best friend, Stacey, agreed, guilt was useless. They intended to use the privilege they had to make the world better and not feel badly about the families they were born into, something they had no control over.

Velvet put her essay aside and decided to get a cup of tea. Her mom had just put on the kettle and was humming to herself. She seemed happy these past few days.

"Hi, Mom," Velvet said warmly. "Is there enough water in there for two cups?"

"I'll add a little more," Tina said as she put more water into the kettle. "What are you up to—homework?"

"Yeah," Velvet murmured thoughtfully, "starting an essay that's due on Monday."

"How's it going?"

"I'm at a loss for the right words. Do you ever think our dreams need a rewrite?"

"I've never really thought about it," Tina replied. "What do you mean?"

"Sometimes I wonder if the things we're told we're supposed to desire don't really serve us very well. Compared to lots of other traditions, it seems like our dreams are kind of hollow." Then she added, "Have you ever heard of Gaia?"

"Gaia," Tina repeated, "I think so, somewhere … refresh my memory, okay?"

"It's a name for our planet, as though it's one big living being that we're all a part of. And why wouldn't our planet be conscious? Many religions believe that everything is part of God, but I think Gaia is considered more female. It's the old Greek term for the primal Mother Goddess."

"Come to think of it, there isn't much female representation in the divinity department, is there? Funny. I wonder why that is." Then Tina said, "Maybe it has something to do with the fact that a lot of women don't feel very divine these days."

"I bet there's a connection," Velvet said, "but I'm hoping that's changing."

"I hope so too. Sometimes it seems like women are just used and spit out, and they're supposed to grin and bear it. And the sad part is women are often complicit. I hope that's changing too."

"Mom, I just want to let you know that you seem so much happier these days, and I'm really glad for you." Velvet couldn't help herself.

Tina gave her a hug. "I'm going through a lot of changes right now, but I think they're good ones." She inhaled the smell of her daughter's hair. "Maybe Gaia is entering my consciousness at just the right time."

CHAPTER 61

Dream Gone Sour

Velvet sipped her cup of tea and got back to work on her paper. Sitting in front of her computer, she did her best to express her thoughts: "Sometimes dreams become derailed and turn into nightmares. How do we change the dreams that guide us so that they take us to a future we all want? The dream we're born into has us inadvertently destroying ecosystems, harming others, making plant and animal species go extinct and perpetuating self-loathing."

She thought about some of the girls at school—some overweight and some dangerously underweight—and some of the boys who seemed trapped by unrealistic expectations about what it meant to be manly. She thought about movies she'd seen that were all about shooting people and songs and videos that treated women as commodities. How did society go so wrong?

"Can we create a new dream? A dream where we get to be ourselves, live on a healthy planet, treat each other with kindness and share our resources? I like that dream. Where do we begin? I wonder if we need to start really listening. We start by thinking of everything as sacred. Then we listen to each other; we listen to the animals and the wind in the trees; we honour the gifts of the seasons; we restore everyone and everything that we can, nothing excluded."

Velvet looked out the window at the rain falling under the streetlight. What's wrong with that dream?

"When I talk to friends or look at environmental sites on the Internet, I know I'm not the only one who has a different dream. My worry is that it's too little too late. Sometimes, though, I think there are a lot more of us than we realize and that our actions are much more powerful than we know. Maybe we're right on the brink of changing things for the better.

"This other dream has been around for a while. As I type, I'm thinking of the words of a visionary of yesteryear: 'You may say I'm a dreamer, but I'm not the only one. I hope someday you'll join us, and the world will be as one.' Thank you, John Lennon, for those words that still inspire people decades after your demise."

Velvet turned off her computer. She had a bath, brushed her teeth and went to bed. She dreamt that she was flying. When she doubted, she started falling, and when she believed, she soared upward.

CHAPTER 62

Guys Sometimes

One evening, Dagmar sat in an easy chair in the bedroom, checking her email and reading an article on the Green Team site. Ross was at his band practice.

A comment leaped out at her:

It's going to take men learning how to deal with their emotions to really get somewhere. Let's face it: men often engage in passive-aggressive behaviour in their blatant disrespect for values associated with women instead of dealing with their own pent-up feelings. Instead of admitting that something hurt them or brought up uncomfortable feelings, they'll pretend those feelings don't exist and seethe inside.

What happens to that seething? Often it comes out in culturally accepted norms that debase women. I mean, where don't we see women debased? Advertising, music videos, movies: many of these involve two-dimensional, sexualized and disposable women.

How does this play out in everyday life? Everything from rape to domestic violence to the more subtle abuses that women are expected to put up with. How often do we see women devalued and demoralized by a society that's internalized these kinds of values?

Here's to the men who have the courage to acknowledge their emotions and to heal. Hopefully we can all create the emotional climate to facilitate this healing that is so badly needed. If we can't heal ourselves, how can we possibly heal our planet?

Dagmar thought about that. She closed her computer and got ready for bed. As she got under the covers, she heard Ross come in.

"Hey, how was your practice?" she asked.

He came in, with beer on his breath, and heaved a sigh. "I don't know about those guys," he said. "Sometimes they really get on my nerves."

"What's up?" Dagmar asked.

"Oh, Donny and his girlfriend split up, and he's in a lousy mood. He treated her like crap, so I don't know why he's even surprised. All he does now is complain about her, and then he wants to sing these songs that degrade women." Ross paused for a moment. "I used to think it was okay and harmless, but I see these guys and how they treat women and maybe even the way I've treated women in the past. I look at the people we're living with and can't help but notice the difference."

"Wow! I was just reading an article—well, actually, the comments about an article—that talked about the way men suppress their emotions and the destructive behaviour it causes. Do you think those guys suppress their emotions?"

"You know, I hadn't really thought about it, but they probably do," Ross said thoughtfully. "I think they just go along with the way things are. I don't know how people get past that."

"How did you get past that?" Dagmar asked.

"For me, it was this whole radical change we both went through—living with these people who pay attention to their feelings, being with you." Ross laughed. "I'm a better person for this and am glad I'm changing, but now it's making it hard for me to spend time with these guys. They're seriously getting on my nerves lately."

"Are all of them like that?" Dagmar asked.

"To some degree or another. It's definitely an old boys' club—country music and all. I mean, there's some great country music out there; I just don't feel like singing songs that are crude."

"Hmm. Sounds pretty challenging," Dagmar said.

"Anyway, I'm glad to be here with you and love what we're doing, the SPIN farming and everything," said Ross, "and I love the way we all work together. What we have is a lot, even if it doesn't look like much. It's great that we all just click and that there isn't a bunch of squabbling." Ross shook his head. "It's really rare. We're so lucky."

Ross got undressed and climbed into bed. "Dagmar, thank you for being here for me. I feel like I can tell you anything and just be myself. I hope you feel the same way about me too."

"I do," said Dagmar. "Thanks for having the courage to go through these changes and for including me in your life." She cuddled up to him. "I agree. We have so much more than so many people, and they don't even realize what they're missing." Dagmar kissed him on the cheek. "Sweet dreams, my love," she whispered.

Ross kissed her on the forehead. "You too."

And they fell asleep.

CHAPTER 63

Online Introduction

Dagmar began her post about the SPIN farm:

Hello, everyone! We're the new owners of the SPIN farm! Most of you have already met at least some of us, but we want to make it easy for you to put names to our faces when we show up at your garden or restaurant or when you see us at the outdoor market.

We'll all be pitching in with the gardening, so you'll see us around. In this picture, from left to right, are Tam, Cammie, baby Bella, Dagmar, Ross, Lydia and Leroy.

We know you'll miss Jon as much as we do, but he'll be keeping us posted online, and we'll be sure to let you know how he's doing.

We look forward to getting to work with and to know all of you, and we hope to maintain the high level of service that Jon's provided.

Thanks for trusting us with your gardens and for supporting us!

"What do you think?" Dagmar asked Lydia.

"I think it's great. Jon told us that he'll send pictures of his grandmother's farm," Lydia said. "I'm glad he's agreed to let us share them on the website. It'll be a nice touch, don't you think? His friends will love to know how he's doing, and it'll give everyone a sense of continuity."

"With so many of us working on the gardens, we'll have time for these types of extra touches. I don't know how he managed on his own—it's so much work for just one person," said Dagmar.

"The picture turned out nicely, don't you think?" asked Lydia.

"Yeah, I like it. It was nice of Phoebe to take it."

Lydia smiled dreamily and said, "You know, with so many of us, we could sell all kinds of things! Cookies, bottles of green juice, upcycled furniture—you name it!"

"Yeah, we could!" Dagmar said excitedly. "Why not? I've got my food-safe licence, so we should be able to sell prepared foods at the market."

"I do too!" said Lydia. "If we do it properly, we can create an element of surprise. People will be expecting a booth beautifully laid out, just like Jon had, so we can build on that experience. If we have a few delicious prepared foods, people will love it! And if we limit the furniture to just one or two beautifully restored pieces, we can keep our booth from looking cluttered."

"Really, the sky's the limit! If we keep it beautiful, high quality and uncluttered, it could work so well. I can picture it now ... I'm getting inspired!"

"Me too!" said Lydia. "Leroy's got a lot to contribute that way. He and his mother used to restore furniture and decorate their house. It might help him to feel connected to her too. It's hard to know how to help sometimes."

"It must be hard," said Dagmar. "Just being there for him does wonders, I'm sure."

"It does; I know," said Lydia. "And I think he's coming around slowly. They were very close, and it takes time."

CHAPTER 64
Dreams for the Future

O ver dinner that night, Dagmar and Lydia brought up their ideas about the other things they could do with their business. Chilli, salad and homemade bread made up their simple meal.

Their ideas got the rest of them going, and they began brainstorming. As they spoke, Dagmar found paper and pen and wrote down their suggestions. By the time dinner was over, she had the following list:

Things to Sell at the Market
- Prepared food items
  - Chutney
  - Green drinks
  - Soup
  - Herbal teas
  - Cookies
  - Dried herbs
- Upcycled furniture
- Bouquets of flowers
- Play music

They agreed to keep the weather in mind and bring warming food on cold days and refreshing foods on hot days.

Dagmar put the list on a shelf and invited everyone to add any ideas that occurred to them later. Then she put on the kettle to make tea.

CHAPTER 65
Vanessa

T here was a knock on the door, and Lydia got up to answer it.

The woman outside said, "Hello, my name's Vanessa. I'm Jared and Ray's sister and just wanted to come by to introduce myself." She smiled at Lydia.

"Pleased to meet you, Vanessa. Come on in. We've just finished dinner. Would you like to join us for a cup of tea?"

"That would be lovely!" Vanessa answered.

The smartly dressed woman followed Lydia into the kitchen, and Lydia introduced her to the rest of the group. Lydia offered Vanessa a chair, and she joined them at the table.

"Jared's said nothing but good things about you! We're so grateful that you're staying here and taking good care of Dad's house," Vanessa gushed. "I'll be staying upstairs with my husband, Mike. He's at a meeting right now, but hopefully you'll get a chance to meet him before we leave." She added, "We'll be here on Sunday, and Jared told us not to miss your performance at the Love Bite, so we'll both be there."

"We really appreciate your family's hospitality and are so grateful to be able to stay in such a lovely place," said Cammie. "How's your father doing these days?"

"The last I heard, he was adjusting quite well to the facility, but Mike and I will check in tomorrow and see for ourselves." Her tone changed abruptly. "I want to apologize to you for Tina's behaviour. She can be so rude and uncharitable, and I truly hope you don't take her actions as a reflection of our family." Vanessa was distraught. "Sometimes she's such an embarrassment to the rest of us."

Dagmar and Ross brought out the teapot and some cups.

Dagmar handed her a cup and said, "Not to worry. Here, have a cup of chamomile tea."

"I appreciate your understanding, thank you. There's a black sheep in every family, I think. Mike and I don't get out this way very often," said Vanessa, "so you won't see a lot of us. We're both overcommitted. Mike's a doctor, and I'm very involved with our church. And this whole ordeal with Dad has been such a strain, bless him." Vanessa bit her lip.

"We understand," said Ross, "and we hope you'll feel free to come and say hello whenever you're in town. This is your dad's place, after all, and we want all of you to feel welcome when you're in town."

"I appreciate how hospitable you all are," said Vanessa warmly, finishing her tea. "Anyway, I should go upstairs and unpack. Lovely to have met all of you," she said and left quickly.

"I think we've met the whole family now, haven't we?" asked Dagmar.

"I think so," answered Cammie, not really sure.

"Any more thoughts on our business venture?" asked Dagmar.

No one could think of anything more, so they cleaned up, went to bed and were all mindful of the list waiting for their ideas.

CHAPTER 66
Dad's Place

Tina pulled into the circular driveway outside her dad's place. She leaned on her horn when she saw two men carrying two large industrial sinks into the backyard.

She rolled down her window and yelled, "What do you think you're doing?"

Tam walked over and said, "Ross and I are taking a couple of sinks into the backyard so we'll be able to rinse produce. We've discussed this with Jared and Ray, and they're fine with it. Is there are a problem?"

She started to react, but Jess put her hand on Tina's arm and shook her head.

"All right. I wish my brothers would keep me posted. Good night," she said rolling up the window, feeling embarrassed at her behaviour in front of Jess.

"They don't seem so bad to me," said Jess.

"I thought he seemed pretty reasonable," added Velvet.

"I still don't trust them," said Tina. She led them up the stairs to the second-floor suite.

CHAPTER 67
Reunion at the Love Bite

Sunday morning rolled around, and the people on the first floor were preparing for their gig at the Love Bite, hoping they wouldn't run into Tina. Tam and Ross had told everyone about their run-in with her, so they all left the house quietly and managed to go unnoticed.

When they arrived at the Love Bite, it was packed! They began to set up and were startled to see Vanessa and Tina with a group of other people. Although Vanessa and Tina had very different personalities, the family resemblance between the sisters was remarkable. They each had prominent chins and noses, full lips and large, dark eyes.

As soon as Tina saw them, she walked over to Tam and said, "I just want to apologize for my behaviour last night." She had told Velvet and Jess that she would apologize, and now she had.

"It's okay. It must have looked odd, and if you weren't kept in the loop, you had no way of knowing." Tam was conciliatory. Tina forced a smile and walked back to her table.

With the energy of spring and exciting plans coursing through them, the music of the Sleeping Dragon was rousing and upbeat. The patrons of the restaurant clapped their hands; some sang along, and a few got up and danced. Warm sunlight streamed through the windows and captured the crystals hanging in them, sending rainbows dancing around the restaurant.

Tam gave a start as the man he'd seen at the food bank with Elly, the woman Glenda and her friends had taken in, walked into the restaurant. He was even more surprised when the man waved toward the group and Ross waved back.

During their break, Tam asked Ross, as casually as he could, "Out of curiosity, who was the guy who waved at you?"

"Oh, that was Donny. He's part of the other band I play with sometimes," Ross said.

Tam changed the subject. "Quite a remarkable resemblance between Vanessa and Tina, eh?"

"Yeah, you're right," Ross said. "I'm surprised to see Tina here."

The second half of their performance was even more boisterous, and they all enjoyed themselves thoroughly. Afterwards, the sisters beckoned the group over. A group of people had just left a nearby table, so they pulled it over to join theirs and arranged six chairs around it.

"Hey, you're great!" Vanessa exclaimed. "I'm so glad I followed Jared's recommendation and came here."

"You caught us on a good day," laughed Tam. "I think we all have spring fever!"

Vanessa went on, "This is my husband, Mike, and you remember Tina? This is Tina's daughter, Velvet, and Tina's friend Jess. And this is Jess's son, Ronnie."

The group introduced themselves and ordered lunch when the server came along.

Tina had genuinely enjoyed the performance and started to warm to the group. She felt good here: the music, the food, being surrounded by people who cared for her. She looked at Cammie and Bella and said, "Your baby seems to really enjoy these performances."

"She's very happy and easygoing and likes all the attention." Cammie was glad to see that Tina looked much better than the last time they'd met.

"That's a rad name for a band, Sleeping Dragon," Ronnie said. "You know what it means, don't you?"

"Yeah, we like that it's a peaceful and powerful form of protest," answered Dagmar.

"Something to keep in mind as they try to ram those pipelines through, eh?" said Ronnie.

"That whole scenario could be a game changer, don't you think?" asked Dagmar.

"I think so," said Ronnie. "There's so much at stake. It's senseless. The way people are adopting new, clean technologies, no one's going to want that dirty oil anyway. I wish they'd just back off and leave it in the ground."

"Me too," Dagmar replied. "Here's another neat term. Have you ever heard of *anima mundi*?"

"No," said Velvet, joining the conversation. "What does it mean?"

"The soul of the earth, as though the earth is a living, sentient being and anima mundi is her soul that we should all be trying to tune into," Dagmar said.

"Wow! That's really cool!" said Ronnie.

"It sure is!" Velvet said. "I just started to write a paper about that very thing, only I didn't realize there was a term for the soul of Gaia. According to what I've been reading, a lot of people feel that the reason we have problems like pollution, global warming, factory farming and so many other things is that we've forgotten that the earth is sentient and sacred. Until we remember that, we'll probably just keep on creating problems."

"That gets right to the heart of things, doesn't it?" said Dagmar. "We have so much to rethink and unlearn."

Jess was talking to Tam and asked, "So you and your group are starting a new business venture. Farming is it?"

"Yes, farming people's backyards, giving them weekly vegetable orders in return for the privilege and selling the rest to restaurants and at outdoor markets."

"Nice arrangement!" Jess answered. "Did you think of this yourselves?"

"No. We're buying the business from someone who ran it successfully for a number of years. He's a friend of ours and a great guy. He's moving, so we'll be inheriting all the goodwill he's created," said Tam. "We're very fortunate that he's been mentoring us and will only ever be an email away."

Tina asked, "With so many of you, are you going to do anything in addition to what Jon's been doing?"

Tam laughed. "Are we ever! We've got a list sitting on a shelf in the kitchen with all kinds of additional things we want to do. We want to keep it elegant, beautiful and uncluttered, with very high-quality products." Then he added, "I hope you'll get a chance to come and see for yourself later in the season."

"We'll make a point of it," said Tina. "Going to the market sounds like a fun thing to do."

Vanessa and her husband, Mike, were chatting with Lydia and Leroy.

"We got in touch with Tina, and she decided to come down with her daughter and their friends. So here we all are," said Vanessa. "And now we get another visit in with you and get to hear you perform on top of that. And eat some great food. I've never been here before. What a great restaurant!"

"We love it!" Lydia smiled. "I think it has the best food in town, and it has a great ambience."

"We really appreciate the gig too," Leroy said. "Maude, the woman who owns the restaurant, does a lot to support the community. All the art on the walls is created locally, and I hear that the staff turnover is practically zilch because people love working here."

"Quite the business model," observed Mike. "It's amazing how well some of these places do. And they grow and sell herbs, which you can also cut into your meal? How interesting."

"Yeah, you won't get any fresher than that!" Lydia giggled.

Vanessa smiled at them. "Your band and the restaurant seem to be a great fit!"

They finished their meals, and all strolled into the warm spring day that awaited them outside.

CHAPTER 68

Setting Up

Tam and Ross set up the sinks behind the house under a small covered area. Ross found some hoses and attached them to the sinks so they could rinse vegetables.

There was a little empty shed close to their rinsing station. After getting Jared's approval, they set it up as a cold-storage room, using large slabs of insulating material on the inside walls. Leroy had discovered online that someone in Silverdale was giving these away to anyone who was willing to pick them up.

Once they'd finished, they looked around the yard, pleased with what they'd accomplished. They walked around to the front and viewed the expanse of lawn that would soon be growing.

"Mowing lawns has always seemed like such a waste of time to me," said Ross.

"Lawns are also the largest threat to biodiversity there is in urban settings," said Tam, shaking his head.

"Amazing," said Ross. "Some of the crazy rituals we've created make no sense."

"I love using creeping thyme in place of grass. It looks so soft and rolling. It smells great, feels wonderful when you walk on it, can be used as an herb to cook with and is drought resistant. What's not to like?"

"It would be beautiful in the front yard, with flower beds here and there," said Ross.

"Sure would," Tam agreed. "Next time we see one of the family, we should run it by them. I mean, do we really want to be mowing the lawn on top of everything else we'll be doing?"

"I can't say the idea appeals to me," Ross said, "but I do like the sound of all that creeping thyme and maybe even some other indigenous ground covers, like wild ginger. You can cook with it too, I think, can't you?"

"Oh, yeah! It's a little different from what we buy in the store but smells and tastes like ginger—a little more peppery though, I've heard," said Tam.

"Some periwinkle might look nice here and there, and it's pretty hardy," Ross said. "There was some growing in a yard where I once lived, and that stuff was almost indestructible." He paused. "Are you hungry?"

"Yeah. Let's go in and get something to eat."

When they got inside, their hunger intensified, as they could smell fresh bread baking. Tam looked in the fridge and saw a couple of large jars of soup. He looked at the clock: 11:45.

"We may as well put on soup for everyone," said Tam. "Great timing with the bread!"

The others trickled into the kitchen, guided by their stomachs. Soon they were sitting around the table, dunking homemade bread into bowls of hardy soup.

"So we got the vegetable washing area and the cold-storage room set up in the back," said Ross, "and we have a revolutionary idea about what to do with the front lawn."

This was greeted with raised eyebrows.

"Well, are you going to tell us your revolutionary idea?" asked Lydia.

"Why not replace the lawn with creeping thyme and indigenous ground covers that never need mowing and are drought-resistant? And maybe throw in some periwinkle just for fun?" asked Ross.

Tam added, "I mean, do we want to be mowing and watering the lawn all summer? There's a lot of it out there."

"We'd have to see if the family would go for it, but it sounds like a great idea to me," said Cammie.

"Yeah, me too," Dagmar said. "Let's run it by the next family member we run into, shall we?"

"On another note, we've gotten most of the glitches out of the website," said Leroy. "We just have a couple of bugs to work out before we show it to you. We should have it done by this afternoon."

"Hey, great!" said Tam. "I can hardly wait to see it!"

"I've set up a bank account in my name and will make sure everyone has access so you can see what's going on," said Dagmar.

"And I've gotten in touch with all the restaurants and introduced myself and made notes of what they'd like this season," added Cammie.

"Now all we have to do is wait for the weather to warm up, so we can get started with the planting," said Ross.

"We've also found some old wooden chairs that we're restoring and repainting to sell at the outdoor market," said Lydia. There was light blue paint on her hands.

"Nice colour!" Dagmar said.

"It'll wear off," Lydia giggled.

CHAPTER 69

Just One Drink

After the meal at the Love Bite, Tina and Jess rounded up their kids, piled into the car and started the long drive back to Amaranth.

Velvet and Ronnie were talking excitedly about each of their school's environmental initiatives, the music at the Love Bite and anima mundi.

In the front seat, Tina and Jess were quiet, their eyes on the road.

About halfway there, Tina said, "So there you have it: the house I grew up in and my sister. Something about being there brings everything back. Right now I feel like a big open wound."

"It's hard to imagine what it must have been like growing up in such an enormous place. By comparison, the house I grew up in was practically a shack," said Jess.

"I guess homes of any size are capable of producing their own form of poison," said Tina. "When you grow up in a big house like that, a lot goes undetected. People get away with things they wouldn't if they had neighbours within earshot. As long as everything looks good on the outside—well, I guess that's the whole point: looking good on the outside. Hey, why don't we drop off the kids and see what's happening downtown?"

"Sounds good to me," Jess replied.

They dropped Velvet off, then Ronnie, and drove back into town. Tina parked the car, and she and Jess walked down the sidewalk, past the many closed shops, until they heard music. A little pub seemed to invite them in. It had dark beams, horseshoes, wagon wheels, cowboy boots, bar stools and loud music.

"I need a drink after a weekend with family," said Tina.

"I could use one too," said Jess.

At first they were going to each order a mug of beer, but then they realized a pitcher wouldn't cost much more. The first went down well, so they ordered another. Soon they were laughing and dancing and having a great time!

CHAPTER 70

Anima Mundi

When Velvet got home, she went to her computer and continued with her essay. After Googling "anima mundi" she wrote, "*Anima mundi* is a term that means the soul of our planet. It implies that earth and all the life she supports make up a conscious, living being and that everything and everyone is a part of her. The term has come into popularity in the past few decades with some environmentalists. Its re-emergence has been associated with the concept of Gaia, the personification of the Earth, the primal Greek Mother Goddess."

Velvet thought about her own mother, Tina—Tina the ballerina—who had had so much invested in being young, beautiful and agile. Her empty dream was just a small part of a much bigger, much emptier dream—the one that was implied in some way every day: movie stars, money, mansions, cruises and limousines, the promise of heaven if we're good, with "good" defined specifically by our culture and having little to do with the well-being of future generations or the health of the planet. Like a late-night infomercial, the dream appealed to people's greed, loneliness and insecurity, to baser instincts, convincing people that there was little more to life. How to express all that?

She wrote some more.

> My interpretation of anima mundi is a voice that speaks through all of us. She's the desire for what's best for everyone. She's the sensibility that runs the household but multiplied

billions of times over, running the "household" of our entire planet: our ecosystems, our interactions with each other and other species and with the rhythms of the seasons. Anima mundi speaks through everyone and everything, and our job is to listen and be attentive, nurturing and responsive to what she tells us—that is, if we're to survive and if it's not too late.

How do we rewrite our dream? How do we write a new story about love and sensibility, a story that blazes a path to a future where we'll all thrive? Not just humans but animals, plants and ecosystems too. How do we translate and honour the story anima mundi has to tell, the story so few have been listening to?

Maybe it starts with tuning into ourselves, since we're all part of this story. When have we felt happiest? For me, and I suspect for many of us, it's when we've been seen, heard and valued for exactly who we are. Maybe that's what she wants for herself and for all of us.

What is Anima mundi saying? I don't think it's as difficult to understand as it may seem. On a warm spring day, do you think she might be feeling happy about all the new life that's springing from her? That would be my guess.

CHAPTER 71

A Hard Morning

"Hello, Jess?" Tina said huskily into her cellphone.

"Yeah, it's me. Are you feeling as lousy as I am?" she asked.

"I can barely move my head. That was fun last night though, eh?" Tina replied before taking two aspirin and gulping down a glass of water.

"I'm getting way too old for this kind of thing," moaned Jess. "It was fun last night, but this morning's hell. I don't even remember how I got home. Please tell me I didn't drive."

"No, I called a cab. At least I had that much sense." She added, "My head is pounding."

"I don't think Ellen's going to be too impressed. When do we meet her again? Tomorrow morning?"

"Yeah, I think so. Let's see. Tomorrow at ten o'clock." Tina paused. "Should we tell her about last night?"

"Of course," said Jess. "Why see her if we're not going to be honest with her? How can she help either of us if we don't tell her the truth?"

"I see what you mean," Tina said, then sighed. "I'm just so used to maintaining appearances. It's hard to know when to stop sometimes. And I blow it all the time anyway."

"Maintaining appearances? You could have fooled me last night! Here's somewhere I can help," said Jess. "Being an investigative journalist, sticking to the facts is a big deal to me. So can we agree right now that we tell Ellen the truth? If not, what are we paying her for? Why are we going to her?"

"Good point."

"It was great to meet your sister and her husband and to see where you grew up," Jess said, "and it was neat that our kids got to meet. And I enjoyed the music and the food at that restaurant we went to."

"That was a fun road trip, wasn't it?" Tina said. "We should have just gone straight home instead of dropping the kids off and going for drinks afterwards."

"Yeah, that would have been the smart thing to do, wouldn't it?" Jess laughed, then stopped abruptly since it made her head hurt. "Ouch! I shouldn't have laughed."

This got Tina laughing and hurting as well. "Okay, I'll let you go so we can stop laughing and take care of ourselves. I hope you don't have too much planned for today."

"No, thank goodness. I'll just lie down, have a bath and take it easy." Before hanging up, Jess said, "See you tomorrow morning at Ellen's office at ten o'clock."

"I'll be there! See you then," said Tina.

CHAPTER 72

Ellen's at Ten

"Good morning!" said Ellen, smiling at the two women in her doorway. She beckoned for them to come in and sit with her at the table by the window. It was overcast outside. "How are you both this morning?" she asked as they all settled into their seats.

Jess and Tina looked at each other.

"Pretty good," said Tina.

"Much better than yesterday," said Jess.

"Oh?" Ellen raised her eyebrows.

"Yeah, we took a road trip, came back, dropped the kids off at home and decided to go for a drink," Jess said.

Tina was looking at the ground.

"A drink?" Ellen repeated.

"Yes, but it turned into more than one," Jess confessed, "and we both felt pretty bad the next morning."

"I see," said Ellen. "Tina, would you like to talk about that a little bit?"

Tina heaved a sigh and looked up sheepishly. "I don't know what to say. It's true. We had a lot to drink, we both felt rotten yesterday and now we're here."

"How do you feel about that right now?" asked Ellen.

"I feel embarrassed, ashamed, and it was hard to tell you. I thought about not telling you," Tina said.

"Can you tell me more about why it was hard to tell me?" Ellen asked.

Tina hesitated for a moment. "It feels like I need to maintain appearances, like I'm afraid of being judged or of letting you down."

"You know I'm here to support you and help you get the most out of life, right? I can only do that when you're honest with me, so I really appreciate your courage in telling me this much." Ellen reached over and gently put her hand on Tina's.

"Thanks," said Tina, her voice becoming small. "I think, in the back of my mind, I expect to be shamed."

"I understand," Ellen reassured her. "Jess, how about you? What's happening for you right now?"

"I'm feeling disappointed with myself," Jess said, "and like my body just can't take this kind of punishment, but how do I get out of this pattern? It just seems so difficult."

"What happened yesterday morning?" asked Ellen.

"Tina phoned to see how I was feeling. She really wanted to know how I was doing, and I was glad to hear from her." Jess looked at Tina and, gently touching her arm, said, "Tina, thanks for caring. I really appreciated your call."

Tina looked up at her and said, "I wanted to know that you were okay. It was so nice to be myself, hungover and reaching out to someone who is my friend. I'm grateful that we can be ourselves together. Jess, thanks." She gently stroked Jess's arm.

"Maybe we can look at what led up to your having drinks and see if we can identify places where things could have been handled differently. Would you be up for that?" Ellen asked.

They thought about it for a minute; then Tina and Jess both agreed.

"Okay, so what led up to your night out?" asked Ellen.

"We took a road trip to the city with our kids to meet my sister and her husband, who were in town," said Tina. "It was a pretty fun trip but lots of activity and personalities to deal with. When we got back to Amaranth, I felt a buildup of stress."

"Yup, that goes for me too," Jess said. "Lots of activity, lots of personalities and settings, and I felt a buildup of tension and welcomed the release that alcohol provides."

"Can you pinpoint some of the things that brought up these feelings?" asked Ellen.

There was silence, and then Tina said, "When I go back to the house where I grew up and see members of my family, I become overwhelmed with feelings of insecurity, fear and self-loathing. That's the way I felt most of the time when I was growing up: those feelings and pressure to appear perfect. Practicing and performing ballet was a welcome focus that helped me ignore those things back then, but it's hard on the body. As I got older, I felt my self-worth plummet as my body was no longer able to perform the way it once did." She paused and then added, "My whole family has always used alcohol to deal with uncomfortable feelings, so that habit comes into play too." She stopped there.

Jess spoke up then. "For me, seeing the mansion where you were raised brought up my sense of unworthiness that came from growing up in a poor family—you know, Kraft dinner, shabby house, my stressed-out single mother who took a lot of her frustrations out on me, never having nice clothes. I don't know. I worked my way through school and became an investigative journalist, but deep down I still feel this sense of inadequacy, like I was just born into not being good enough." She stopped for a moment and then continued, "I've tried to honour some of my good qualities, but really I sometimes feel like there's nothing I can do to be a worthwhile human being. No matter how hard I try, it seems that feeling still lurks beneath the surface." Jess laughed. "What a facade we create, eh? No matter how much or little we have, so many people our age feel worthless for some reason or another. Then we smile and invite each other to have a nice day."

Tina shook her head slowly, and Ellen smiled sympathetically.

"Since you're becoming a team, can you see places where you can ask for help or be of help to each other when you're triggered?" asked Ellen.

"You know, I'm feeling better already just openly expressing what goes on for me and still feeling valued," said Tina. "Jess and Ellen, thank you."

"I feel the same way, Tina," said Jess. "We really value each other. That means so much! It might be a foundation for some major healing. I think a lot of women our age aren't acknowledged and valued for who we are, and consequently we devalue ourselves. It's almost habitual."

"I know what you mean," said Tina. "When we were growing up, both boys and girls were fed degrading stereotypes of women. Our parents were of the generation whose own parents went by the 'spare the rod, spoil the child' philosophy. Issues of self-esteem were non-existent back then. What can you expect from children who grew up getting beaten for the slightest thing? We had it better than them, but let's face it: they were pretty damaged. As parents they were probably doing the best they could."

"When I met your daughter, Velvet, I could see right away that you've raised her to value and respect herself," Jess said to Tina. "I've tried to do the same with my Ronnie, and I think we both deserve a pat on the back for caring about how our children feel about themselves."

"How do you feel about that, Tina?" Ellen asked.

"That feels so true!" Tina replied. "Something I know deep down is that the way I feel about myself causes more problems than anything. I don't want my daughter to have the same kinds of feelings to grapple with."

Ellen glanced at the clock on the wall and got up. "Tina, Jess, I'm delighted with the progress you're making," she said. "It feels like we're really getting somewhere, and it feels like you're becoming an amazing support system for each other."

Outside, the sun was starting to peek between the clouds.

"Ellen, thanks for putting us together," said Tina from her heart. "I feel like my whole focus is changing. I feel less concerned with what other people think and care more about doing what's best for myself."

As Jess got up, she put an arm around Tina, looked at Ellen and said, "Thanks for being such an intuitive therapist. I'm really glad we all took a chance on this arrangement and feel like I'm at the beginning of a very important healing journey."

"Thanks both of you for your trust and for your hard work," Ellen said. "I think we all have a real opportunity to make changes for the better. I hope this coming week you'll have more of these kinds of conversations. Same time, same place next week work for you both?"

Tina and Jess nodded, and the three of them walked out the door feeling relaxed and whole.

CHAPTER 73

Community Currency

Tam was in the vicinity of the food bank, so he popped in. Mary was preparing food as usual, and Glenda was rinsing a bunch of dandelion greens, chickweed and lamb's quarters in the big industrial sink.

"Hi, Mary. Hi, Glenda. How's it going?" he asked.

Mary stretched backwards and put her hand on her lower back. "Pretty good," she said. "How's everything with you?"

"Great!" he answered. "Just getting things set up for gardening season. Are there any vegetables you need? I'd like to bring you some over the course of the growing season."

"Oh, the usual. You know: potatoes, carrots, beans, zucchini—anything you've got really."

"Thanks. I'll just bring any surplus, and I'm sure you'll find a use for it," Tam replied. He looked over at Glenda and asked, "Glenda, what's up?"

"I've been helping some of the neighbours weed their greenhouses, and they've been throwing these away," she answered, gesturing to the plants she was washing. "I've done a lot of wildcrafting, and these greens are so nutritious, often more than the plants they're being weeded out from. I couldn't stand to see it go to waste. We've been eating lots of these at home, and I just thought it would make a nice addition to what the food bank has to offer."

"Have you thought about giving a small talk on wildcrafting?" asked Tam. "Your knowledge could help a lot of people. We've been raised to consider all this stuff weeds, and most people throw it out."

"I'll keep that in mind and maybe just discuss it informally with others when I'm here," said Glenda.

"Say, Tam and Glenda, could you give me a hand moving that couch? My back's not up to it, and I think it would be so much nicer by the window," said Mary. "I can even pay you."

"Pay us?" exclaimed Tam. "There's no need. I'm happy to give you a hand."

"Yeah, me too," added Glenda.

"No, really—I'm trying to get rid of this money," insisted Mary.

"What?" said Tam. "Trying to get rid of money? I thought you were looking for money."

"No, this money's different," she said. "I get it all the time, and I actually look for opportunities to spread it around." She pulled out a stack of bills and put it on a nearby bench.

"We got a few of these in the hat when we were playing at the Love Bite on Sunday. What are they anyway?" asked Tam.

"It's a community currency, and it can only be spent here in Silverdale," said Mary.

"How does it work?" asked Tam.

"In a nutshell, local businesses pledge a certain amount of this currency to a local community group or groups of their choice. So a number of local businesses have chosen the food bank. We're given a certain amount of this currency, and when people make monetary donations to the group, we can offer them a tax receipt *or* the same amount of money in community currency, which they can then spend at participating businesses. It's an excellent fundraiser, since donors get to spend their money twice: once as a donation, then again as a local currency. It makes donating more affordable, so it's easier for community groups to raise money."

"Whoa, what?" said Tam, confused. "So you have a bunch of this money that you can donate or spend at local businesses or wherever else you want, is that right?"

"That's right," Mary replied. "Participating businesses pledge to accept a certain percentage of payment in this currency. When people spend it at a business, the business can re-donate it, spend it at other participating businesses or pay anyone who's willing to accept it. Does that make sense?"

"Not really," Tam said, trying to understand her explanation. "I don't get how businesses can afford to spend all that money to get the currency started. Aren't they taking a huge financial risk?"

"They don't pay any regular money; they pledge the amount in community currency, and that brings it into existence," Mary said. "They don't pay a penny, but they agree to accept a certain percentage of the community currency in payment for their goods and services. Their pledge starts the whole process."

"So how do businesses benefit from it?" asked Tam.

"Well, it's free advertising, for one thing, since their businesses are listed on the website and on these flyers." Mary handed one to Tam. "And it gives businesses something to offer community groups besides money or their goods or services, so it's easier on them, especially in these tough times. One community dollar is equal to a regular dollar. And since just a percentage of a purchase can be made in local currency, regular money comes with it, so it helps their businesses to become more profitable."

"Wow," said Tam. "I'll check out the website."

"Yeah, it takes a while to really grasp it, but once you do, you can see how much it does for the community. It can never leave Silverdale the way regular money does, so it just sticks around, stimulating the local economy all the while." She smiled. "Can I offer you $10 each to help me move the couch and rearrange a couple of things?"

"Sure," said Tam. "Thanks very much!"

CHAPTER 74

Chloe

P hoebe heard a meow at the door and let in Chloe, a cat the people living in the fourplex shared. She was a beautiful calico with golden eyes and tended to spend time with people when they were feeling sad. Was Phoebe feeling sad? Maybe a little blue this time of year just before spring. This was always the most challenging time of year for her. She just wanted the warm weather already! She stroked Chloe, who sat on her lap purring. Such a comfort!

In the last couple of weeks, she'd gotten the attentions of not one, but two men and didn't know how she felt about her situation. She'd been widowed about five years earlier—a freak boating accident—and after a short grieving period she'd thrown herself into her work. It was the only way she knew how to cope with, or at least not confront, her deep feelings of loss. Since then, she'd dated once or twice but nothing very serious.

She promised herself to get to know these men better and let things progress organically. She knew them only superficially and was aware that people could be quite different from the way they appeared at first. She promised herself she'd take her time getting to know them, maybe as friends, even if neither went any further than that.

She was working with one of the men, Liam, on designing a bedroom since he was having trouble sleeping. He was in the environmental technology field, and she'd collaborated with him on some of the houses she'd worked on. She had gone to his home, which had three bedrooms, and had a consultation with him. The master bedroom, where he was sleeping, was very large and white and cold. It didn't surprise her at all that he was unable to sleep there, since rooms that were small, warm and cozy were much more conducive to sleep, at least for most people.

When she'd mentioned this, he'd thought it made a lot of sense. She'd told him that she would present him with a couple of options: one was to section off a sleeping area in the master bedroom and the other was to use one of the smaller bedrooms.

As Chloe purred on her lap, she thought about their conversations and the options she could provide. She'd enjoyed the consultation. Liam had been able to relax and tell her what colours he found soothing. He'd also given her a few more details that would help her to design something beautiful and unique that suited his needs. The colour he found most relaxing was sage green, which she knew would be calming in a bedroom. She also felt that she could find an antique room divider that would work well with that shade if they were to use the master bedroom.

He was engaging and professional, but she could feel a mutual attraction between them. It was restrained but quite delicious. She loved her profession, but there was an added element of excitement to this particular project because of the dynamic between them. She would carry on with it, make sure she did a great job and see where things went.

She'd gone to a potluck earlier that week and met the other man, Cole, who seemed to be fun. He'd asked her out for a hike on the weekend. She liked to get out in nature, and it was a popular trail they'd be taking, so she accepted his invitation, knowing there'd be lots of other people on the trail. He'd left a message on her phone the other day, and when she'd called back, a woman had answered. He'd told her it was his roommate and that they were just friends. Anyway, a hike couldn't hurt.

She put Chloe down, got up and put out some kibbles and water for her. Then she sat down at her computer and started the renderings of the two bedrooms.

CHAPTER 75

Dollars and Sense

After lunch, Tam and the rest of the household sat around the table in front of his laptop. They went to the web address that was on the bottom of the ten-dollar bill he'd gotten from Mary. It was a simple site decorated with similar artwork to what was on the bills. There were bees, flowers, hearts and other images in pen and ink. The homepage said, "Welcome! You've discovered a currency that cares! Instead of leaving town at the first opportunity, it sticks around and builds community. We hope you'll join us."

"Currency that cares?" said Ross. "Isn't that an oxymoron?"

"I've never heard of anything like it before," said Tam. "But the way Mary explained it made it sound pretty good. Now that I've got some, I want to see where I can spend it."

Dagmar added, "This seems like great advertising for businesses. As soon as you get some of this stuff, you check the website to see which businesses are participating, just like we are."

"You don't think it's some kind of scam? Why would people trust this stuff?" asked Ross.

"It begs the question, why do we trust any currency? Currency is all about trust. Do we trust the system that creates our currency?" asked Leroy. "I know it's something we've used our entire lives, but economies sometimes crash, then what? Yet we continue to use the stuff because it's what we know how to use. I'm intrigued by the idea of someone designing a currency to stimulate local economies."

"I love the tone of this site," Lydia said. "Creating our own money! Who would have thought? Let's see what it says under each of the tabs."

There were only three tabs: "About Us," "Get Involved" and "Contact Us." Its simplicity was easy on the eyes. On the homepage it said,

> Wouldn't it be great if money had a heart? What would it be like if it actually cared about us, our community and all the places where we volunteer to make life better in our communities?
>
> Regular money doesn't care, because it's designed not to. But it doesn't have to be that way. We offer a currency that supports all the things that most people value: each other, community groups and our local businesses.
>
> Be patient with yourself as you try to wrap your head around this. It takes a shift in our understanding of how money works. But it's worth it, not just to you but to everyone you care about. The more you use it, the more it will make sense and the more you'll want to keep using it.

The other two tabs described how the currency worked in more detail, the businesses and community groups involved and how people could get involved.

"Sounds great!" said Leroy after they'd read through the tabs. "You want to sign up?" He looked around at the rest of them.

"I think it's worth at least finding out more," Cammie said. There was a phone number and an online form to fill out. "We've got a speakerphone, so why don't we give them a call? That way we can all ask questions."

They dialled the number.

CHAPTER 76

Money Talk

"Hello?" a woman answered the phone after a couple of rings. "Hi! I'm calling to get information about the community currency. Is this the right number?" Tam asked.

"Yes! I'm so glad you're interested! How can I help you?" the woman asked.

"My friends and I are taking over a SPIN farming business and want to see how we can get involved," Tam said. "I'm going to put you on speakerphone, if that's okay. That way, we can all ask you questions."

"That's fine with me," said the woman. "My name is Janet. What are your names?"

They introduced themselves, and then Janet asked, "How did you hear about our community currency?"

Tam said, "Mary at the food bank gave me some and told me about it, so now we're all looking at your website trying to wrap our heads around how this works. It's intriguing, but we want to be sure we understand it and maybe sign up."

"Great! What questions do you have for me?" asked Janet.

Dagmar asked, "So how much of this money do we donate?"

"We recommend a donation of $1,000 in community currency per employee and a 10 percent administrative fee to the administrative body," said Janet. "How many of there are you?"

"Six," Dagmar said.

"It is a lot of money, but don't forget it's not federal money; it's community currency that costs you nothing, nothing except your agreement to accept a percentage of it for the goods and services you sell. When you pledge, you're putting community currency into circulation and not spending a cent of regular money. And since you're committing to accepting a certain percentage, it'll keep coming back to you. You can spend it, offer it to customers as change, give it to local musicians you happen to like—"

The household burst out laughing.

Ross said, "We sing at the Love Bite every Sunday morning, and someone's already left us some."

"I'm glad you've received some. That makes it much easier to explain. Now that you have it, what are you going to do with it?" she asked playfully.

"Well," Cammie said, "I'm going to go to your website and see where I can spend it."

"Exactly!" said Janet. "Doesn't having this currency make you want to go to these places of business?"

"Yes, it does. It's great advertising," Cammie said.

"Okay, so we go to one of these businesses and decide to buy something," Lydia said. "What happens next?"

"Let's say you find something for $10, and they take 20 percent of the community currency," explained Janet. "Then you give them $8 in regular money and $2 in the community currency."

"So it works just like real money, then?" said Leroy.

"Yes, but it never leaves the community. You can't put it in the bank; you have to recirculate it. So the business will have to find a local business or person to spend it on." Janet laughed. "Kind of like a hot potato."

"Mary at the food bank was actually trying to spend it," Tam said. "I guess that's why."

"It encourages our generosity and nurtures the qualities we want our society to have. We can also offer it to people as change and get them involved in the adventure too," Janet said. "So can I sign you up, or do you want to think about it some more?"

They all looked at each other and nodded in agreement.

"Okay," said Dagmar, "I think we're agreed."

"Now you have a couple of decisions to make," Janet said. "You need to decide which community group or groups you'd like to donate to, and you need to decide what percentage of community currency you'll accept. I'd recommend 30 or 40 percent, since you don't have a lot of overhead. Also, at first very few people will be using this currency, so it'll make up just a small fraction of your earnings."

"Very few people know what a SPIN farm is," said Lydia. "It just dawned on me that we didn't have to explain it to you."

Janet giggled. "It's similar in the sense that it creates value in a very innovative way. Besides, Jon's a friend of mine. You must be the ones who bought his SPIN farm business, which is great!" Janet paused, then added, "The people who rent out the tables at the market accept community currency, just so you know."

Tam had gone to the "Community Groups" tab on the computer. "All the groups look worthwhile to me," he said. "Are there any that are more in need than the others?"

"The animal shelter could use some love," Janet replied. "Other than that, they're pretty evenly split."

"How about if we each choose a group to donate to?" asked Tam, and everyone nodded in agreement. "So I'll take the animal shelter."

The rest of them each chose a community group and agreed to accept 40 percent.

CHAPTER 77

On a Hike

The day was overcast as Phoebe and Cole climbed up the mountainside. It was an easy slope, and many passed them coming down the trail.

"Have you climbed this trail before?" asked Phoebe.

"Only once, but I've always wanted to do it again—with someone special," Cole said.

Phoebe wasn't sure what to make of the "someone special" part of his remark. "So what makes you think I'm someone special?" she asked.

"Oh, I don't know," he said. "You just seemed like someone kind of special when I met you at the potluck the other night."

She didn't know how to answer that. "It's nice to be out in the wilderness," she said as she held on to a rock and pulled herself partway up a segment of the trail. "I hope we're all able to live so harmoniously one day—people, that is—the way natural systems do. They're so intricate, honest and beautiful."

"Yes, it's nice to be in the great outdoors!" Cole exclaimed. "I don't know if people are capable of living the way the rest of nature does. People are so selfish and keep having wars and destroying the planet. Maybe we'll just go the way of the dodo bird. Good riddance to us, the blight that we are."

"Is that really what you believe?"

"Well, yeah," Cole said. "All you have to do is look around, read the news or even look at people's relationships these days."

"When I look around, I see a lot of people doing their best to improve things," Phoebe said. "Maybe that's just one of the perks of having colleagues who do environmental restoration work." She laughed. "Plus I don't watch TV and very rarely watch movies, most of which give the same depressing messages. I believe in people's innate goodness." She continued her climb and then added, "I mean, have you ever seen an evil baby? That's what we all start as."

"You don't really believe that, do you? Even if there are some good people, there are always a few bad apples, and they often wind up running the show. How do you account for them?"

"Maybe they've just learned to believe all the negative programming they've received. So much of what we see in movies shows us that people aren't as they present themselves and are out to take advantage of others. I think when we internalize those messages, we feel alone and like we're not accountable to anyone. When we believe this, lying, cheating and stealing are normalized, so some of us do what we think everyone else is doing." Phoebe reached for a large rock and climbed up a root system that had become a kind of stairway. She looked over her should into Cole's eyes and noticed that they were focused on her behind.

"Don't you think that's a little naive? To me it seems like everyone puts on a show but ultimately is in it for themselves. Aren't we all just looking out for number one?" he asked, scrambling up the root system. Then he sighed. "Maybe one day someone from another planet will come and make things right. Do you believe in extraterrestrials?"

"I've never given them a lot of thought," Phoebe said, "but shouldn't we take responsibility for the mess we've created instead of counting on beings that may or may not exist?"

"I suppose," Cole answered nonchalantly.

They climbed silently for a while and then took a little break on a flat rock at the side of the trail.

"So tell me about yourself," said Phoebe as she took off her daypack and got her water bottle out.

"What's there to tell?" Cole laughed. "I live here in this beautiful valley, do a number of things for a living—everything from carpentry to online stuff to playing music to marketing. I love the outdoors. What about you?"

"I lead a pretty quiet life. I enjoy my work as an interior designer with a focus on sustainable materials, and it takes up a lot of my time. I have a few good friends and a cat the people in my fourplex share," she said. Cole pressed up beside her. "I'm curious about your roommate, the woman who answered the phone," she said. "Are you lovers?" *Why not ask point-blank?* she thought.

Cole laughed, embarrassed. "She's just a friend from one of my jobs. My partner and I split up about six months ago, and she and I both needed a place to stay, so we decided to share a place and split the rent."

"So you're not sleeping with her then?"

"Why do you women always assume things?" Cole answered teasingly. "Shall we get back on our hike?"

"Actually, I'd like a little snack. Want some trail mix?" Phoebe asked, rummaging around in her daypack.

"No, that's okay. I'm not hungry right now."

Phoebe got out her trail mix and ate some. After she'd chewed a mouthful, she said, "You didn't answer my question, did you? Are you sleeping with Alice?"

"What is this, the third degree?"

"So you are," said Phoebe. "How does she feel about you dating other women?"

"Wow! You're really jumping to conclusions!" Cole said.

"If she's a friend, why didn't you bring her to the potluck, and why won't you answer me directly?" Phoebe was feeling increasingly upset by this encounter.

"Well, we're friends, but we don't run with the same crowd," Cole said. "We have different sets of friends."

Phoebe put away her trail mix. "Cole, I'm sorry we've gotten off to such a bad start, but you know what? I just want to go down the mountain now and go home. I'm not enjoying this anymore."

"Wait a minute," Cole said. "Don't you think you're overreacting? She means nothing to me! She's just my roommate."

"So you're just using her for sex, but she doesn't mean anything to you. How do you think she feels about that, or do you care?" asked Phoebe.

"Stop with the leading questions," Cole pleaded, stoking her arm.

"Please! Get your hand off me!" said Phoebe. "Do you care about her feelings?"

"Well, no, she's just a friend," Cole said in an exasperated voice.

"I care a lot about my friends' feelings," said Phoebe indignantly. "It's hard for me to relate to someone who doesn't care about the feelings of their friends." She stood up and started climbing down the mountainside.

"Phoebe!" Cole exclaimed. "You're overreacting! Come on; let's just finish our hike. The view from the top is lovely."

She continued walking away as she said, "As we've been chatting, I've realized that we have very different values. I care about the feelings of the people in my life and have a hard time understanding people who don't, especially when it's someone they're sleeping with."

"What can I say to make things right?" asked Cole.

Phoebe sighed. "I don't know if there is anything you can say. I'm just not getting a very good feeling about the way things are going, and I would rather be home right now." She looked at him and saw a man who looked sheepish and evasive. Suddenly he was unattractive to her. "Goodbye, Cole," she said, climbing down the slope more quickly.

When Phoebe reached the bottom, she hopped in her car and drove home.

CHAPTER 78

Home Again

P hoebe drove into the driveway of her fourplex and undid her seat belt. She sat in the car for a second. Had she overreacted? Somehow she didn't think so. She got out of her car, grabbed her daypack and walked into the entrance of the fourplex. She opened the door to her unit and put the kettle on.

Outside a storm started brewing. The rain blew against the windows. Just as well she wasn't up the mountain with Cole. She was content to be in her cozy home.

She sat down and looked out the window, sipping a cup of tea. She heard a meow at the door and let Chloe in. When Phoebe sat down, Chloe jumped on her lap and started purring. It was comforting, and she stroked Chloe as she thought about what had just happened with Cole. The experience on the mountain had left her feeling unsettled. Why? First of all, she knew in her bones that Cole was sleeping with his roommate and didn't care about her feelings. He wouldn't come out and deny it, because he didn't want to lie. She didn't like that he would use someone that way.

She also didn't like how he sexualized everything—from the vague statement that she was someone special to the way he pressed up against her. All these things communicated his attitude toward women. Maybe he didn't realize how cheapening his behaviour was. No matter. He was in the past.

The phone rang. "Phoebe?" It was Cole.

"Yes. Hi, Cole," she answered coolly.

"I don't understand what just happened," he said in a quiet voice, as if he didn't want to be overheard.

"Are you at home?" she asked.

"Yeah, I'm in my room."

"So what would you like to talk about?"

"I want to apologize for whatever it was I did," he said.

"No need for an apology. You were just being yourself, and we got to know each other a little better. I think I know you as well as I want to."

"You don't forgive me?" he asked.

"There's nothing to forgive. We have different values; too different for me I'm afraid. Let's just leave it at that," she said in a clipped voice.

"Well," sighed Cole, "I guess I'll see you around."

"Goodbye." She hung up the phone.

She took a deep breath and let it out, then relaxed into her chair, had another sip of tea, closed her eyes and listened to the storm outside. She was happy to be safe, warm and in her home, being soothed by the tea, Chloe on her lap and the sound of the rain.

CHAPTER 79

A Short Walk

Alice had a lump in her throat and was holding back tears. She and Cole had made love an hour earlier, or "had sex" as he liked to put it. He'd been out that morning but had come back early in the afternoon. He'd told Alice that he had started to go on a hike in the woods but had realized that the weather was going to change so had come home.

"It's just sex," he said.

"Not to me," she answered.

"It's like we're having a chocolate bar together, nothing more than that."

"Cole, I only got into a sexual relationship with you because I thought you wanted a relationship. Even other people told me that they thought you were interested in me. Can you understand how heartbreaking this situation is for me?"

"You shouldn't have had so many expectations," he said. "Hey, pull yourself together. I didn't mean to do anything to mislead you. It's just a part of my personality. I don't realize I'm doing it, but I inadvertently give everyone that impression."

"You want to keep this a secret, and you barely acknowledge me in public. I do the housework and pay more than my share of the bills. Do you really not have a conscience?" At this point there were tears streaming down her face. "Do you know how hard this is? Do you even care?" she sobbed. She put on her coat. "I'm going for a walk," she said, slamming the door behind her.

The rain had stopped a few hours earlier. It was getting dark, and the streets were quiet. Alice was glad no one could see her swollen, tear-stained face. She walked a short ways up a steep slope, gradually coming to a place with a three-storey drop into a ravine beside it.

Alice sat down, dangling her feet over the edge of the ravine, and took some deep breaths. It had been about six months that they'd had this living arrangement. They both had needed a place to live so thought they'd share a place and the expenses. She'd always been empathetic, and Cole had told her how hard his life had been. She'd melted. She had done everything she could to help him, and when they had finally made love that first time, she had been over the moon.

But then he'd told her he only wanted sex. She wasn't the one, but why not just have a sexual relationship and nothing else? And he meant nothing. Practically the only time he talked to her was when he wanted something from her. No friendship, no camaraderie, nothing.

A few days earlier a woman had phoned and said she was returning his call. He had been a different person on the phone to her: laughing, chatting. Who was the real Cole, anyway?

She thought about her friends and all the people in her life who cared for her. "I'm sorry," she said quietly. "It's not about you; it's just too hard for me to go on." Then she thought of her daughter, Janey, and started to cry again.

She took one more breath, held herself very still for a moment, and then let herself fall over the edge of the ravine.

CHAPTER 80

Sirens in the Morning

Cole woke with a start to the sound of sirens. He hadn't slept well. *Where the hell is Alice?* he wondered.

He got out of bed, got dressed, went downstairs and made a cup of tea. As he took his first sip, Cole looked out the kitchen window into the morning fog.

There was a loud knock on the door. He answered it to find a police officer with a notepad in his hand.

"Hello, Officer, is there a problem?" Cole asked.

"Is this the home of Alice Johnson?" he asked.

"Yes, it is," Cole said.

"And what relation are you to her?" he continued, pen poised to write.

"I'm her roommate. Is something wrong?" Cole was starting to get worried. He gave the officer his name, which the officer then wrote down.

"I'm afraid she was found unconscious in the ravine this morning by a man who was walking his dog," he said. "I have to ask you to come with me to the station."

Cole put on his shoes and walked to the police car waiting outside. As they drove off, Cole said, "I can't believe it. She was just here last night. She said she was going to go for a walk. When she didn't come home, I thought she'd gone to a friend's house."

"Sorry to have to be the bearer of this news," said the policeman. They drove to the station in silence.

When they got out, the policeman took Cole into a waiting room and asked him to take a seat. About 10 minutes later the officer called his name and beckoned him into an office.

A man in his fifties, around the same age as Cole, invited him to sit down in a chair across the desk from him. He reached out and shook Cole's hand. "Hello, Cole," he said. "I'm Lieutenant Barkley. I'm sorry to be meeting you under such distressing circumstances."

Cole just hung his head, not knowing what to say.

"Alice is your roommate?" he asked.

"Yes," Cole said.

"She had sex about an hour or two before her fall," Lieutenant Barkley said. "Do you know who she would have had sex with?"

Cole sighed, "Yes. It was with me."

"Did you have any idea that she might attempt suicide?" asked Lieutenant Barkley.

"It really didn't occur to me that she would do anything like that," Cole said. "To tell you the truth, I'm stunned."

"Do you know her next of kin?" asked Lieutenant Barkley. "We'll have to notify them."

"She has a daughter," Cole said. "She's going to school back east."

"Thanks for your time," Lieutenant Barkley said matter-of-factly. "I'll need you to fill out some forms."

"Thank you, sir," Cole replied. "How is Alice doing?"

"She's in serious but stable condition."

"Can I see her?" Cole asked.

CHAPTER 81

Getting Things Straight

Cole sat in the waiting room at the hospital and tried to process what had just happened. What was he going to do? What would people think? He knew this private part of his life would be blown wide open, and he wasn't going to come out smelling very pretty. The bills were all in her name. She'd done all the housework and a lot of other things to make him feel better. Alice was a very empathetic person, and he knew he'd completely tapped into that, but he hadn't expected her to pull something like this. The police had probably already looked him up online and found his many online dating accounts. That would make him look even worse.

A nurse walked out of Alice's hospital room. "How's she doing?" Cole asked with a look of deep concern on his face. He noticed the nurse's shapely legs.

"She's had a concussion and has a few broken ribs, but she's in fairly stable condition," the nurse said. "Would you like to go in and see her? She's regained consciousness."

Cole walked into the hospital room and looked down at Alice lying on the bed. Her face was swollen, and she was hooked up to various monitors and tubes.

"Alice," he said, "it's me, Cole. How are you?"

Her eyes welled up with tears, and the heart monitor quickened.

He touched her arm. "Hey, relax. Everything's going to be okay," he said in a soothing voice. Her eyes continued to water. He stroked her arm gently.

"Go away!" she said.

The nurse came in and said, "I think she needs to be alone right now."

"Okay, thanks for your help," said Cole in his warmest voice, giving the nurse a grateful smile. Then he whispered, "Goodbye, Alice," and left the room.

He walked home, his mind racing. One of the guys in his band, Donny, recently had his girlfriend leave him. Maybe he'd be looking for a living situation.

CHAPTER 82

Band Practice

Ross walked up the steps to Cole's house and knocked on the door, guitar case in hand.

"Hey, Ross," said Cole. "How're you doin'?"

"Not bad. How about you?" he answered as he took his guitar out of its case and started tuning it.

"Well, I've had quite a day, actually," he sighed. "Alice is in the hospital. She's always been kind of unstable. Seems she fell last night as she was walking over by the ravine. She has a concussion and maybe a few broken ribs. She was lucky some moss broke her landing, thankfully."

"Wow! That's awful!" Ross exclaimed.

"I saw her in the hospital this morning, and she was hooked up to monitors and everything and looked pretty bruised, but she was talking, so that's a good sign," Cole said. "I'll check in again on her tomorrow."

"I'll be sure to stop by and see her," said Ross. "Is there anything she needs?"

"I can't think of anything," Cole said, opening a can of beer.

There was a knock on the door, and Donny peeked in. "Hey! What's up?" he asked as he took his banjo out of its case.

"Alice is in the hospital! Had a fall down a ravine last night," said Ross.

"Is she okay?" asked Donny. "How'd she manage to fall down a ravine?"

"I don't know. I wasn't there," Cole said. "She said she was going for a walk and then didn't come back. I thought she'd gone to spend the night at one of her friends' or something. Then in the morning, I heard sirens, and the police came to the door. Someone found her unconscious while walking their dog."

"Man! Women can be so crazy sometimes, can't they?" It was more of a statement from Donny than a question.

They all started tuning their instruments.

"Hey, you guys, I was thinking of a couple of new songs," said Donny. "It might be fun to do 'It's Cheaper to Keep Her.' Do you know that one?" He laughed.

"Yeah, that's a good one!" said Cole.

"The other one, since summer will be here in a few months, is called 'In the Summertime'—you know, the one that has these sort of rhythmic grunts. Some of the words are hilarious! 'You've got women on your mind. Have a drink; have a drive—go out and see what you can find.' And 'If her daddy's rich, take her out for a meal. If her daddy's poor, just do what you feel.' I love it!" Donny laughed. "It would be nice to have some material for the summer. It's not really country, but we could do a country-sounding cover."

"I'm not really keen on either of them, to tell you the truth," said Ross in an apologetic tone. "I'm sure we can find some other new stuff."

"Aw, come on!" said Cole. "You're not yourself these days. Dagmar got you whipped?"

"Nah, I just don't really like either of those songs. I wouldn't be comfortable singing them," Ross said.

"Yeah, it's got to be all peace and love, like the stuff at the Love Bite, eh?" said Donny. "Where's your sense of humour, man?"

"Does it have to be insulting to be funny?" Ross asked. "Why do we have to put women down in our music? I have a daughter, you know."

"It's just a bit of fun. No one takes it seriously," said Cole.

"I just don't like those songs, and I don't want to sing them," Ross said.

"You know, you're really changing, Rosco. Ever since you got mixed up with the people in that house, you're just not yourself," said Donny. "I mean, lighten up!" Donny grabbed a can of beer and opened it loudly.

"Yeah, I guess I have been changing," Ross sighed. "Look, I'm going home. I have things to do tomorrow to get ready for farming. You guys do what you want." Ross put his guitar away and walked toward the door.

"Hey, it's not that big a deal. We can play some other songs if you really don't like those ones," said Cole.

"No, really. I just want to go home and get a good sleep," Ross said as he opened the front door. "I have a long day ahead tomorrow. Bye."

He ran down the steps and walked home briskly.

CHAPTER 83

Insights

Ross walked into the bedroom and found Dagmar lying on the bed at her laptop. When she heard him, she smiled at him and said, "You're home from your practice awfully early."

"Dagmar." Ross sat down beside her and gently stroked her hair. "I just want to say thank you."

She looked into his face and could see that he was struggling with some intense emotions. "Hey, what's going on?" she asked quietly. She'd finished her post about SPIN farming and had been checking out her social media. She turned off her laptop, rolled onto her back and stroked his hair.

"I'm so glad I'm not like those pigs I play music with!" he exclaimed.

"What happened?" she asked.

Ross sighed. "Well, first of all, Cole's roommate, Alice, fell down a ravine last night, and she's in the hospital recovering. She's always sort of been in the background at our practices, but she's really kind. Cole just ignores her. He said it was an accident, but she always seemed so sad." He paused. "I can't help but wonder if she did this to herself. Then Donny wanted to learn a couple of new songs, and they were both just put-downs of women." He paused again. "I mean, I have a daughter, you know? I don't want to sing those kinds of songs."

"Sounds like it was really upsetting for you," she said.

"Dagmar, before everything that's happened with us, I think I would have just gone along with them," said Ross, "but now I can't. I don't even know if I want to play with them anymore." He lay down beside her and held her hand.

"Ross, you've been going through so many changes. It must be really hard for you sometimes," Dagmar said, holding his hand up to her lips and kissing it. "Is there anything I can do to help?"

Ross sighed. "Just be here for me, okay? I don't know what I'd do without having you to talk to. You're helping me to realize that just being myself is all right. It's such a gift. I don't have to pretend the way those guys do."

"What are they pretending?" asked Dagmar.

"That they're tough, that they don't have any feelings, that they're being big men by being jerks," Ross said. "I'm going to visit Alice in the hospital tomorrow and see how she's doing. I feel so sad for her."

"I do too, and I don't even know her," said Dagmar, stroking his chest.

"I'm so grateful for you and for everything that's happening for us," said Ross. "I never would have guessed that deep down the way we're living is everything I ever wanted." He kissed her cheek.

Dagmar kissed him back. "I'm so grateful for you too and so glad that you're figuring all this out. It's wonderful being with you."

They helped each other undress and made love tenderly, then shared the deliciousness of sleeping beside each other. As they fell asleep, they looked up and saw clouds outlined by the glowing silver of the moon.

CHAPTER 84

Green Connections

Phoebe sat at her laptop drinking her morning coffee and scrolled down her Facebook page. She had a loose collection of people who were interested in social and environmental issues who kept each other up to date with what was going on in their community and around the world.

She noticed a picture of Alice with a caption from a mutual friend saying that she was in the hospital after a serious fall down a ravine. Phoebe and Alice often commented on and shared each other's posts even though they didn't know each other well, and Phoebe hoped that Alice would be all right. She typed in the comments section under the caption, "Get well soon, Alice. I'm rooting for you!" Something about the incident rattled her more than it would have normally, but she couldn't put her finger on it.

After scrolling down her Facebook wall, she got back to work on Liam's bedroom. She had a healthy budget to work within and was enjoying the rooms she was working on. She was just adding the finishing touches to the smaller of the two rooms.

After about an hour's work, she sent him an email asking when she could present her ideas to him. Ten minutes or so later, he emailed back asking if she'd like to join him for lunch at his place and show him what she'd come up with.

She accepted eagerly. Rumour had it that he was an excellent cook, and eating lunch together would be a great way to have a relaxing discussion about the pros and cons of each of her prepared options—and she enjoyed his company.

At noon, she drove up to his house, a large, sturdy three-bedroom built in the 1930s, which he had retrofitted with solar panels and geothermal energy. It was a lovely, environmentally friendly house with heritage features: the best of both worlds.

She walked up the steps, briefcase in hand, and rang the doorbell. Liam answered the door and invited her in with a friendly smile. "How are you today?" he asked after giving her a warm hug.

"Pretty good. I'm pleased with what I've come up with so far and look forward to hearing your thoughts. Did you sleep well last night?" she asked.

"I got a little sleep, but it was still pretty fitful. I've been drinking chamomile tea and reading before bed—trying to take your advice. Maybe it's just all that space around me. I don't know."

"Hopefully feeling more enclosed will help."

"Are you hungry? I've made pasta with tomato, basil and mushroom sauce, and it's ready any time you are." Liam led her into the kitchen.

"Now that you mention it, I am getting a little hungry," she said, "and it smells awfully good!"

He had the table nicely set with place mats, salad and homemade bread in the middle of the table. Liam pulled out a chair for her. "Please, have a seat," he said warmly.

Suddenly Phoebe found herself feeling pampered and cared for. "Liam," she said, looking into his eyes, "thanks for going to all this trouble. I'm so grateful."

Liam blushed. "Oh, it was no trouble. Having you over was an excuse to make things a little special. It was fun, actually," he said.

She couldn't help but smile. He dished spaghetti and sauce onto their plates and then sat across from her.

"Mmm, this is delicious!" Phoebe said between mouthfuls. Then she asked, "How was your morning?"

"Uneventful. I'm either between things or caught up on the jobs I'm working on, so I reviewed some new geothermal products online. Actually, it's great timing to be working on my bedroom. I'm glad the timing's worked out for you too."

"Say," said Phoebe, "this whole meal is vegan, isn't it?"

"Yes."

"We didn't even have that conversation. Did you know that I'm vegan?" Phoebe asked.

"I think so, and I'm not sure why," Liam said thoughtfully. "What made you become vegan?"

"Oh, I saw a film years ago that left me with no more appetite for meat, although I never was much of a meat eater as an adult anyway," she confessed. "What about you? When did you become vegan?"

"Oh, about eight years ago or so. I worked close to a slaughterhouse for a while and could hear the cows. It just made me not want to eat meat anymore. It's part of the different direction I took that eventually broke up my marriage. Anyway, it's neat that we're both vegan."

"Yes, it is," she said. "And I'm getting pretty excited about this project. Whichever room you choose, I think we can do a great job of making sure you have a cozier, more-sleep-inducing bedroom."

They ate and talked leisurely, discussing the pros and cons of the large room and the small room. By the end of the meal, they were both leaning toward the large room with a partition between the bed and the rest of the room, which could be used as a sitting room full of plants, wicker chairs and a table. The smaller bedroom could be used as a studio and double as a spare bedroom.

"Can we go in and take a look, and I can show you my ideas?" asked Phoebe.

They walked into the large bedroom. The queen-size bed was in the centre of the room with the headboard against the inside wall. Across from it was a large walk-in closet. At the far end, there was a set of three large windows with built-in cupboards underneath and a fourth large window around the corner from them. This area contained a rocking chair, large fern and umbrella tree, as well as a number of houseplants on the ledge. On the other side of the bed was a chest of drawers, and there were nightstands on either side of the bed.

"I propose that we put the bed and nightstands in the area where the dresser is. The dresser could come out, and we could put a partition between the bed and the rest of the room," said Phoebe. "This way you'll have a dark, enclosed sleeping space on the other side of the partition and a comfortable semi-private room where you can relax." She stopped for a second and said, "Hmm. I'm just trying to remember where I saw a partition that would work beautifully. It was a dark-lacquered antique with a peacock painted in the panels."

Liam smiled. "I'm enchanted already!" he said. "And it sounds like the wicker furniture I already have would work well in the sitting area, don't you think?"

"Yes, I think it would. We could get a few more pieces and a table. It would be a great place to have a peaceful breakfast or to read."

"And you think the sage green would work?" he asked.

"Yes, perfectly. It would set such a calming tone, which hopefully would help with your sleeping problems. The wood floor is lovely the way it is, so my suggestion would be to not touch it."

"Phoebe, with what you've suggested, I think we'll be well under budget." Liam smiled. "That's always good news."

"I like to work with what people already have. This room has a lot going for it," she said. "We just need to make it feel warmer and cozier and utilize the space a little differently."

She brought out some paint samples, and they looked at a range of shades of sage green, eventually settling on one that was greener and less neutral than some of the others.

Without realizing it, they'd both become quite relaxed talking about the peaceful space they'd be creating. As they finished up the consultation and walked to the door, Liam asked, "Say, do you enjoy theatre?"

"As a matter of fact, yes, I do," Phoebe said, "but I haven't seen a play in years."

"There's one coming up on the weekend at the playhouse. It's a comedy. Would you like to come and see it with me?"

"You know, I'd love to," she replied.

"Great! I'll pick us up tickets at the box office. It's playing Friday and Saturday evening, and either works for me. Do you have a preference?"

"How about Saturday?" she asked. "I feel more refreshed on Saturday evenings, having a day to recuperate after the workweek."

"All right! Saturday it is! Can I pick you up?"

"That would be lovely!" she said, smiling. "Can I offer you dinner at my place beforehand?"

"I'd be delighted!" Liam said.

She gave him directions to her place, and they gave each other a hug before Phoebe left. As she drove away, she felt excited about her upcoming date.

CHAPTER 85

A Daughter's Love

R oss entered the hospital waiting area outside Alice's room. Just then a woman who looked to be in her twenties came out of the room, looking distraught. Her eyes were puffy, as though she'd been crying, and wisps of her brown hair fell across her face. He approached her and said, "Hi, my name's Ross, and I'm a friend of Alice's. Are you her daughter?"

"Yes, I'm Janey."

"How's she doing?" asked Ross.

"Physically she's okay, but emotionally she's a wreck," Janey said. "She needs to have somewhere to go when she gets out of the hospital. That man she's living with is bad news."

Ross nodded and sighed. "I'll put some feelers out. She deserves better than that."

"How do you know my mother?"

"I used to play guitar with the man she shares a house with," Ross admitted reluctantly.

"Do you know what happened?" She searched his eyes.

"I can put two and two together," he said.

"How could he be so mean? I know her. She'd do anything to help someone out. He just took advantage of her. He didn't care at all about her feelings, did he?" Janey was wringing her hands.

"Janey, I'm so sorry." He stroked her arm gently. "I promise you that I'm going to look out for her and see what I can do to find a situation where she'll be valued," he said. "I want to go in and say hello and let her know that I'm going to do all I can to help her."

"Okay," said Janey, "she was still awake when I left her."

Ross walked through the door and up to Alice's bed. Her cheeks were still stained with tears.

He touched her shoulder. "Hi, Alice. It's Ross." He felt awkward.

"Hi, Ross," Alice said. "I'm embarrassed that you're seeing me this way."

"Don't worry about it. I just want you to know that I've quit the band and will do all I can to help you through this. You look like you need some rest, so I'll keep this visit short and come and see you again tomorrow. If there's anything at all I can do to help you, just let me know, okay?" Then he added, "I appreciate the kindness you've always shown me, and I want to help you get back on your feet."

Tears started streaming down her cheeks again.

"I'm going to go now, and I hope you get a good sleep." He gave her arm a gentle squeeze and left the room.

Janey was still in the waiting area. When he came out, she said to him, "I really appreciate your concern and your help."

"We'll help your mother get through this. This is a caring community, despite the few bad apples. Those bad apples will never know the kind of simple love and goodwill of people who trust and can be trusted like your mother. She's the one who's hurting now, but at least she's for real." He paused, choosing his words. "People who use and manipulate others hurt inside and don't know what to do with their pain. So they just inflict it on the people who get close to them. They're on their way to being lonely and bitter. That's just what happens to people who are uncaring and selfish. We have to protect ourselves from them and wish them healing."

"It's hard to do when you see the pain they cause, isn't it?" said Janey. "But I know Mom would be the first to agree."

"I know she would too," said Ross. "Janey, it was great to have met you. Do you have a place to stay while you're here? We have an extra bedroom if you need it."

"I appreciate the offer, but I'm staying with some friends."

"Good," said Ross. " Hopefully I'll see you again. If there's anything I can do, please let me know. Here's my phone number." He wrote his number down on a piece of paper and gave it to her.

"Thanks," said Janey. "I'm glad there are some decent people in my mom's life."

CHAPTER 86
Realization

Dagmar sat across from Phoebe at her place. She'd brought over some oatmeal cookies she'd made. She asked, "So how are you? It feels like it's been a while since we've had a chance to catch up."

"Pretty good," Phoebe said. "I'm working on a room that's quite inspiring and going to a play with a very nice gentleman on Saturday evening."

"Hey! That's exciting!" Dagmar smiled. "About time you had an evening out with a very nice gentleman, I'd say."

"How about you?" asked Phoebe. "You seem really happy these days."

"Yes, I'm feeling pretty good about everything," Dagmar said, dipping a cookie into her cup of tea. "Lots of excitement with the SPIN farm operation.

I'm getting to blog and take care of the banking. And Ross is a sweetheart. Things couldn't be much better."

"What a change from a few months ago, eh?" said Phoebe. "I was so worried about you, and you've come through with flying colours."

"Thank goodness Ross and I stopped in front of that abandoned house!" Dagmar exclaimed. "I can't believe the transformation Ross is going through. He's quit the band and is helping a woman who lived with one of the band members. She threw herself down a ravine. If you hear of a situation where someone needs a caring, responsible person, let me know."

"Threw herself down a ravine … you don't mean Alice, do you?" asked Phoebe.

"Yes, Alice. She shared a house with a guy named Cole," said Dagmar.

"Cole! Oh, wow!" said Phoebe. "It's all just falling into place. I met a guy at a potluck a couple of weeks ago, and he invited me to go for a hike. I started the hike, but the more we talked, the more I realized we weren't on the same page at all. For one thing, I just knew he was sleeping with his roommate, and he was really evasive about it. Then on Facebook I read that Alice, who I'm friends with but don't know very well, had fallen down a ravine and was in the hospital. I only put the two of those things together this second."

"Ross was distraught when he came home from band practice the other night. The day after Alice's fall, the other band members wanted to learn a couple of songs that were degrading to women. I guess with what happened to Alice, the fact that Ross has a daughter and all the changes he's been going through, it was too much for him. He's quitting the band. Actually, I'm so proud of him," Dagmar said. "He's become the most wonderful, caring person you could ever imagine."

"Amazing, isn't it? He must be so grateful for you," said Phoebe. She added, "I'm still trying to come to terms with the connection I just made between Alice and Cole and what happened." She paused for a moment and gazed out the window. "You know, I actually just read about this organization that's supposed to help people who've been taken advantage of by those close to them."

"Would you mind emailing that information to me?" Dagmar asked. "I'll pass it on to Ross. I know he'll want to call and check to see if Alice would be a good fit."

CHAPTER 87

Green Property Value

"Thanks, Jess," said Tina over the phone. "I really appreciate being able to talk to you about these things. Sometimes it feels like our kids and the people living at Dad's house are ganging up on us. I don't want Dad's property to turn into a freak show, with weird plants in the front yard instead of a lawn. It's a very respectable neighbourhood, after all."

Jess chuckled. "You're welcome. So why don't we break this situation down into its pros and cons," she suggested. "You and Ray like lawns. You don't want to have some weird-looking front yard. Vanessa and Jared are open to the suggested ground cover. The house-sitters say the pros are an indigenous ground cover never needs mowing, needs very little water and upkeep and adds visual interest to the property. You and Ray are afraid it might bring down the property value. Vanessa and Jared think it might raise the property value."

"Another family squabble! We go through things like this all the time, and it's so infuriating!" Tina exclaimed.

"It must be frustrating," Jess said. "Why do you and Ray think it would drive down the property value? It sounds very green, and whatever you believe about that, it's the up-and-coming thing."

"I suppose," Tina conceded. "Velvet and her cousins love the idea because, as you say, it's good for the environment. It could be the thin edge of the wedge—next thing you know they'll want to install solar panels or something."

"Would that be so bad?" asked Jess. "I read somewhere that there were more solar panels sold in the last year than in the previous 30 years. Greening your dad's house could make it attractive to celebrities who are advocating for all things green if and when you decide to sell."

"That's true," said Tina. "You never know which movie star is going to jump on the environmental bandwagon these days."

"Would you like me to do some research on what kind of impact greening a house and its yard has on its property value?" she asked. "I could write an article on it for homeowners who are going through similar dilemmas."

"Really, you'd do that? Sure, I'd love to hear what you come up with," said Tina. "If it brought up the property value, I'd go for it, and I bet Ray would too. Jess, thanks for putting things into perspective. Sometimes my family just goes around in circles. Looking at facts with a cool head is really helpful."

"Here, I've got my laptop in front of me. I'll do a quick search right now." Tina could hear typing in the background; then Jess came back on the line. " From the looks of it, greening a property can actually bring up the property value significantly."

"Seriously?" said Tina, sounding skeptical. "Would you mind forwarding those links to me and Ray?" She gave Jess their email addresses. "If we're both convinced, we may wind up doing exactly what you've suggested. We both love a good investment." Then she added, "How's your day looking? Do you feel like getting together for a coffee and a dessert at the Phoenix this afternoon?"

"I'm just finishing up this article and should be done by late morning, so, yeah, why don't we get together at the Phoenix? See you there—what, one-ish?"

"One-ish works for me," said Tina. "See you then, and thanks for the heads-up about how to increase the property value of Dad's house."

CHAPTER 88

Sunday

The sun streamed in like honey through the windows of the Love Bite.

"The heart brings you back. I ain't telling you no lie," the members of the Sleeping Dragon sang straight from their hearts. These days they were productive, fully themselves and loving what they were doing. They were aware of the charmed lives they were leading and were grateful.

Jared and Ray were at a table near the back and looked as if they were enjoying the music and their food. They seemed to be getting used to this setting and becoming more comfortable, infected by the warmer weather and the uplifting music. They both looked happy.

At the end of the set, Jared walked over to the group's table and asked if he and Ray could join them. The group welcomed the brothers, and Ross pulled chairs up for them both.

"Your music matched the weather this morning: warm and joyous," said Ray.

They all laughed and thanked him.

"Your asking about replacing the lawn with indigenous ground covers got us looking at how adding green features to a house adds to its property value," he said. "Now I want to find out more about how I can upgrade the house; green it, if you will. I thought you might be able to recommend someone locally who could take this on. Any suggestions? I'm out of my league here."

"Actually," said Dagmar, "I have a friend who is an interior designer whose focus is on using environmentally friendly materials. She's been in the business for about 10 years and knows many architects and green-energy specialists. She'd be able to point you in the right direction. Would you like her card?"

"Yes, I'd appreciate that," Ray replied. "Thanks very much, Dagmar."

Dagmar rummaged around in her purse and eventually found her wallet. Then she rummaged around in her wallet and found Phoebe's card. As she handed it to Ray, she said, "Shall I let Phoebe know that you'll be giving her a call?"

"I'd appreciate that," Ray said.

"It's funny how one thing leads to another," said Jared. "Ground cover got us thinking about green features for the house; then it had us thinking about our investments. It's surprising how well stocks in green technologies are doing. We're looking at moving a considerable portion of our investments from conventional funds to companies invested in green technologies. It seems to be the way of the future."

"That's what I've heard," said Dagmar. "It makes sense that it's up-and-coming. I understand that there's been a huge growth spurt in these types of investments, and it's expected to continue."

Jared and Ray got up, thanked them again, said their goodbyes and left the restaurant.

After a pleasant meal together, the group got up and strolled into the early-afternoon sunshine.

CHAPTER 89

Targeted

"Hello, Alice," said a woman sitting next to her hospital bed. She had soft eyes and looked to be in her sixties. "My name's Amber, and I'm a counsellor."

"Hello," said Alice. She was more composed after being in hospital for over 24 hours and felt somehow reassured by this woman's presence. Still, Alice's ribs hurt, and her head ached.

"How are you?" asked Amber.

"I'm—" Alice sighed. "I don't know, a whole bunch of things. I'm ashamed, confused and really sad. And I'm in some physical pain."

"I'm sorry to hear that," said Amber, placing a gentle hand on Alice's arm. "A friend of yours, Ross, got in touch with our organization, and I'd like to ask you a few more questions. Would that be all right?"

Alice nodded.

"Can you tell me what happened before your fall down the ravine?" Amber asked.

"I had a heated discussion with Cole, my roommate, about what was going on between us, and then I just had to get out of the house," Alice replied. "I felt so worthless, confused and crazy—I just didn't want to go on anymore." Her voice broke.

"And what was going on between the two of you?"

Alice sighed. "We had a sexual relationship for about six months. He wanted to keep it secret, and it was all about sex for him, but for me ..." Tears welled up in her eyes. "It was more than that."

"How did it begin?"

"We met each other when he had a temporary job at a school where I was working. Then we ran into each other at different cultural events—holistic health presentations, meditation sessions, that sort of thing. He was very charming and friendly, and it seemed like he was interested in me. Some of my friends thought so too. He and his girlfriend had split up a few months earlier, and he was looking for a place to live. I needed to move too, so we decided to rent a place together, as friends." Alice sighed again. "Eventually, though, we wound up in bed, and I thought that was going to be the beginning of a romantic relationship. But he made it clear soon afterwards that he just wanted sex."

"What about the bills and the housework—did you split those equally?"

Alice shook her head. "No. He was going to put the hydro in his name but didn't get a chance and asked if I'd mind putting it in my name along with everything else. Housework? He often worked during the day, and as a substitute teacher, I worked less regularly and wound up doing almost all the housework. It seems crazy, but he had a way of getting me to feel sorry for him, to the point where I'd do things for him. I think part of me hoped he'd want more than just sex."

"And he knew how you felt?"

"Yes, I told him."

"Did he show any concern for your feelings?" Amber asked.

"No. He trivialized them, didn't take them seriously at all."

Amber paused. Her tone changed and became more probing. "Tell me a little about your childhood, Alice."

"It wasn't the easiest," Alice replied. "My parents had a very unhappy marriage, and I was the oldest child so felt responsible for everything. Eventually they had a long, drawn-out divorce."

"You know, it sounds like you may have been the target of someone who is predatory," Amber explained. "People with these tendencies are very good at recognizing people who are empathetic and who have emotional scars from their childhood. Unfortunately, it's quite common. People like this don't experience emotions the way most people do, and they actually derive pleasure from controlling others and inflicting emotional pain." She paused to let her words sink in. "They're often charming and good at manipulating others."

Alice thought about this information and its implications.

"Alice, would you be interested in staying awhile in a special place that was set up by others who have had to recover from similar experiences? An experience like this can be emotionally devastating, and having people around who have been in similar situations can really help a person to recover."

Alice slowly nodded. "I'll mull it over," she said, sighing again. "I sure can't go on the way I have."

"Give it some thought, okay? Getting back on your feet can be tough, and there's help for you if you're willing to take it. Empathy is a very special quality, and our world needs it now more than ever. Our hope is that we can help people like you to heal and learn to put their empathy where it'll be valued and appreciated."

Amber stood up and said, "I'm going to let you rest. Thanks for talking with me and being open to getting help. I'll come by again tomorrow."

"Thanks for sharing this option," Alice said. "I feel so stuck and am really grateful for what you're offering me."

"Have a good sleep, and I'll see you in the morning." Amber gave Alice a tender smile as she left the room.

CHAPTER 90

Lament

A lice closed her eyes as she sat in the warm sunshine. When Amber had come back the next day, Alice had decided to go with her to the place she'd spoken of.

Alice had warmed to the facility where she was staying. She found it calming and comfortable. Her first few days there she'd spent mostly sleeping in her room, but today she'd wandered through the hallways, finding the cafeteria, library, lounge and the garden at the centre of the complex. There were lawn chairs in the garden, and she was sitting in one of them now.

Amber had helped Alice to cancel the accounts for the phone, gas and hydro at the house she'd been sharing with Cole. Amber had also spoken to Cole briefly to let him know that Alice wouldn't be moving back, since Alice had agreed not to have contact with Cole as part of her healing process. Alice had deleted Cole's contact information from her cellphone, email and other online sites where they were associated.

Alice had contacted the schools where she worked to let them know that she'd be taking a leave of absence for the rest of the school year. She had some money saved and felt she'd need the time to recover.

After relaxing for a while, she took out her laptop and checked her email and social media. She'd had a tasty and nutritious breakfast with a few other people in this facility. Meeting them, she felt a little less crazy. They were so obviously kind and empathetic, and she could see what someone who was predatory might see. It helped her to understand how she would have been a target just as they had been.

Her assignment this morning was to write. It could be anything, as long as it expressed the emotions she was feeling as completely and as accurately as possible.

She took a sip of chamomile tea and opened up a document. After staring into space for a few minutes, she started to type:

> I understand that you don't feel things the way I do or the
> way most other people do.
> My head understands it at least; my heart still struggles.
> My heart still aches for you, for the crumbs you might throw
> to me.
> Unaffected, you cut through the tender feelings in my heart,
> manoeuvred your way in so you could
> take only what served you, discarding—blind to—the
> numinous.
> You've trivialized the most primal of impulses,
> casually pasteurizing the sacred elements out.
>
> Inside, a little girl weeps, hoping to be noticed, hoping for
> an encouraging smile.
> My head knows it will not come,
> that you're incapable of giving me what I need, only of
> taking what you want.

A predator who tricks the guardian,
taking the choice bits and destroying the rest.

Something has extinguished your ability to value context:
childhood trauma, the drip, drip, drip of cultural stereotypes
in movies, in the news, in popular music, in a society that
values manliness
and leaves little room for what happens in an open heart.

Somewhere in eternity, the love and kindness I've given you,
the love and kindness you've taken without even a thank you,
will change your orientation;
just as rivers erode mountains, you'll begin to question your
need to inflict harm,
and you'll grow some tentative feelers, experience the beauty
of an emotional reality where caring and nurture are normal.

You'll grow a flower or two as your heart begins to open.
Little shoots of appreciation here and there, the deep
comfort of being transparent,
no need to manipulate or mask the truth.
Slowly fear will disintegrate as you realize that you're capable
of intense feelings,
feelings other than rage and jealousy.
Somehow love will creep in and find you.

I leave you now with this blessing,
as I learn to heal the wound that you entered through,
I hold the door open and ask you to leave—easier said than
done.
Goodbye, farewell, and I hope the path you're on changes.
I hope that you are detoured from that lonely, bitter road
and that you discover love and joy
somewhere along the way.

Is that a small gift you've left?
Perhaps it's the ticket to my own healing.
Maybe it's an invitation to the little girl who's weeping
to wipe her eyes, look around and find what she needs
to heal, to love, to participate in life fully.

CHAPTER 91

Vortex

"Okay, so next time we go to your dad's place together and start to get triggered, what are we going to do, and how can we support each other?" asked Jess before taking a sip of her coffee. They were sitting in a booth at the Phoenix.

"Maybe a good place to start would be to share where we go in our own minds that gets us triggered," Tina said, taking the first bite of her orange poppy-seed cake with chocolate glaze. "Mmm! This is delicious! Want a taste?"

"Sure," said Jess. "Wow! This is good. I'll give you a taste of my banana cake when it gets here. We are literally having our cake and eating it too—it's hard to believe this stuff is so healthy! Anyway, where we go in our own minds …"

"Yeah," said Tina. "When I get together with my family, so many memories come up, and it's like I'm sucked into this vortex of pain. It feels so big that trying to name it is even hard."

"I know what you mean about the pain being big," Jess said. As her piece of cake arrived, she said to the waiter, "Oh, thank you! This looks beautiful!" Looking at Tina, she said, "Go ahead! Have the first bite."

"Heavenly!" said Tina after she'd finished the mouthful. "The desserts are so good! We'll have to try some of the other things on the menu one of these days. Anyway, where were we? Big pain, I think."

"Even trying to reach out from that place feels like it's impossible. We both know the feeling. Should we try to communicate from that place or see if we recognize it in each other and throw a lifeline or both?" asked Jess. "Maybe we should have a code word. Something simple, something like—I don't know—*vortex*?"

"*Vortex* … I think that would work," Tina replied. "I wonder if instead of talking about what brings up these feelings, we should bring notebooks with us and write a few notes when we feel like we're getting sucked into the vortex. What do you think?"

"I like the idea. That way when we come back, we can sit here eating something delicious, get our notebooks out and have something more concrete to work with," Jess said. "I think Ellen will be impressed with our plan."

CHAPTER 92

Line in the Sand

R oss and Dagmar sat near the back of a packed boardroom. They were at a community outreach meeting sponsored by the oil company that would be building pipelines from the Alberta tar sands to the west coast of British Columbia. A dignified-looking man in a grey suit got up to address the audience. "Hi, my name's Al, and I want to talk to you about the benefits of our proposed pipeline. Like you, we care about the environment, so you have our commitment that we will do everything in our power to do our work in a way that respects nature. But let's face it, folks: we need oil for our cars and our homes, and we need the jobs these pipelines will give us. Our company is providing these things in the cleanest way possible. We care about the same things you care about. I see a hand raised. Sir, do you have a question?"

An Aboriginal man stood up. "According to your own public records you've had many spills over the years that still haven't been cleaned up. Also, your company has not adequately consulted with First Nations affected by these pipelines. The routes go through unceded Aboriginal lands. Will you please address these issues."

"Technology has improved since those spills, sir, and we've learned from our mistakes. And we're in negotiations with First Nations whose territories are affected and are offering jobs and compensation for the use of the lands we require. Next question?"

The questioning continued, and community members became increasingly hostile, citing broken promises and contaminated lands and water.

Dagmar and Ross left early, since it felt as if the meeting was going nowhere.

"That guy sure was smooth, wasn't he? He didn't miss a beat," said Ross as they headed toward home. "If someone wasn't up to date on that company's terrible track record, he'd have them convinced."

"Things are sure heating up. Hopefully enough people are aware of the problems the company's caused," said Dagmar as they walked up the hill. The late-afternoon sun was shining.

"It feels like a line in the sand," said Ross, "environmentally, democratically, for the First Nations …"

"I know what you mean," Dagmar said as they walked up the circular driveway. "This pipeline is like the oil industry's last stand. They're going to try to force it through despite citizens' objections. Our political leaders all have vested interests in the oil companies, even though they're supposed to be representing us. We're finding this out at the same time we're finding out how much more serious climate change is than we thought initially. So much is at stake, and people are scrambling to prevent it from going through."

"Hey, Ross, Dagmar, you're just in time!" called Leroy as they walked through the door. He and the rest of the household were in the TV room.

"Let me guess!" Dagmar exclaimed. "The latest from your friends who make that cartoon?"

"Bingo!" Lydia affirmed. "And we've got popcorn."

Dagmar and Ross curled up together on a loveseat with cups of tea and a bowl of popcorn. Leroy pressed play on the remote, and there on the big screen was the unlikely hero they were becoming accustomed to. Lav, the hero, stood chatting with a woman who had short hair, was heavyset and wore utilitarian clothing. Lav was in a red-and-white-checked shirt and blue jeans. They were both in a garden leaning on their shovels.

"Time for a break. Feel like a cup of tea?" the woman asked Lav.

"Yeah, that would be great. Thanks, Cat. I've got some lemon loaf. Why don't we sit outside at the picnic table?" he suggested.

"Okay, I'll get the tea; you get the lemon loaf; and we'll rendezvous at the picnic table," she said as they both started walking in different directions. They both returned shortly.

Looking over at the garden and sipping on their tea, Cat said, "I don't think it's too early to plant as long as we mulch well. That'll protect everything if there's a frost."

Lav nodded in agreement.

"Lav, you seem a little distracted. Is something bothering you?" Cat looked at him closely.

Lav heaved a sigh. "Yeah, this whole pipeline thing is getting to me. They're going to destroy our land and pollute our waterways. No one wants the pipelines, and they're not even legal! They violate First Nations agreements, but our politicians have been bought." Lav sighed again. "I don't know what's going to happen."

"I know," Cat said. "It's pretty grim. To me it's like a literal line in the sand."

Dagmar and Ross gave each other a long look, silently acknowledging they'd said the same thing moments ago.

"On one side of that line, there are bought politicians, destroyed ecosystems, dirty oil contaminating our lands and waters," Cat said. "On the other side, if we can beat this thing, we'll have a renewed democratic process—maybe even some elected officials who actually represent our interests—clean water, intact ecosystems, better relationships with First

Nations and green solutions." She took a bite of lemon loaf. "Hey, this is pretty good."

"You don't think there's too much baking soda?" asked Lav.

"Maybe just a little bit, but it still tastes great, especially after turning soil all morning," Cat said. "It's all so complex, isn't it?"

"Isn't what so complex?" asked Lav.

"The soil, growing plants, how it all works together. Also, what people are doing. Everyone has different ideas, different ways they stick up for our environment."

"Yeah, both are complex," said Lav. "I wish people could work together the same way the processes of nature do. We need everyone's approaches and actions. If we and our small groups do what's important to us and try to work with others who have different ideas, we can achieve so much." Then he looked at Cat conspiratorially. "I've been meditating on these things, and I don't know how to describe it, but a part of me is becoming really focused and strong."

"Really? How do you mean?" Cat asked.

"Well, it's like I have these feelings of rage and powerlessness, but when I meditate, they seem to gel into something powerful and constructive, like they're transforming into a force for positive change. Does that make sense?" he asked, picking a piece of lemon loaf out from between his front teeth. "Do you think we'll ever figure out how to work harmoniously together to create change?"

"I think it's starting to happen," Cat said. "More and more, people are learning to support each other where they can, and more people are using the tools at their disposal more effectively. They're voting with their dollars, going to demonstrations, signing petitions, donating to organizations that are working to stop the pipelines, divesting their retirement funds if they have them and probably lots of other things I haven't even thought of. Plus they're organizing in new and better ways. People are collaborating and sharing information. I think it's having a cumulative effect."

"We're recognizing the places where the systems that support pipelines are weak, where we can make a difference. Whole institutions are divesting from dirty technologies, and we're letting each other know every time we find a weak link. And we're supporting alternatives. But it's a race against time," Lav said. He took another bite of his lemon loaf and a sip of tea. "Spearmint—very nice! From the garden?"

"Yeah, I dried a bunch of it last year," replied Cat.

"I wonder about anima mundi, the soul of Gaia, of our earth," Lav said. "Sometimes I feel like she's communicating with me when I meditate."

"What do you mean?"

"Well, I don't think she's very happy these days. I mean, we haven't been treating her very well for a long time now. I think she's pissed," said Lav with conviction.

"I would be too if I were her," Cat said.

"I wonder what she's going to do," Lav said. "There's so much going on: fracking that is contaminating our groundwater and causing sinkholes and heavy machinery that's digging up the land to get to the oil sands. I wonder about sinkholes and heavy machinery, and I wonder about earthquakes, landslides, drought, weather events and who knows what."

"Fracking makes my blood boil!" Cat exclaimed. "Contaminating all that clean water when we need it so badly, just so we can have natural gas. We need to get our priorities straight."

"What would you do if you were her?" Lav asked.

"I'd be pretty upset; that's for sure."

"Ultimately we're her allies. We're all anima mundi—we're part of her," said Lav.

"Yes, we are. As much as people like to think we're separate from nature, we're not, and the sooner we realize it, the better."

"To me it's something we should celebrate. I don't know why so many want to deny such a vital connection."

"Yeah, I know what you mean," Cat said. Then, popping the last bite of lemon loaf in her mouth, she said, "Well, back to work I guess."

Lav looked up at the sky and watched the clouds roll by. "Hey, Cat!" he exclaimed. "Does that cloud look like it's giving us a thumbs-up?"

"Yeah, kinda," she said.

"I wonder what she's got up her sleeve," Lav said as he got up from the picnic table and grabbed his shovel.

The group in the TV room giggled as they finished their popcorn.

CHAPTER 93

Put to the Test

"I didn't think we'd get to try out our new system so soon, but let's stay vigilant, okay? I've got my notebook. Have you got yours?" Jess asked Tina, who was driving down the road toward Silverdale. Their kids, Velvet and Ronnie, were in the back seat.

"Sure do—it's in my purse," Tina said. "As much as I go through a lot of complicated feelings, I like to make the effort to see my sister, Vanessa, when she comes to Dad's. Thanks for coming along. This'll be the test run for our code."

In the back seat, Ronnie asked Velvet, "So what's your group doing about the pipelines?"

"A number of things," she said. "We made a list of actions that takes people's comfort levels into consideration. Some people are afraid of going to demonstrations and things like that, so we're offering them a variety of tools. They can choose to help stop the pipelines or even just help the environment generally."

"What's on your list?" Ronnie asked.

"Let's see … donating to groups that are working on keeping the pipelines from being built; if they have a bank account, switching to a credit union that invests in the community and not in things like oil companies and pipelines; discussing the issues with friends and family; buying organic food; eating less meat; joining demonstrations; sending emails; writing letters to the editor; supporting clean energy in any way they can— things like that," she said. "What about you and your group?"

"We're creating an alternative model. We're looking at what percentage of our tax dollars is going toward everything to do with the pipelines and demonstrating the kind of clean energy we could be creating with that money. Since we're near the coast, we could have turbines generated by the currents in the ocean, as well as solar, wind and geothermal. We're also helping a group that's organizing a citizens' referendum on the pipelines. We're seeing if we can get people of voting age to sign a pledge to endorse it, since we'll need 10 percent of eligible voters for it to go ahead." Then he added, "You know what would be neat?"

"What?" asked Velvet.

"If our schools collaborated. That way, we could each double our impact."

"Hey, that's a great idea!" agreed Velvet. "We could credit each other's groups and make collaborating with groups who are like-minded part of both of our projects."

"It's all great information, and it would increase everyone's options and vision for what's possible," said Ronnie.

"We should all get together sometime, maybe at one of our homes. We could have an evening of collaboration and fun!" said Velvet.

"Okay, let's do it!" They were pleased with their idea and chatted enthusiastically about the logistics.

"Our kids are really hitting it off, aren't they?" Jess said.

"Yeah, sounds like they're plotting the revolution together," Tina laughed.

"It's great that they have a common interest. Seems like everywhere you turn there's something about the environment, going greener and all that. What do you think of all this green stuff?" Jess asked Tina.

"Well, I used to think it was a lot of hot air, but I'm beginning to see things differently. Velvet's been very persuasive. She's adamant about environmental issues. I think learning about the increase in property values swayed me somewhat as well. It's become a big part of the consciousness of the times. What about you?"

"The older I get, the more it makes sense to me. I have a friend who's always been that way, and I thought she was way out in left field. But more and more, with the way the weather's been changing, how oil spills aren't getting cleaned up and what the scientists are saying—I guess it's all been turning me around. As much as we see ads and hear politicians talking about it, their arguments make less sense to me all the time. Why wouldn't we want to adopt clean technology and leave our children a world that's inhabitable?"

"When you put it that way, it makes me wonder what we're clinging to," Tina said. "The way things were? Why are we so attached to oil when it's causing so many problems? The sane thing to do would be to adopt clean technologies. From what I understand, the alternatives are there, but there isn't the political will to implement the changes needed."

They cruised down the road silently for a while. "Look!" said Velvet. They slowed down to watch two bears loping along the side of the road. "I bet they're hungry. They would have just come out of hibernation recently."

Soon they pulled into the circular driveway of Tina's dad's house.

CHAPTER 94

For the Children

It was a rainy day, and there wasn't much the house members could do in the gardens, so Tam and Cammie decided to see what was happening at the food bank. They entered the room adjoining the kitchen and sat down with Glenda and her friends, who took turns bouncing baby Bella. When Tam noticed Elly, he did a double take: Was this vibrant person the same woman he'd first seen with the older man who had seemed so indifferent to her feelings? The transformation was remarkable. She looked strong enough to handle any situation, and no longer appeared to be hiding from anyone.

"I'm so excited about this new project we're taking on!" said Glenda. "Bella, I hope you'll come when you're a little older," she said as she bounced Bella on her lap, the baby laughing with each bounce.

155

"How did all this start?" asked Cammie.

Glenda told them about Ceri, an elderly neighbour they'd met who, like Glenda and her friends, had a background in childcare. Ceri owned a large house and garden that she was finding difficult to maintain as she aged. She'd recently tried to sell it but hadn't received any offers. One day Glenda and Ceri explored the idea of using a portion of the house as a daycare centre. Ceri became so inspired that she invited Glenda and her friends to move into her six-bedroom house and establish a daycare centre in a portion of it. Between them, they had daycare licences, food-safe certificates and grant-writing experience. Ceri's kitchen was food-safe approved, since she had prepared and sold food from her garden up until a few years ago. Thinking it might come in handy one day, she'd maintained the licence.

The daycare would encourage free play where the kids would learn about respect and co-operation. The children would each have small garden plots and bring the food they'd grown home to their families. They would be fed nutritious meals, much of the food coming from the garden. Glenda and her friends wanted to take children in on a sliding scale so that parents who shared their vision wouldn't be turned away. The arrangement would provide Glenda and her friends with a home, and Ceri would get help with the maintenance and upkeep of her house and garden.

"One more thing you could consider throwing into the mix is accepting local currency. Have you seen it?" asked Tam, reaching into his pocket.

"No," said Glenda, taking the ten-dollar local-currency bill Tam handed her, turning it over to see both sides.

"More people seem to be using it all the time," Tam said. "Basically, it helps to fund community groups like the food kitchen here, increases people's spending power, stimulates local businesses and helps to keep money in the community. I'll explain it to you sometime, or you can ask Mary to. She loves it!"

"Hey, thanks for the heads-up," Glenda replied. "I'm open to hearing more about it, for sure!"

"It's money that behaves in a way that can make things better for a whole lot of people. We often get it when we perform at the Love Bite, and we accept it at the market, and so do the people who rent out the stalls. It's quite the thing!" Cammie said.

"Really!" said Glenda. "I'll have to look into it!"

"You can keep this money," Tam said. "Consider it payment for listening to our half-baked explanation. If you want to know more, check out this website," he said, pointing to the bottom of the bill. Then he winked. "Don't spend it all in one place."

"I can't accept this!" said Glenda.

"Why not?" asked Cammie, smiling.

"I didn't do anything to earn it," she said.

"This money's really different. If you love someone's intentions or just feel like saying thank you, this money works really well," Tam laughed. "It just keeps on coming back like a hot potato but does a lot of good as it circulates. Consider it a donation to your daycare facility!"

CHAPTER 95

Historical

"So that means our old abandoned house will be empty again soon, eh?" Tam said. "Do you have people in mind you want to pass it along to?"

"As a matter of fact, we do," Jay said. "We've found some people—a couple of guys and one of their girlfriends—and they've been helping others to find or create accommodation. You'd love their energy!"

Rose interjected, "Ceri has lived in the neighbourhood for decades—raised her kids here and everything—so she knows a lot of local history. The house that you passed along to us belonged to a couple who were community outreach workers. They did a lot to help this town become the caring, resilient community it is. No one's sure what happened to them, but rumour has it that they took a trip to Africa and never came back. Some speculate that the poverty they found in the region they visited broke their hearts, so they were compelled to stay and help in whatever way they could. They'd probably be thrilled at what we've all been doing. I wonder if the house has some special force that intensifies what we do for the betterment of the community."

Tam shook his head incredulously as Rose handed Bella back to him. He cuddled her on his lap. "Amazing, isn't it? I guess we never know what kind of energetic impressions we're giving off and taking in all the time."

Cammie said, "We really have been propelled into a very special kind of life. Moving in with Leroy and Lydia was easy, since we're all good friends. But having it work out with Dagmar and Ross, who were total strangers and are much older than us—well, it's amazing that it's gone so smoothly."

"It's almost as though the energy transfers to us and heals us while helping us to make our community a better place," Elly said. "I wouldn't have believed that I'd be doing this well, even a month ago."

Tam said, "Elly, I can barely believe you're the same person I first saw here. It's inspiring to see how much better you are now."

"I feel like a different person." Elly thought about it for a moment. "Well, maybe just more of who I really am. Before, I always felt like I wasn't good enough, that I had to justify everything about myself, and now I know I'm appreciated for just being me. It makes me want to contribute. The more I contribute, the better I feel and the more I'm appreciated. Funny how that works, eh?"

"It's like we're all being called to give our best and being provided with the opportunity if we're willing to step up and take it," Cammie said. "These times we're living in demand so much from us. Thankfully, many are rising to the challenge."

CHAPTER 96

Ground Truthing

Sitting in her dad's house, Tina looked out the window at the tilled yard that used to be a lawn. She sighed and hoped the indigenous ground cover wasn't a big mistake.

"Jess," she said, "vortex."

Jess nodded in acknowledgement of the code word and asked, "What's happening for you right now?" She tried hard to focus on Tina over the excited voices of their children in the other room. They were planning a joint event between the environmental groups of their two schools.

"I'm feeling indecisive and panicky and distrustful." Tina sighed again. "I'm looking out at what used to be a nice lawn that is now a pile of dirt and feeling panicky: What will the neighbours think? Should we really trust these people? Am I too old-fashioned and uptight? It feels like all the options are negative."

"Sounds like you're in a pretty scary place." They sat silently for a moment, excited teenagers' voices in the background. Then Jess said, "May I offer some thoughts?"

"All right," Tina said.

"I just want to remind you that this is a process and that so far the people who are doing this have done a good job maintaining your dad's house and have done nothing to damage the trust they've earned. Do you think you'd be able to give yourself permission to give them and the yard time?"

"I guess so," Tina said in a voice that wasn't particularly convincing.

"After all, seeds take time to grow," said Jess, "and these people know what they're doing. Didn't you say one of them is trained in permaculture?"

"Yes, but I don't even know what permaculture means."

"Then maybe we should look it up on the Internet," said Jess. "It might help to understand what their philosophy is."

They got onto Tina's laptop and searched the word *permaculture*. The Wikipedia definition that came up was "a branch of ecological design, ecological engineering and environmental design that develops sustainable agriculture and self-maintained agricultural systems modelled from natural ecosystems." They both read the definition over.

"What comes up for you after reading that?" asked Jess.

"It makes me feel a little better. It's even in line with what our kids are talking about."

"You're sounding much better," said Jess. "Amazing what a little reality check can do, isn't it?"

"It sure is," said Tina. "I feel much better already. It's so easy to get caught up in uncertainty and become paralyzed by baseless fears."

"I'm going to keep this in mind for when it happens to me," Jess said. "Sometimes it just takes a little reality check to turn our feelings around."

"I've heard that called *ground truthing*," said Velvet, who had quietly entered the room.

"Ground truthing?" said Tina. "What's that, hun?"

"It's a technical scientific term that means checking to see what statistical models look like on the ground, but it's sometimes used to describe any situation on the ground compared to what we think of it, if that makes sense. What were you talking about anyway? I only heard the last little bit."

Tina laughed. "We were literally talking about the ground outside and my mixed feelings about what it looks like out there where it used to be a beautiful lawn."

"I know it's a little distressing right now, Mom," Velvet said, "but it'll look better when things start to grow. And since it's drought-resistant, it'll look way better than the parched lawns of our neighbours. They'll be wanting to do what we do if we have a hot summer, maybe even if we don't." Then she added, "Are you getting hungry? Ronnie and I are."

"Why don't we head over to the Love Bite?" Jess suggested. "It's almost lunchtime."

CHAPTER 97

Candle

A lice sat on a sofa, wrapped in a warm shawl with her laptop in front of her. Despite the caring and support she was receiving, the healing process was difficult. Her body still ached, and she felt emotionally fragile. Still, it was comforting to listen to the rain outside and sip a cup of tea.

Although she'd learned about how predatory people could be, she didn't want to believe that about Cole. She wanted to believe that her love would bring him around, even though she knew deep down that it probably wouldn't. She also realized that her own healing had to be her priority.

The ritual of checking her social media was also comforting to her. Although she was quite introverted, Alice had many caring relationships online that had developed over the years. She had a lot of different interests and had become part of a supportive online community.

She was stunned to see how the word had gotten out about what had happened to her and all the caring messages of encouragement and concern she'd received.

She sat back, looked out at the rain and sighed deeply. Processing how many people knew and how much they knew was hard to fathom. Part of her was afraid to look at the messages she'd received. Alice felt exposed, which was especially hard when feeling this vulnerable.

She looked again and saw supportive posts from Phoebe, Ross and some of her other online friends. Finally, she scrolled down and liked all the supportive comments. She took a deep breath and posted a message to her page.

"Thank you, friends, for your encouragement and support. I feel grateful but also exposed and vulnerable right now. As I struggle to retrieve the parts of myself that feel far away and try to put my life back together, I will remember all your kind words. My recent experience has made me realize that most of us tend to put on a happy face, even when our lives are falling apart. We never know what secret pain others might be in, so we need to be kind to each other. Thanks for your gentle and caring words. They mean so much. Love and best wishes to all of you."

The rain was drumming loudly on the roof outside. Alice closed her laptop and walked into the kitchen. She made herself a snack of crackers and peanut butter. As she brought her plate over to the table, she saw another woman drinking a cup of tea. The woman looked to be in her sixties and appeared tired and weak.

"Hello," said Alice, "do you mind if I join you?"

"No, not at all. My name's Celeste. What's yours?"

"Alice," she replied, pulling up a chair.

"You're quite new here, aren't you?"

"Yes, I just got here a few days ago," Alice said. "How long have you been here?"

"Just a couple of weeks. It's great that we have a place to go. Before the alternative involved being heavily drugged. I'm so glad we're able to heal this way."

"Yes, me too," Alice said. She hadn't thought about what the alternative to this place might have been. "How's your recovery coming along?"

"It's taking time, but I feel safe and understood here," Celeste said. "I often feel impatient with myself—I just want to be better! But then I remind myself that it's hard to breathe life into the emotional flatness we're left with after the kinds of things we've experienced."

"Emotional flatness," Alice repeated. "That's a good description of my inner state too."

"Yes, most of us know the feeling all too well. The lack of interest, how hard it is to pay attention, the longing to sleep and inability to do so a lot of the time."

"What you're saying is helping me identify my inner territory," said Alice. "What do you do to remedy it?"

Celeste sighed. "I don't know. I try to connect the dots between what I went through recently and the childhood trauma I experienced. That way I can understand my part in what happened. The group work helps a lot too. Sharing this stuff with others who have had similar experiences not only validates our experience but also gives insights into what we do unconsciously that allows us to be targets for people who will, well, you know …"

Alice saw the feeling, or lack of feeling, she was experiencing herself on Celeste's face. Celeste seemed unreachable. *How do we come back to life after this kind of trauma?*

"Have you seen people recover?" asked Alice.

"Yes," said Celeste.

"What happens to them, do you know?" Alice couldn't imagine the journey from where they both were now to emotional health and some kind of happiness.

After thinking for a moment, Celeste said, "It reminds me a little bit of trying to light a candle that doesn't have much of a wick." She paused, then smiled. "We have some pretty bright sparks here in this place doing what they can to help, but it takes some adjusting of the wick too."

"So they've been through what we've been through? I like that feeling of being deeply understood," said Alice, "but the wick part—it's a tough job, isn't it?"

"Sure is," said Celeste. "It helps to see people at different stages of recovery. That way you can see an emotional pathway. I mean, some days I feel better than others. I guess gradually we start feeling a little better a little more of the time."

"I see what you mean," Alice said. "I've only been here a short time, but sometimes I don't feel so bad and others …" She sighed. "Others are pretty hard." Alice looked down as tears welled in her eyes. She noticed her crackers. She had little appetite for them but knew she should eat.

"We have to accept the painful times too and realize that they will gradually diminish. We just have to be with them when they come up," said Celeste. "I know it's hard, but if we deny them, they intensify and sneak up on us. It's like they never go away unless we can just be with them and allow them to flow through us."

"I wonder if that's why sad songs sometimes feel so healing," Alice said. "It feels good to know that others have had as hard a time as we have but were then able to make something beautiful out of their experience."

"Yes," Celeste said. "That's why we're always encouraged to express what we're feeling. Sometimes what we can get out of ourselves helps to put things into perspective and helps us to find what we need to heal." Then she added, "We're often reminded that the source of our pain, which is our vulnerability and ability to love deeply, is a gift the world needs now more than ever. If we can heal ourselves and give this gift in a way that's healthy, we can do a lot for the world."

"That makes sense," Alice said. "The challenge is to heal and learn to give our gift where it's appreciated."

"Not to say that our gift hasn't already been of use," Celeste cautioned. "We never know what healing we've helped to bring about, even when we've experienced pain. Love is never wasted, even when it hasn't been returned. It may bring some good, even if we don't see it, even if it's in another time. Life is mysterious, and love is powerful."

"Thanks for that comforting thought," said Alice. "I feel much better after talking with you." Alice was aware of the pain in her body. She still felt tired a lot and napped frequently. "I need to go and lie down. I'll see you again."

"I hope you sleep well. Nice to talk with you," Celeste said.

As Alice walked away, she noticed that Celeste looked a little more alive than when Alice had first joined her at the table. Alice walked back to her room and crawled into her bed. She'd try to get some sleep for a few hours before her daughter, Janey, came to visit in the afternoon.

CHAPTER 98

Family

Leroy and Tam were turning the soil in one of the backyards they were gardening. The soil was quite loose from the previous year, so the work was going quickly and easily.

"Jon sure left things in good shape, didn't he?" said Tam. "It feels like we've slipped into a well-oiled machine, in a way."

"Yeah, it does to me too," Leroy said. "It's great that he took such good care of the land and established such great relationships with the people involved." He pitched his shovel in the dirt and wiped his hands on the front of his jeans. "Feel like taking a little break?"

"Sure," said Tam, getting the thermos of tea out of his backpack and some chocolate spice cookies Lydia had made the night before. "These cookies are delicious!" He handed Leroy a cup of tea and offered him a cookie, which Leroy accepted.

"Thanks," said Leroy. "A lot of life doesn't feel very real for me right now, but there's a part of me that's intensely aware of how lucky I am to have Lydia and you and the rest of our household." Leroy paused for a second, then leaned against his shovel. "Can I tell you something? It's kind of personal." He studied Tam's face intently.

"Yeah, of course," Tam said.

"Remember that cartoon Simon and Lester dedicated to my mom?"

"Yeah."

"Well, ever since she passed away I've been having these intense dreams about her that sort of remind me a little of that cartoon. It's like she wants to tell me something, but I can't figure out what it is," Leroy said. "I wake up from these dreams, and what she's telling me is just on the edge of my consciousness, but then it disappears."

"What kinds of feelings do you have when you wake up?" Tam asked.

"Of course, I'm glad to see her; then I realize that she's dead and kind of don't know what to do, how to relate to her, but there's something else ..." Leroy stopped. "I don't know how to put it. It's not bad or anything; it's like she wants to tell me something, but when I wake up, it's gone."

"Are you sleeping all right?" Tam asked. "I know it's a practical question, but if it would help you to get a better sleep, I know Cammie could put together some Chinese herbs that might help. Maybe that way you'd be able to hear what your mom is trying to say."

"Think so? Maybe I should give that a try. I'm a pretty light sleeper, but I think I'm waking up more often than usual. Do you think my mom's trying to tell me something?"

"I don't have any set ideas about all that stuff, but why not?" Tam replied. "You were very close, and why wouldn't she want to communicate with you still?"

"Thanks, Tam. That's what Lydia says too. Sometimes it makes me feel kind of crazy, and I know I'm not myself these days," Leroy confessed. "It's such a confusing time, and I really appreciate being able to tell you this stuff without you treating me like I'm nuts or something. I'll talk to Cammie about herbs to help me sleep. It couldn't hurt."

Tam put his arm around Leroy and said, "Hey, we all just want to help you through this, Leroy. We're in this for the long haul. You know we're here for you, whatever you're going through."

CHAPTER 99

Busy Times

As the days gradually became warmer, life became much busier for the household on the first floor of the mansion. It was slow in coming, but when the weather started warming up, it reached high temperatures quickly. The front yard had grown in nicely and, as promised, was drought-resistant and attractive. They were glad they'd taken the time to do this early on as it saved them a lot of time and energy, not having to mow and water it.

The local currency was circulating rapidly. Each week, they paid for their tables at the outdoor market with the local currency they received when they performed at the Love Bite or sold their wares at the market. Since they always seemed to get so much of it and had so few expenses, they were generous with it, giving it to panhandlers, buskers and people at the food bank who looked like they could use some extra spending power. It was fun getting and distributing this money. It felt like a boomerang, always coming back, doing good things for everyone along the way.

Leroy had discussed his sleep problems with Cammie, and she'd given him Chinese herbs to help him sleep. She also started to give the others in the household acupuncture and acupressure treatments, moxibustion and Chinese herbal remedies to help them stay well during this busy time. The massage table was useful, and everyone benefitted from her care.

Baby Bella was getting bigger, and sometimes Cammie and Tam would drop in to see Glenda and her friends as they prepared the daycare. When the time came, they wanted Bella to feel comfortable in the place and with the people running it. Glenda and her friends were willing to accept a large percentage of local currency for their daycare fees so it would be accessible to everyone who needed it.

The SPIN farmers' table at the outdoor market was a source of pride for all of them. Jon was still in town and helping when needed, but that was very seldom. He loved what they were doing and reassured them that they were on the right track.

With bouquets of flowers, fresh vegetables, Lydia and Leroy's occasional piece of beautifully restored furniture and trays of prepared foods, they often had very little left over to give to the food bank. A volunteer from the food bank would take a wagon around near the end of the market and ask for donations from the vendors, who were happy to help out that way. Often the other vendors would donate some of the local currency as well as vegetables, fruits and soaps they hadn't sold. The food bank gratefully accepted all donations.

Cammie had made a point of asking the restaurants they were supplying what kinds of foods they wanted, which turned out to be mostly salad greens, onions, zucchini and cucumbers. They grew plenty and staggered their plantings so the restaurants could count on a steady supply.

Dagmar kept track of the money, doling out some to each of them and giving all of them the ability to see the online banking records. She and Ross did the grocery shopping from a bulk, organic food outlet. Anyone in the house could add to the list that was stuck on the kitchen door with a magnet.

Although busy, things were flowing smoothly: the gardens were growing well, and the group was developing good relationships with the landowners, the vendors and customers at the outdoor market and the people at the restaurants they were supplying. The washing station worked well. They all felt enriched by the interactions they were having with the people in their community.

When they performed at the Love Bite on Sundays, they'd often see Jared or other members of the family there. The family members seemed to be feeling more relaxed in that environment. The household stuck to their Sunday rule and always made sure they had a relaxing afternoon after their performance.

If one of them was tired or under the weather for any reason, he or she would take the day off. Since there were so many of them, it was never a problem. Generally no one wanted to take a day off, since they enjoyed each other's company and the things they were doing.

They all made time to meditate in the meditation room with the stained glass dragon window. Maybe it was the change in the spring sunlight, but somehow the dragon appeared a more radiant shade of red than it had in the past. They all noticed that they felt especially recharged after meditating.

CHAPTER 100

Soup for Cole

"Ross? It's Cole. Are you busy?" Cole's voice on the other end of the phone sounded urgent.

"Why? What's up?" asked Ross.

"I'm sick—a cold or something. Donny's at work." He paused. "I'd really love it if you'd come over. I need someone to talk to."

"Okay, I'll be right over," Ross said and hung up the phone.

"That was Cole," he said to Dagmar as they finished cleaning the kitchen. "He doesn't sound very good and wants me to come over, and I said I would. I think we've got some soup in the fridge; maybe I'll bring him a jar."

"That sounds like a good idea," Dagmar said. "See you when you get back, hon." They gave each other a quick kiss, and Ross left the house.

When he got to Cole's house, he knocked on the door, opened it and walked in. What was that smell? It was like a combination of stale beer and body odour. Whew!

"Hey, I brought you some homemade soup," Ross said.

"Hey, thanks, man," said Cole, coming out of the living room. He looked haggard. "Want a beer?" he asked.

"Okay," Ross said. It was still early in the afternoon, but he wanted Cole to feel at ease. "So what's up?"

"Oh, I don't know. Living with Donny sucks, and after this business with Alice, I feel like everyone's avoiding me."

"Yeah?"

"Yeah, you wouldn't believe the snarky comments I'm getting on social media. I've had to increase my privacy settings; they're so embarrassing." Then he added, "How's Alice doing anyway? I saw her once since her accident, but she's blocked me from her email and other sites, so I don't know how she is."

"From what I hear, she's pretty fragile but in a good place and getting help."

"Do you think you could tell her something from me? She hasn't blocked you, has she?" Cole asked.

"No, she hasn't, but if she doesn't want to hear from you, I feel I should respect that. Sorry, bud."

"I wonder how I can reach her," Cole pondered.

"Maybe you should just let her go," said Ross gently. "If she doesn't want to see you, you should respect that."

"I feel so embarrassed!" Cole exclaimed. "I want to patch things up."

"So you won't have to feel embarrassed anymore or because you're concerned about Alice?" Ross asked, feeling a surge of anger.

"I don't know; it was so much better when she was here," sighed Cole.

"Better for you or better for her?" asked Ross. "It doesn't seem to have been all that great for her—she attempted suicide."

"Yeah, why would she pull something like that?" Cole shook his head incredulously, chugging back some beer.

"Pull something like that? Are you serious?!" asked Ross. "You think she pulled something? She's lucky to be alive right now, and you're complaining about being embarrassed."

"So it's my fault? Everyone is responsible for their own happiness. I can't help it if Alice is unhappy. That's just the way she is."

"Spare me the crap, Cole. Yeah, there's a grain of truth about each of us being responsible for our own happiness, but if you're being treated like garbage by someone you care about, it's pretty hard to feel happy." Then Ross added, "And you know it."

"So what was I supposed to do?" asked Cole.

"Oh, I don't know. Maybe treat her like a human being, maybe show her a little concern, help with the housework? Maybe when she leaves the house crying after you've just made love, go and see what happened when she doesn't come home all night? That's for starters."

"I don't know why I called you!" Cole exclaimed. "I thought you might be a little understanding."

"I do understand," said Ross, "and I'm embarrassed that I do. I used to be a lot more like you. Women are not disposable objects here solely for our pleasure and use, and I'm finally getting that. I hoped maybe you were too. From what I'm hearing, you just don't want to feel embarrassed. I don't detect a whit of genuine concern for Alice's well-being, and to tell you the truth, it's upsetting me."

"Donny's right about you. You're just pussy-whipped," Cole huffed.

"No, if it wasn't for the environment I've been living in, I might have tried to treat Dagmar the same way. But, you know, I noticed that everyone's happier when both men and women are on the same footing, and that includes the men," said Ross. "Treating women like dirt doesn't do anything for anyone. And speaking of Donny, have you seen Elly around town lately?"

"Donny's ex?" Cole asked. "Yeah, she looks like a different person."

"Exactly!" said Ross. "You got it. She seems like a different person because she's spending time with people who value and respect her." Ross stood up. "Anyway, I hope you're feeling better and enjoy the soup, but I don't want to be here anymore. This conversation isn't doing anything for either of us." Ross walked to the door, leaving his unfinished beer behind him.

CHAPTER 101

Another Try

"Ross, wait!" called Cole from the porch. "I'm miserable and lonely and stuck, and I have no idea what to do."

Ross stopped and stood in the walkway for a long moment, then walked over and sat on the porch steps. "I get how you must feel, really."

Cole sat down beside him. "Thanks for understanding."

They sat there like that for a while, looking off into the blue sky.

"You don't know how lucky you were to have wound up with Dagmar and those people," Cole said finally. "I haven't been so lucky. I know I've been a jerk, and I haven't the slightest idea what to do about it."

"You're right; I have been lucky," Ross said. "And, you know, it was really hard at first. I didn't know who the hell I was."

"I wonder if I could change like that. Where would I even begin?"

"You could sing songs that don't put anyone down, for starters," said Ross. "But the main thing is you need to see the value in that and actually want to change yourself."

"What do you mean?"

"Do you want me to tell you what happened to me? Maybe that'll be some help," Ross offered.

"Yeah, sure."

"Well, at first I felt glad that I had food and a roof over my head after Debbie changed the locks on me, but I thought I'd just gotten in with a bunch of losers," said Ross. "Then living with them day to day, I slowly came to see the value in what they were doing, which was helping the community get by; treating each other and Dagmar and me with honesty, kindness and respect; and doing their best to make sure we were feeling okay, and not just physically either."

"What do you mean?"

Ross paused for a moment, then said, "They made sure we ate well, but I remember them watching us closely to see how we were adjusting, and I know they were aware of the inner adjustment I was going through. They said they'd each gone through something kind of similar themselves. I don't know if they were like me, but it's scary suddenly being without a home. These people weren't just talking about changing the world; they were doing it in the most down-to-earth way you could imagine. And it deeply made sense."

"Donny and I both noticed that you changed a lot," Cole said. "Was it hard for Dagmar too?"

Ross laughed. "For some reason, Dagmar took to it like a fish to water, but for me it was a huge shift in the way I'd always seen things. She helped me to see the value of that way of life, and eventually I … well, it was like the lights went on. Dagmar called me on my crap, I remember, and I wanted to be more like her and these people we wound up with. They're so kind and non-judgemental, and they just help to take care of the community."

Ross looked at Cole. "Say, that's something you could do. You could start volunteering somewhere, like maybe at the food bank."

"Yeah, you think that would help?" asked Cole earnestly.

"It might, but only if you want it to and only if you let it," Ross said. "Just look at all the ordinary people doing their best to get by and helping each other out, and see what you can do to pitch in. And maybe sing songs that help people to feel happy and good about themselves."

Cole said, "I've been thinking a lot about how I treated Alice …"

"Yeah?"

"Yeah, I don't want to treat people that way anymore," Cole said. "It's like I want to see how much I can get out of them by convincing them that I care when really I'm just looking out for myself. Know what I mean?"

Ross sighed. "Yeah, I do, and it's so normal for some of us and so not okay—and not just for the people unlucky enough to get sucked in by our behaviour but for us too. I've realized that everyone's happier and more relaxed and able to just be themselves when we actually do care about each other." He added, "There's so much freedom in being authentic, even though we're taught that we're all just looking out for number one." Ross laughed cynically. "What a joke! I don't know how to put it, but you don't have to keep your story straight; you start actually wanting to know how others are doing and what you can do to help out."

"Hey, Ross, thanks for coming back and hanging out with me, eh?" said Cole. "I really appreciate it."

"You're welcome. Oh! Something else we did, and still do a lot, is meditate. Just sit comfortably and pay attention to your breath and let your thoughts float by instead of getting caught up in them. When you do get caught up in a thought, as soon as you realize it, just let it float away, and go back to paying attention to your breath," Ross said. "I'm not sure why, but it helps to calm the mind." He leaned forward, preparing to stand, then added, "Anyway, take care of yourself, buddy, and I hope I've been some help. Enjoy the soup."

"Okay, I'll think about those things. Thanks for bringing that soup over. I'm feeling a little better already. It felt great to talk about this stuff."

"Glad to hear it," said Ross. "Good luck with everything, eh?"

"Yeah, thanks, Ross, you too. Thanks for giving me a place to start at least." They both stood up, and Ross slapped Cole on the back before heading off for home.

CHAPTER 102

Reminiscing

On the way back, Ross walked by the old abandoned house. He hadn't really looked at it closely from the outside, oddly enough. It still appeared to be abandoned, although Ross knew it had occupants. He thought about the transformation he'd undergone there and about Cole. The house was tall and rundown. There were hints of brown paint that were mostly worn off its wooden exterior. He could see where the window was that he and Dagmar used to look out of, and he smiled involuntarily.

On his way back to the mansion he'd pass by the labyrinth, and he felt a need to walk it after his and Cole's discussion. Cole had made him realize just how lucky he'd been, and he could understand how stuck Cole might be feeling. He hoped Cole would find a way to—to what? To reclaim his humanity the way Ross had.

When Ross got to the labyrinth, the sun was shining in a hazy, languid way. All of a sudden, the day felt mystical. He felt he was exactly where he was supposed to be. Ross went with the feeling and walked leisurely to the centre of the labyrinth. As he stood there, he thought about Cole and sent out a little prayer for him.

Ross strolled back to the mansion, knowing that he had a life he was happy to return to. As the sun warmed his back, he realized how much he'd changed and how remarkable his personal journey had been.

He quietly entered the mansion through the front door and walked into the bedroom he shared with Dagmar. He saw the velveteen rabbit he'd given her for her birthday perched in its usual place on top of the chest of drawers. He walked over to it and gave it a hug, embracing all that he had become and what he was becoming.

His heart full, he walked into the kitchen where Dagmar and the rest of their household greeted him. He pitched in with the preparations for lunch. What could possibly be more wonderful than this?

CHAPTER 103

Consultation

Ray had called Phoebe for a consultation about greening the mansion, and she had offered to bring along a colleague, Liam.

"You said it was a house," said Liam. "This is more like a mansion in my books."

She smiled at him. "Look. That must be Ray." She gestured to a man standing on the steps.

Liam parked the car, and they got out. Phoebe walked over to the man and said, "Hi, you must be Ray. I'm Phoebe, and this my colleague, Liam." She held out her hand.

"A pleasure to meet you, Phoebe, Liam." Ray first shook Phoebe's hand, then Liam's. "Thanks for coming out on such short notice."

"You're welcome. This is a lovely old building," said Liam. "What do you have in mind for it?"

"Well," said Ray, "it belongs to my dad, who, unfortunately, has dementia and lives in a facility. None of our family wants to live here, so we're considering having it fixed up and eventually selling it. It hasn't received a lot of care recently." He paused, and they all looked at the building's faded exterior. "I've been reading about the increase in market value that renovating in an environmentally friendly way can have on a home."

"So since the building needs some upkeep anyway, you're thinking you may as well make it more environmentally friendly while you're at it. Am I getting that right?" Liam paraphrased.

"Yes, that's what I'm thinking," Ray confirmed.

"And you'd like to renovate both the interior and exterior in a way that reduces the building's environmental impact and makes it more marketable?" Phoebe added.

"That's right," said Ray.

"Would it be all right then if we took a look around the building, took some pictures, made some notes and got back to you with a few options?" asked Liam.

"Certainly, as long as it's all right with the people on the main floor," Ray answered.

Phoebe smiled at him. "They're friends of mine and are expecting us. If you can let us see the top two storeys and the basement, we can go in and see my friends on the first floor afterwards."

"Very good," said Ray. "Let's walk around the yard and then go upstairs."

CHAPTER 104

Contemplation

Cole finished the last of the soup Ross had brought him. He felt stronger, his health almost restored. Looking around, he was tired of the dirty house he was living in. He picked up a few beer cans and put them in a pile by the door. Then he got a dishcloth and wiped off the counter and felt at a loss about what else to do.

Thinking about his life, he couldn't help but compare himself to Ross and Donny. Of the two of them, Ross seemed much happier, although he was no longer playing music with them. Cole wondered who he was really and who he wanted to be.

He thought he'd seen a broom in one of the kitchen closets. There it was, with a dustpan. He swept the floor. It felt comforting to get the dirt swept into little piles and then throw them in the garbage. There was a mop in the closet too and a bucket. Checking under the sink, he found some liquid soap that looked like it might work for the floor. He put some of the soap in the bucket and then ran some hot water into it. As he mopped the floor, he enjoyed the scent of the soap and how clean it made the place smell.

Cole felt angry, betrayed—all these years, trying to act like a man, all those action-adventure flicks, the idiotic things that guys were supposed to buy into. He guessed women were supposed to buy into their own brand of idiocy too, but at least they could express their feelings. Guys were just supposed to be tough and not have any feelings.

How did he feel about what had happened to Alice? He didn't even know, really. Embarrassment was the first thing that came to mind. Under that? Anger that she'd expose what he'd wanted to keep secret. Concern for her? To be honest, he wasn't sure. He knew he was supposed to, but did he?

Did he miss her? He missed having sex and having a clean house. All her tears and pleading had left him feeling contempt at her emotional outbreaks. What the hell did she want anyway? Sex was good enough for him, but she wanted all that other stuff—a relationship, some kind of emotional connection. He didn't even want to try. What did he want in a woman? He wasn't sure, but it was someone alluring and mysterious and sexy, like in the movies. Alice was just, well, Alice. Nothing special.

He sat down in the living room, picked up his guitar and played a quiet tune.

CHAPTER 105

Clothes Swap

Silverdale was experiencing heavy rains. It had been coming down for days, and there was a major landslide on the main road to the valley. Thankfully, no one had been hurt, but food supplies were dwindling since delivery trucks were unable to drive in.

The people on the ground floor of the mansion were doing all right with their stocks of dried food and the fresh food from the gardens they were tending. They'd gone in on a bulk, wholesale order with Phoebe and Sophie, so their households were in good shape too.

People who shopped week to week at the grocery stores had to be creative and buy what was available to feed themselves and their families. Road crews were working around the clock, but the slide was difficult to clear. It took a good two weeks to finally open the road.

Relative to the rest of the country—and the rest of the world for that matter—their little town had been lucky so far. Other places had experienced tornadoes, hurricanes, arctic cold and drought, with indications of more drought this summer. Anima mundi had been relatively kind to Silverdale. Hopefully this valley would remain in Gaia's good graces.

Phoebe was in organizing mode. She'd cleaned out her kitchen cupboards and put her winter clothes away. As she got out her summer things, she realized there were some items she was just tired of. The rain was getting everyone down, so she thought it might be fun to have a clothing swap.

She invited Dagmar, Lydia and Cammie to participate and asked them to bring friends. She also invited Sophie, who lived across the hall, and the women who lived upstairs in their fourplex.

Lydia and Dagmar were both good at finding clothing in the free boxes people left at the side of the road and at second-hand stores when there were sales or free days. Lydia was also good at altering clothes and did a lot to keep people in her household fairly well dressed. Cammie paid less attention and had fewer clothes than the other two women, but her body was regaining its pre-pregnancy shape, and some of her pants and tops were becoming looser than she liked.

Cammie invited Glenda and her household to come along as well. Ceri, the woman whose house Glenda and the others were living in, brought some classic suits. She had worn them to business meetings in her younger years when she was advocating for childcare that was more grounded in real life skills.

"I don't wear these anymore and haven't known what to do with them, but I'd love to pass them along to a group of incredible women like you," she announced. After choosing a few items of clothing for herself, she took a seat and enjoyed watching the others trying things on.

Luckily, Phoebe had a large living room. The women who came brought desserts and snacks, and Phoebe provided coffee and tea.

Dagmar was happy to see Phoebe, Sophie and the rest of the women. It felt great to have this diverse group of wonderful women all together. Despite the dreary weather, there was lots of laughter as they tried things on that sometimes fit and sometimes didn't.

Phoebe was sitting down sipping a cup of tea and watching the antics of the women trying on clothes. Dagmar sat down beside her and poured herself some tea too.

"Hey, Phoebe, thanks for organizing this!" She smiled at her friend. "It's fun to participate and to be a spectator." They laughed at the pile of clothing and the women helping each other with zippers in the back. Dagmar had a small stack of what she'd chosen on her lap, and Phoebe had put a few items inside her bedroom door.

Everyone pitched in to do the dishes after they'd taken the items of clothing they liked and had a bit of a visit. Since Dagmar was the last to leave, she put the clothes that weren't taken into a box. Once the rain stopped, Phoebe could put it beside the sidewalk so people could help themselves to what they wanted. When Dagmar finished, she sat down at Phoebe's kitchen table.

"Thanks, Dagmar, and thank you for hooking me up with Ray," said Phoebe. "This is going to be a pretty exciting project."

"And we'll get to see more of each other." Dagmar smiled. "Nice perk!"

"And you'll get to know Liam," Phoebe said with a twinkle in her eye.

"Is he the fellow you've been seeing lately?" asked Dagmar with interest.

"Yes, and he's a sweetheart," Phoebe said with conviction.

"So glad to hear it, my dear. You deserve someone special. I hope he has as big a heart as you do."

"At least as big, maybe bigger." Phoebe blushed. "He really goes out of his way to be good to me, and he's kind and mature and shares a lot of my values. We've been colleagues for a long time, so we're comfortable with each other and have a lot of history."

"Why don't the two of you come by for lunch next time you're over?" asked Dagmar.

"We've taken pictures and measurements and just have to come up with a couple of options for Ray. It should take us about a week. What about the end of next week, say Friday tentatively? If we're not ready, we can just reschedule."

"Okay, next Friday for lunch unless I hear from you otherwise," Dagmar confirmed. "Say, when you were cleaning out your cupboards, did you find any food you're not going to use? We're collecting for the food bank. They're struggling right now."

"Yeah, I've got a few dried goods that I'd be happy to donate. Thanks for thinking of it," Phoebe said, getting up and taking jars of various beans and grains down from the shelf and putting them in a bag. "This should help a little."

"It's Tam who looks out for them mostly, but I'm glad to be part of it. People have to eat," said Dagmar.

"Right you are," said Phoebe. "We're both lucky to be in good situations in these crazy times, and it's nice to help."

CHAPTER 106

Presentation

Jess and Tina found chairs together in the crowded gymnasium of Velvet's high school. Parents, friends, teachers and students were awaiting the presentation organized by Ronnie's and Velvet's high schools. The loud chatter made it difficult to hear.

Jess shouted to Tina, "They've gotten a great turnout!"

Tina just nodded her head vigorously. She didn't even want to try to compete with the hubbub around her.

Soon the lights dimmed, and the noise turned into a soft murmur. When the lights went out and the spotlight shone a circle on the stage, the room became quiet.

The school principal walked into the spotlight and cleared his throat. "Thanks, everyone, for coming to this joint presentation by the environmental groups of these two high schools. I want to commend you for showing them your support, and I want to thank them for their collaborative efforts. We hope this is just the beginning of many more! Sharing our talents, resources and bright, young minds can only be a good thing. Without further ado, here's their presentation."

Velvet, Ronnie and the members of their environmental groups walked onto the stage. Behind them was a silhouette of a large branching tree.

Velvet stepped to the front and spoke into the microphone. "I want to thank all of you for coming to our two schools' joint presentation. We also want to thank the Indigenous people of this land, of this unceded traditional territory, for doing so much to defend it and for their graciousness in allowing us to be here. We will do all we can to support you in your vision for a land that's whole and healthy." She paused for a moment. "We hope you enjoy our presentation."

The light dimmed, and the spotlight narrowly shone on Velvet.

"How does it feel to be alone in a hostile world?" she asked. "A world where you can't trust anyone and everyone's in it for themselves? There's so much conflicting information out there, and you don't know what to believe. Everyone's trying to be cool, to get in with the right crowd, to manage their image. What does this feel like?"

The spotlight widened to include the tree. There was blackness behind the tree onstage, making it look fragile and isolated.

Velvet stepped back, and the spotlight shone on one of her classmates wearing baggy jeans and a hoodie who was standing beside a large boulder. The classmate said, "From this place of feeling we can easily be manipulated. When we feel isolated, when we have little hope for a better future, when it's demonstrated repeatedly that we can't trust anyone, what do we do? We try to fill the void in our souls with habits that don't serve us, habits like drugs and alcohol or buying stuff or overeating. That void we're compulsively feeding is our humanity seeking acknowledgement.

"We're presented with options that don't hold a lot of promise, a set of labels that don't honour the fullness of who we are. We need to broaden our options, make them more inclusive, authentic and kind. Anima mundi needs all of us in our fullness. Anima mundi, the soul of our planet, is shattered. Just like us, Gaia wants to be acknowledged and is vulnerable right now. She is pleading for our help."

The spotlight shone on a girl with curly red hair from Ronnie's school who sat beside a brook that appeared to be moving toward the crowd. She said, "In reality, we have so many options, and we're privileged to be living in a time when we can sample as many as we want. When we really listen to anima mundi, we can hear her in the wind and the rain and the babbling of a brook. We can see her in the stars and the sunshine. Physically and emotionally, we no longer honour her or treat her as the sacred life giver she truly is. She's the source of everything we know and love.

"This is the time when all of us are being called to rise to the challenge, to change our way of being so that future generations will have a planet to support all they've come to know and love. Our lives are fleeting, ephemeral; every one of us will die one day. With this one precious life of ours, we each have a chance to seize this incredible moment and see it for what it is. Fear of our own vulnerability has left the very planet we depend on vulnerable. Our earth is what we rely upon for everything; it's the place that holds everything we've ever collectively known and accomplished."

The spotlight shone on a boy of Asian descent from Ronnie's school, and fruit appeared on the branches of the tree. He asked, "What happens if we continue on the path we're on? We're looking at a world with more greenhouse gas emissions, more climate change and more and more extreme weather. Sea levels will continue rise; there will be more droughts and wildfires; more species will become extinct, and eventually maybe human beings will become extinct too.

"But we have alternatives, and many of us are embracing them. There are so many things we can do! Whatever your comfort level or personality type, there's a way you can contribute." He started walking slowly under the branches and picking some of the glowing fruits from them. "Some of the low-hanging fruits are things we can do with our money. Things like buying local, organic and fairly traded goods or not buying disposable junk or reusing, buying second-hand, repurposing. All these things help our world to become cleaner, healthier and fairer. We can bank at credit unions where money stays in our community instead of putting it in big banks where it supports all kinds of dubious things.

"We can sign online petitions to politicians and industry leaders. We can stay well informed by investigating our news sources and finding out who funds them and which interests they're representing. We can join groups that help to make the world a better place for all of us. And we can share and celebrate our collective victories."

The spotlight shone on Stacey, Velvet's best friend, who had long, dark hair. A bright full moon appeared through the tree branches. Stacey said, "Doing things like this might inspire you to do more. No one has all the answers, and the world needs all our creativity, all our commitment, all our best efforts to turn things around. Do you hear the voices of your children's children's children calling you? They are the timeless voice of anima mundi. They are the voice of our future. Please heed the call."

As the light on the stage expanded and revealed the whole scene, Ronnie stepped to the front of the group and said, "This is our invitation to you to embrace your own humanity and to join us in this commonsensical quest for survival. Because, make no mistake, that's what it is. In the process, you'll find a sense of purpose and belonging. You'll discover what it truly means to be alive right now. The world is counting on you and me and all of us to wholeheartedly embrace this critical time, see it for the grand opportunity it is and do everything we can to turn things around.

"Our schools have joined together to find solutions to these major problems. There's a new world emerging through the rubble. We need to nurture it together while creating space for it to grow. Gargantuan industries and institutions are crumbling. Let's protect each other while they fall. Let's focus our intentions on the beautiful world we're helping to create.

"Imagine if our governments chose different priorities. We've prepared an alternative federal budget, to demonstrate what's possible. What if our priorities were clean energy, healthy food, sustainable agriculture and a healthy and well-educated population? Our tax dollars would be distributed in a much different way.

"We invite everyone to take a look at the materials on the tables at the back. We hope you'll sign the petitions, take whatever literature interests you and begin or deepen your journey in the direction of making the world a better place. All action starts with a step. We hope it leads to more steps, steps that will save our beautiful planet and will honour the rhythms of anima mundi. Thank you."

Spotlights shone at the back of the gym onto tables with brochures from various environmental organizations.

The lights dimmed, and the crowd roared with applause and whoops. As the lights went on, people milled around, talking excitedly, and many headed to the back of the gym to the tables that were laden with brochures, petitions and sheets of information.

Tina leaned over to Jess and said, "You know, I really heard where they're coming from, but a few months ago I think I would have been too wrapped up in my own suffering to have this material penetrate. Know what I mean?"

"Yes, I do," Jess replied. "I guess it takes healed people to heal a sick world. Let's go check out the material on the tables at the back."

CHAPTER 107

Visit With Amelda

Leroy bolted upright, sweating. He looked at the clock beside his bed: 3:00 a.m. What had his mother been saying just then, in his dream? He reviewed it in his mind: They had been sitting together at the kitchen table at his mother's house with the sun shining in. She had been laughing and talking and seemed to be in good spirits. His heart warmed thinking about it.

She'd leaned across the table, put her hand on his and looked into his eyes. What had she just said? Each time he dreamt of her, he was getting a little closer, but he still was not quite there.

He looked at Lydia sleeping deeply beside him, her gentle, rhythmic breathing calming him. Lydia and his mother had always gotten along well, and he was grateful for that, for the fun times they'd all had together. He wondered how Dan was doing and promised himself he'd give Dan a call the next day. Last time they'd spoken, Dan had sounded as if he was doing not too badly.

Leroy got back under the covers and curled up against Lydia, who automatically snuggled against him. He lay there for awhile, smelling the moist, intimate fragrance of Lydia's sleeping body, before drifting back into a fitful sleep himself.

He woke up that morning feeling unrested. When Lydia curled up beside him and asked him how he'd slept, he told her about his dream. "It's like something on the tip of my tongue. Every time, I almost hear her but then miss it somehow," said Leroy, frustration in his voice.

"It'll come to you one day," said Lydia as she stroked his hair. "Maybe you need to reframe your question. Maybe there's something else you need to understand."

"Maybe." Leroy pondered her remark. "Maybe I'm looking for words when I should be looking for something else."

CHAPTER 108

Clarity

It was a warm spring day, and Alice was working in the garden with Celeste. After the recent rains, they'd had to do some replanting. The quiet, easy activity was its own kind of therapy. As she planted seedlings in the ground, she thought about her relationship with them. It was so direct and mutually beneficial. Shouldn't all relationships be like that?

That morning, she'd gotten an email saying that Cole had added her to one of his social media accounts—this after she'd cut him out of all of her social media. She felt angry and confused. Why would he want to be connected with her after clearly demonstrating that all he wanted from her was what benefitted him?

She thought about the seedlings and how her other relationships had much more in common with the relationship she had with these small plants. Genuine concern, mutual benefit—all those things came naturally to her and the people she was close to. Her friends and her daughter all tended to each other the way they would seedlings. They wanted the best for each other, and those relationships enriched all their lives.

It dawned on her that she and everyone else was entitled to relationships based on those things. She said to Celeste, "I've been thinking: all relationships should have to pass what I call the seedling test. If there isn't the kind of care and mutuality like what's between these seedlings and us, we shouldn't have those relationships in our lives. What do you think?"

Celeste stood up and arched her back. "I like it. So often we feel obligated to be helpful when that isn't being reciprocated, especially people like us."

Alice continued, "It doesn't mean that we won't have problems in some of our important relationships, but if there isn't a basis of genuine caring, transparency and honesty, that should be our signal that those relationships are unhealthy and we should let them go."

"Yes, I agree," said Celeste, down on her knees planting again. "That even goes for bigger, less personal relationships, like the news we listen to. What's the source? Who's paying for it, and what are their vested interests? If we're being manipulated, then it's time to find another source, don't you think?"

"Good point," Alice replied. "These little pea plants will feed us one day. We need real news and real people in our lives because they feed us and we feed them too. We give them our attention and depend on them to be true. As soon as trust is gone, the relationship should be as well. There are too many demands on our attention and too much good stuff—and good people—out there to waste our attention on manipulative energy of any kind."

"Truth is beauty and beauty, truth," laughed Celeste.

"Maybe part of the upside of the glut of what we experience these days is that it makes us develop discernment. Everything is going to be put to the seedling test in my life!" exclaimed Alice. "And I'm happy to add that most of my relationships pass with flying colours."

"Me too—and mine too!" Celeste agreed.

The pea plants glowed green in the morning sun.

CHAPTER 109

A Gift

C ole said into his phone, "I've been thinking of sending Alice a gift. What do you think of that idea?"

There was silence on the other end, and then Ross said, "Why do you want to send her a gift?"

"I don't know. I just thought it might help to smooth things over."

"So let me get this straight," said Ross. "You were happy to use her for sex, housework and whatever else you could get out of her, and now you want to send her a gift. Don't you think it's a little late for that? Do you even know her well enough to be able to buy her something she'd like? As far as I could tell, you barely gave her the time of day."

There was a long pause. "Well, what am I supposed to do?" Cole pleaded.

"I don't know, but I don't know that Alice would appreciate a gift from you right now. The most important part of gift giving is the relationship it's built upon. A gift has to come from a place of genuine caring and concern, or else it's meaningless. Where would a gift from you to Alice be coming from?"

More silence. "I'd have to think about that."

"You know, Cole, I got something for Dagmar for her birthday that was inexpensive, but it symbolized something really important to both of us, something very intimate in our relationship. It represented a common bond and understanding."

"I don't think a second-hand negligee would be appropriate," Cole said.

"It wasn't a negligee," said Ross, exasperated. "You're missing the point. Being able to give and receive gifts is like a pathway that's created by a special bond. If you don't have that bond, no gift is appropriate. But if you do, then people can give and receive freely, and part of the receiving is welcoming and honouring the inner place the gift is coming from. Does that make sense?"

"What was it then?" asked Cole.

"It's none of your business," Ross said. "The point is, it's not the gift but where it's coming from. Why would Alice want something from you? You ignored her, you didn't care about her feelings and you took advantage of her."

"She enjoyed having sex just as much as I did," Cole snapped.

"That's not the point either," Ross said. "She wanted more, and you were willing to take only what you wanted and ignore her wants and needs. Would you like it if you were treated that way?"

"No, I guess not."

"Don't you think you've had your chance with Alice? Why would she want anything from you? What reason would she have to trust you at this point?" Ross asked. "My guess is that a gift from you would just bring up sad feelings and confusion for her. You probably don't even know what she likes anyway, do you?"

"Not really," Cole said. "Do you?"

"No, I don't know Alice that well." Ross paused for a moment. "But it has less to do with what you get someone than where it's coming from. When people say, 'It's the thought that counts,' it means that someone is showing that they genuinely care, and that's what's important. I'm not convinced that you do genuinely care, and I doubt that you're convinced of that either."

"Am I really such a bad guy?" asked Cole.

"What do you think?" Ross asked. "How do you feel about the way you behaved toward Alice? I can't figure out if you feel badly because you used her without any regard for her feelings or if you're just pissed off that you got caught and are trying to make it look better. Judge for yourself. When you treat people like a commodity, you reduce everything and everyone to a commodity, including yourself. That's why the world's in the miserable state it's in."

"Anyway, I've got to run. Bye," Cole said and turned off the phone. He leaned back, heaved a sigh and ran his fingers through his hair.

CHAPTER 110
Recommendations

Phoebe and Liam joined Ray in the driveway in the sunshine. They each said hello and shook his hand. The front yard that had been dug up now had a covering of indigenous plants and looked very nice.

Ray said, smiling, "The yard's starting to look good, don't you think?"

Phoebe smiled back at him and then looked out at the yard. "It sure is."

"Why don't we sit out here and discuss your findings?" Ray said, gesturing toward a table and some chairs on the veranda in the sunshine. They went to the veranda and sat down.

Liam said, "Taking a first look at your place, we have a couple of different options for you, but we'd advise an energy audit first through the hydro company here. The cost is very reasonable, and it gives an accurate picture of where you're losing energy. I'd be happy to arrange that for you, or, if you prefer, you can arrange it. I'd be happy to pass along their contact information."

Ray thought for a moment. "I think I'd like to leave that to you, since you'll be able to answer any questions they have with more accuracy."

"All right, I can arrange that," Liam said. "Another issue that might be a little more difficult to resolve is what you want to do with the building itself. Would you like it to remain one large household, or would you prefer the option of turning it into separate suites?" Liam handed Ray a manila envelope. "I've prepared a report with drawings of the layout of suites."

"Suites …" Ray said. "I hadn't thought of that option. I suppose we could keep one for the family and rent the rest of it out. Does the zoning allow that for this area?"

"Yes, it does," Phoebe said. "That option would bring in revenue each month and provide much-needed housing to this area. You could also try to sell it as a single residence, but as you probably know, the housing market hasn't been very good lately and isn't showing signs of improvement, even for grand homes like this one." She handed Ray another envelope. "I've prepared a budget for each of the interior design of each of these options."

Ray was taking notes on his iPhone. "That decision may take some time, since the family will need to discuss it and come to an agreement. We'll review your proposals and get back to you. Is there anything else we'll need to consider?"

"Yes," Liam said, "and that's how far you want to go with the green renovations. Do you want to just make what you have more efficient? Do you want to have things like heat pumps and solar panels? It's a matter of degree. My report outlines costs and benefits of each of these."

"That's a lot to consider," said Ray thoughtfully. "In the meantime, though, please go ahead with the energy audit. I'll get back to you after I've discussed it with the rest of the family. Thank you both for your time." Ray bowed his head graciously to Phoebe and Liam and then stood up, signalling the end of the meeting. Phoebe and Liam stood up and shook Ray's hand again.

They went their separate ways, Ray heading for his vehicle and Phoebe and Liam heading to the front door in anticipation of their lunch date with Dagmar and the rest of her household.

CHAPTER 111
A Luxuriant Lunch

A smiling Dagmar greeted Phoebe and Liam at the door. "Wonderful to see you!" she said, giving Phoebe and then Liam a hug. Dagmar stood in the sunshine for a moment and then suggested, "It's so beautiful outside; why don't we eat lunch on the veranda?"

"Sounds like a great idea to me," said Liam, smiling. "Can we help you bring things out?"

"Sure, come on in, and we can bring everything outside. We have plenty of hands, so it'll take no time," said Dagmar.

The whole household liked the idea of eating outdoors and brought out plates, cutlery and the soup, bread and salad. Ross pushed two smaller tables together on the veranda and put eight chairs around them; then he helped Cammie spread out a blanket so that Bella could crawl around on it. She'd recently learned this skill and was enjoying her newly found independence. So far there had been only a few casualties to Bella and her surroundings.

She had a safe distance where she could explore between the far wall of the veranda and the table where they were eating lunch.

"This feels like a big family meal, like people used to have generations ago," Liam said happily. He was from a small family, and this felt like something out of a myth.

"Yes, we enjoy it," Ross replied. "We take turns cooking and all pitch in with the clean-up, so we eat really well without cooking that often. It's as much fun as it seems."

They all looked over at an orange-and-white cat that had jumped up onto the sill of the veranda and watched Bella's reaction to it. She was cooing and laughing. The cat jumped down and walked toward the baby. Bella reached out and touched the cat's fur. The cat jumped back, then moved cautiously toward Bella again. Tam got up and walked over to the cat. He held out his hand so the cat could sniff it and then patted its head. The cat started purring.

"Nice kitty," said Tam. "Bella, do you want to pat the kitty too?" Bella reached out her hand, and the cat sniffed at it. "Like this," said Tam as he continued to stroke the purring cat. Bella got excited and laughed, and then she reached out and touched the cat's fur again.

"I love the purity of the reactions of babies, don't you?" Liam said to Phoebe. "This is how we start off; then we're trained to behave in certain ways and, after a point, do our best to regain that kind of purity in our interactions."

"I know what you mean," Phoebe said. "After all the conditioning we go through, being authentic can be a challenge."

Turning to Dagmar, Phoebe asked, "Did you make this soup?" She dunked a piece of homemade bread into it and took a bite.

"Yes, do you like it?" Dagmar asked.

"I love it! Bean and barley, eh? The flavour's exquisite," she said.

"Beans, barley and whatever needed using up in the fridge," Dagmar confessed. "I don't know why, but often that's what makes the best soups." They both laughed.

"This is good! And I know what you mean about leftover soup—always the best!" Liam said, smiling broadly.

Afterwards, they had tea and strawberry-rhubarb crumble made from fruit that Phoebe had frozen the previous year. She'd made it up ahead of time and brought it over, so it had been warming in the oven as they'd eaten their soup.

"Simple and sumptuous!" said Liam. "It's amazing how well we can eat using what's around us. Thanks, Phoebe, for this amazing dessert—a taste of where we live."

They finished their lunch, enchanted by the first days of warmer weather and by the antics of Bella and the cat who had joined them. Spring was in the air and breathed happiness and optimism into the gathering on the veranda.

CHAPTER 112
Jess's Vortex

"Vortex," Jess said into the phone.

"Okay, what's up?" asked Tina.

"Well, another trip to your dad's sounds great. I know Ronnie and I will have a wonderful time with you and Velvet," Jess said. "Only these feelings of inadequacy keep coming up for me. I can't imagine what it must have been like growing up with so much wealth and everything that goes with it. My family was so different growing up, so much more—I don't know—nuts and bolts, I guess." She took a breath. "I know it's my problem, and I shouldn't compare myself, but it's tough not to. I get these feelings of being not good enough no matter what I do, but especially when I go to your dad's place with you."

Tina thought about that for a moment. "Jess, I hear you, even though I can't fully understand, since my experience was so different from yours, even though it left its own scars. But what if you looked at it in a different way?" Tina was doing the dishes as she talked into the phone that was squeezed between her ear and her shoulder.

"Okay, shoot. Show me a different way, and I'll see if I can convince myself."

"Remember what we were both like when Ellen first got us together?" Tina asked.

"Yeah, we were both a couple of wrecks."

"Right. And we're both doing so much better because of each other, and for me, that's because of you. I care that we have this amazing friendship and that we've developed so much trust and helped each other up from the abyss, even though those big holes are slightly different for each of us."

"Yeah, it's really special," Jess acknowledged. "And we both really are doing so much better."

"And seeing how much better you're doing helps me to feel good about myself," Tina said. "However we've been treated in the past, we're invaluable to each other. Whatever it takes, I want to throw you a lifesaver when you're feeling this way. What can I do for you right now?" She finished the dishes and started wiping off the stove and countertops.

Jess sighed, curling up in her chair and relaxing a little. "What you're saying is true, and looking at our situation that way helps. Knowing that you value me makes me feel like I'm not all alone with this. The fact that you're not judging me and genuinely want me to feel better is validating. I realize that whatever's going on inside of me is my internal issue and not something that other people see. Sometimes when I feel like crap, it's as though the whole world can see my humble roots and not whatever's right about me. Do you think everyone experiences this kind of inner junk?"

"My guess is probably," Tina said, "but maybe to different degrees. We both seem to have pretty dark inner places."

"It's funny how exposing them makes them less dark, isn't it?" Jess said. "Like when we can share the hard stuff, it becomes less hard."

"We really are our worst critics, aren't we?" Tina said. "I bet we wouldn't dare talk to others in the harsh and demeaning ways we talk to ourselves. Wouldn't it be great if those voices were a little bit kinder and gentler?"

"Sure would. Mine are unrelenting when they get going."

"Yeah, mine too. Why don't we ask Ellen if she knows how to tame those voices a little bit. I bet she has some ideas." Tina folded the dishcloth and draped it over the faucet of the kitchen sink.

CHAPTER 113

Preparations

George sat at a table on the beach, sipping an iced tea and looking at his laptop. He'd just finished buying his airline ticket to Silverdale and was searching the town to see what was new. He checked out the tourism site, read lots of press releases about the proposed pipeline and then stumbled on a community-currency site.

George's mother sat down across the table from him. "So you'll be off to Canada soon, will you?" In her late sixties, she was tall, slender and agile.

"Yes, just got my ticket," George said. "I'm glad we've had a bit of time together."

"So am I," she said, smiling at him.

"Here's something you might find interesting: a community currency. Take a look." He turned the laptop to face her and showed her the page. He pulled his chair around so he could sit beside her.

"I've never heard of this. They have this currency in Silverdale?" she asked.

"It looks like it," George said. "The site's current."

186

"Encourages generosity," she read aloud. "Do you understand how it works?"

"Not really, but I'm curious to try it out."

"Is it even legal?" asked George's mother. "I'm surprised the organizers of this scheme haven't been arrested. Who do they think they are creating their own currency?"

"It can only be spent locally, so maybe it works the way coupons do," said George. "It looks pretty innocuous to me."

"Wouldn't it undermine legitimate currency?" she asked. "I can't understand how it could possibly be legal."

"They have a website, and lots of businesses and groups are participating, so if it's illegal, they're being pretty open about it," said George. "I guess I'll find out more when I get there."

"Just don't get yourself mixed up with a bunch of counterfeiters," George's mother warned. "Who knows what else they might be up to."

"Oh, Mom!" said George. "It looks like this currency was designed to stimulate the local economy. I wouldn't read all that into it."

George's mother looked over at him and sighed. "George, you could have absolutely anything you want. Why do you waste your time on these crazy schemes?"

"Because it's not just about having anything I want. There's a whole world out there, and so many aren't being served by the way things are now. I'm drawn to systems like this that peacefully alters the structure of the economy in a way that enriches so many."

"I guess giving to charities doesn't do that?"

"There are charities that address the roots of some problems, but I'm concerned about getting to the deeper structural root," George said.

CHAPTER 114

Circle Time

Alice had had a good sleep for a change and then had a pleasant visit with her daughter over breakfast on that sunny morning. She was starting to feel a little better and finally felt up to participating in the group work at the facility. She decided to join what they called the healing circle.

The small room held chairs and cushions in tones of beige, peach and cream. There were simple paintings on the wall that added to the overall calming effect of the room. Alice slowly sat down on a large, comfortable, peach-coloured cushion. She was still recovering physically, and it took some effort for her to move. There were 12 other men and women sitting in the chairs or on the cushions, and it didn't appear that anyone was leading the circle.

When they were all comfortably seated and settled, a woman help up a large, brown feather. "Hello and welcome, everyone. My name's Mayzie, and I'll start. I want to acknowledge that we who've found ourselves here are a caring bunch. In our hearts, we want to help humanity, and that's a good thing. We have a certain empathetic quality in common that makes us especially vulnerable to people who are willing to take advantage. We know lots about their personality types but less about people like us who are taken in by these people."

Alice could relate to what Mayzie was saying.

Mayzie continued, "Call them takers or whatever you want—it doesn't matter. We in this room know the type all too well: their ability to engage our empathy and then take advantage of us. As I said, they're not our focus, as much as we're inclined to be concerned about them. We need to heal so that we no longer allow ourselves to be partners in the dance that ultimately doesn't help people like us."

Mayzie passed the feather along to the man on her right. He said, "My name is Steven, and I want to acknowledge how difficult it can be to shift our focus to ourselves when we've put so much energy into rescuing someone else, because often that's how it feels. We've done our best to be there for someone whose distress has hooked us. I realize we need to unhook and take care of ourselves and learn to share ourselves with those who are willing to give back and not just take."

As each person held the feather and took a turn speaking, Alice realized that her situation with Cole wasn't unique. The people sitting in this room were all empathetic and had all been in situations that were somewhat similar to hers. Looking around at the faces in the room, she could see eyes filled with concern and understanding. Celeste, who had also joined the group, brought up the issue of childhood trauma, something this group had in common with the people who were willing to take advantage of them. Both groups had boundary issues; one overstepped boundaries, and the others allowed their boundaries to be violated.

When the feather reached Alice, she said quietly, "This is my first time participating in the circle, and I find it chilling to hear all your observations because they hit so close to home for me. Like many of you, I had a difficult childhood, and, like you, I was involved with someone who didn't seem to value me or care about my feelings. It'll take a while for me to process this information, but hearing it from so many different perspectives will help, I know. I want to thank all of you for your courage in exposing your personal traumas, and I look forward to healing with you."

Alice shifted on her pillow. "I value the empathy we all have. As much as it makes us vulnerable, empathy is said to be the most revolutionary of emotions, and I believe our world needs our empathy now more than ever. I hope each of us learns to channel it in better directions."

CHAPTER 115
Community Power

Communities didn't want the pipelines; First Nations didn't want them; people were concerned about the dangers to lands, air and waters. But none of it seemed to matter. The politicians at the highest levels of government had ties to the oil company that wanted to build pipelines to the coast where oil would be put on giant tankers and carried through some of the most treacherous waters in the world. These waters provided habitat to salmon, whales and other marine wildlife.

The many groups in opposition to these pipelines were organized, and the law was on their side. Indigenous people all over the province were lodging lawsuits against the governments that were going ahead with plans to compromise Native lands without the consent required under federal law. Community members were supporting protesters by donating food and giving lots of moral support. Some protesters were being arrested while peacefully blockading pipeline construction in particularly vulnerable areas.

Locally, the Green Team and other environmental groups were collaborating. They'd discovered the usefulness of the community currency that had recently been launched and were putting it to good use. People were making donations to the Green Team and receiving the amounts of their donations in community currency. Since so many small businesses were opposed to the pipeline plans, they were signing up as a way to support the work of the Green Team. Since this currency increased people's spending power, participating businesses were benefiting. Citizens were happy to be finding more businesses that accepted the new currency that was helping to fund this important cause.

The Love Bite, which had been an early adopter of the community currency, was even busier than usual. They were making generous donations of food to people who were demonstrating on the front lines, enabling the protesters to hold their ground. The Love Bite used the local currency it received to buy fresh produce from the markets and the local greenhouse.

Printers and filmmakers adopted the community currency and assisted the Green Team and other environmental groups in preparing educational materials like leaflets and short videos. Many of the videos were going viral.

One that was particularly popular outlined the financial contributions oil company executives made to politicians. In turn, the politicians were granting licences to oil companies and changing laws and relaxing environmental regulations to make it easier for them to go ahead with their plans.

Someone else had created a video game where people tried to manoeuvre an oil tanker through clusters of islands during gale-force winds, typical of the conditions the oil-filled tankers would be exposed to in reality. This sensitive wildlife habitat was extremely difficult to navigate. To date no one had won the game, and it effectively illustrated the near impossibility of the planned tanker route.

The local credit union began to offer homeowners credit to replace their furnaces that depended on oil and natural gas with heat pumps and solar panels. The payments homeowners made to the credit union for this were equivalent to the amounts of their heating bills. This was effectively costing homeowners nothing while dramatically reducing greenhouse gas emissions. For that reason, a lot of people moved their mortgages from traditional banks to the credit union. This increased and added value to the credit union's housing stock. Creating a cleaner community helped everyone win, while diverting funds from dirty technologies to technologies that were environmentally friendly and to a more community-oriented way of banking.

The forces of healing were operating like an ecosystem: people were doing what they could and co-operating and collaborating with others who had similar goals. It felt like a giant dance to change things for the better.

Many who were out of work and who usually spent time at the food bank were spending time supporting Indigenous people and their supporters, bringing food or physically blocking the oil companies from compromising the land.

Community life was evolving in a positive direction, even though no one could tell where it would go. There was excitement in the air; people were hopeful; local businesses were thriving; everyone played a role in making their home a better place. What was this momentum building toward?

CHAPTER 116

House Plans

P hoebe and Liam sat down with Ray in the wicker chairs on the veranda in the early spring sunshine. The crisp air seemed to hold fresh promise. Phoebe laughed, "Ray, you certainly got us at a good time—there has been such an upsurge in demand for what we do that we now have a pretty long waiting list."

"I consider myself lucky," Ray said. "And it hasn't been nearly as difficult as I'd imagined getting agreement from the rest of the family," he added in an upbeat tone.

"Oh?" said Liam.

"Well, when you talked about the difficult market and the high demand for rental accommodation, it just made sense to turn the house into rental units," Ray explained. "The place will need upgrading anyway, so why not divide it into suites at the same time? That way we'll have a steady income that will keep Dad well looked after, and we can write the upgrades off as a business expense. We can keep one large suite for family when we're in town and see if we can convince the people downstairs to be the caretakers for us. That way, they can stay here indefinitely." He paused for a moment and then said, "I don't know how to put it, but it just seems like things have been getting better for the whole family since they've moved in, and we want them to stay."

Phoebe grinned. "Sounds like a wise choice. They are lovely people."

Liam added, "Ray, thanks for taking this time to plan. I know it feels like a lot of talking and decision making without much progress at first, but it's so important for us to be on the same page. Once it gets going, it takes a relatively short time to get everything renovated. I have an excellent crew, and we've worked together on these kinds of projects for years."

"I appreciate your taking the time as well," Ray said. "I also understand the value of planning and am grateful that you're so respectful of what we want."

Phoebe said, "We're also committed to making sure that what we come up with won't be disruptive to you and your family. You can stay where you normally do on the second floor until the end of the renovations; then you can stay in one of the new suites until we've upgraded yours, and then you can move back."

"So shall we draw up some plans and present you with options in, say, two weeks?" asked Liam. "That will give us time to get the results of the energy audit, do some planning and create a budget."

They agreed and set up a time to meet.

CHAPTER 117
Food Bank Transformation

T am popped into the food bank and immediately noticed a difference. The walls were freshly painted, the atmosphere was upbeat and there was even something different about Mary. The people playing cards seemed happier, livelier and more energetic.

"Hi, Mary," said Tam. "You've made some changes, eh?"

"Yes, what do you think?" Mary asked.

"It's great! It feels fresh and energized—quite a transformation. There's even something different about you, but I can't put my finger on it."

"We've been putting the local currency to work," Mary replied cheerily. "Once you get the hang of it, it's great! And probably what you're noticing about me is that I no longer have a sore back. A local chiropractor accepts community currency, so I'm not limping any more. My sciatica's virtually gone."

"That's wonderful!" replied Tam.

"You're telling me! It's made such a difference to my quality of life. The currency's also stimulated the chiropractor's business like crazy," Mary said. "I'm so glad we got on board with it."

"Shall I just put these greens in the fridge?" Tam asked.

"Sure," she said. "There should be some space on the bottom shelf. Thanks for bringing it. And how's everything with you and your family?"

"Just great! Bella's learned to crawl, so that's a whole new can of worms for us. Cammie's doing well, and so is everyone else."

"Glad to hear it, and always good to see you," said Mary, moving easily between the stove and the fridge.

"You too," Tam said before heading out the back door. "Take care, and see you again soon."

"Bye for now." Mary waved.

CHAPTER 118

Butterfly

At the facility where Alice was staying there was a crafts room with everything from paints to paper to wire, Post-it notes and felt pens—almost anything imaginable to help people express themselves. Being in this room with tables, chairs and people immersed in self-expression reminded her of high school art class. The sound of the rain outside was comforting and somehow made the space even more conducive to expressing her creativity.

Something in her mind had been brewing since she'd participated in her first circle, and it had to do with symbolically representing her journey to recovery. How to represent the transformation she was beginning to experience? She thought of the cocooned caterpillar becoming a butterfly. How could she represent ideas and attitudes that were part of the cocoon that held people in and gave them wings? she wondered.

She found a large sheet of blank paper and sat down at a table beside Mayzie, from the healing circle, who was working with clay. Alice then found a pencil and drew a large butterfly that took up the whole piece of paper. Next, she found some square, white Post-it notes. She sat down and closed her eyes. In a few minutes, she took a felt pen and wrote, "I am not worthy of love," on a Post-it and put it on the body of the butterfly. She sat back and closed her eyes again, and in a few minutes wrote, "I am too sensitive," and added it to the butterfly. Alice gazed out the window and watched the clouds lazily roll across the blue sky and wrote, "My life has no value," and stuck that one on too. Looking out the window again, she thought about her childhood and wrote, "My feelings don't matter," and put it with the other Post-it notes.

Alice got up and found a paintbrush, some water and some watercolours, then sat back down and looked at her butterfly. Right now it was a cocoon of self-criticism. She thought about her experience with Cole and about her childhood. Neither her parents nor Cole had paid attention to her feelings. It was as though her more recent experience with Cole was a newer reflection of how she'd felt as a child growing up.

Alice felt trapped. How does an intelligent person break the emotional pattern imprinted from childhood? she wondered. She found another Post-it and wrote, "I am doomed to repeat the emotional reality of my past," and stuck it onto the cocoon of her self-criticism and negative feelings.

She looked at the words on the Post-its and assessed the feelings they brought up for her. What if a good friend of hers was experiencing these kinds of thoughts? What would she want to say to them? How could she become a good friend to herself?

"I am doomed to repeat the emotional reality of my past"—is this true? she wondered. From deep within, she heard, *No.* Why not? Alice realized that even though her recent experience with Cole was similar emotionally to what she'd experienced growing up, she also had friendships based on deep caring and concern and a loving relationship with her daughter, Janey. Based on this evidence, she saw that she had healed enough from her childhood to establish these healthy relationships. She knew she'd be able to heal even more, enough so that deep caring and concern could be the basis of an intimate relationship.

Alice picked up that Post-it note and on the other side wrote, "I am healing. My next intimate relationship will be based on deep caring and concern." Around the words, she painted spirals, stars and hearts in shades of magenta, red, blue and burgundy. It looked beautiful! She folded the sticky edge of the Post-it and put it on one of the butterfly's wings.

Mayzie asked her, "Say, what are you making?"

Alice said, "A butterfly. The middle part is a cocoon and contains the words of my inner critic. I'm going to take each one and think about what I would tell a treasured friend who had the same thoughts and replace it with that. Then I'll decorate it and put it on the wing of the butterfly as part of a transformation process. What are you making?"

"I don't know," Mayzie said. "Just letting my hands do what they want and seeing what they come up with. My name's Mayzie, by the way." The freckle-faced, curly-haired woman smiled at Alice.

"Hi, I'm Alice. I remember you from the healing circle the other day." Alice looked at the piece Mayzie was making. It was a curving hourglass shape with a heart-shaped cup on top. It reminded her of a woman's body and a fish with its tail on top. "It's beautiful," said Alice. "It conjures up so much for me."

"Does it?" asked Mayzie. "It does for me too. I'm going to glaze and fire it later. When it's finished, I'd like to put water in the top part and have a fresh flower floating in it."

"Wow! I really hope it turns out," Alice said.

The woman was now looking more closely at Alice's butterfly. "You know, this looks like a great healing tool. I can think of a few beliefs I'd like to change," she said.

"Feel free to write them down and add them to the cocoon," Alice said, handing her the pad of Post-it notes. "I'd be honoured to see it help you and anyone else turn their thinking around."

"Really?" Mayzie asked.

"Really. It's the way it works as a tool that interests me more than its artistic value," Alice replied. "Go ahead."

Mayzie picked up a felt pen, thought for a moment, then wrote, "I'm ugly and stupid," and put it on the cocoon.

Alice heaved a sigh. "Yeah, I feel like that sometimes too."

"Do you?" asked Mayzie. "Sometimes it feels like I'm the only one."

"Those kinds of thoughts make us feel so alone, don't they?"

They both looked down, pondering the butterfly in front of them.

"Hey, I couldn't help but overhear some of what you were saying," said a thin man with black hair. "Can I add something?"

"Of course," said Alice, smiling. She liked that others were finding her butterfly useful too.

The man picked up a marker and wrote, "Nothing I do is ever good enough," and placed it on the cocoon.

The three of them stared down at the butterfly, whose cocoon was becoming fuller.

"The challenging part is transforming these statements into something constructive," said Alice. "The easiest way for me to do it is to imagine that a good friend is telling me these things and then to think of what I'd want to say to them. For me anyway, it's much easier to see what's good about my friends than what's good about myself, but deep down I know I deserve the same respect and appreciation they do."

"Okay," said the man, "so if a friend of mine said that to me, I'd probably say something like, 'Hey, don't be so hard on yourself. You did your best, and that's the main thing,' or something like that, and I'd mean it too. Why can't I lighten up on myself the way I hope my friend would?"

"Our inner critics can be so ruthless," Alice said, "especially when we've come from families that have been highly critical."

"Which means most of us here," said Mayzie.

"Yeah, how do we subdue that voice or at least make it a little gentler?" asked the man, looking down with his hands in his pockets.

"This is my attempt. We can see what happens," Alice said.

"Okay," said the man decisively, picking up a marker. "If it was a good friend saying this, here's what I'd say." On the other side of his Post-it note he wrote, "Thanks for giving it your best shot!" Then he got out the paints and painted orange smiley faces around his words and attached it to the wing opposite the one where Alice had put hers.

"Great job!" she said, patting him on the back.

"Yeah, nice one!" said Mayzie. The three of them smiled down at the butterfly.

"Okay, I'm going to give it a try," said Mayzie, who had been working on her clay sculpture. "What would I say to a friend who felt like she was ugly and stupid? First of all, I don't really think anyone's ugly or stupid. Why should I be so special? Second of all, when we believe these kinds of things about ourselves, we behave in ways that reinforce them. So knowing these things, here's what I have to say." She picked up her Post-it note and wrote on the back, "I am a worthwhile human being." Then she painted blue, green and purple stars, hearts and circles around her words and stuck it on one of the wings. "This is really fun!" she exclaimed.

The afternoon flew by as they identified and transformed the messages of their inner critics.

CHAPTER 119

Songs

"Donny, I don't really want to learn these songs," said Cole, half pleading, at their practice.

"Hey, what's gotten into you?" asked Donny. "They're good songs, and we should learn some new material."

"I feel embarrassed to play them. After this stuff with Alice, I think people would be really put off hearing them. I just don't think this is the time for them," Cole said. "I mean, right now everybody's mad at me, and those songs would just make them madder. We want our audience to like us, don't we?"

"Aw, come on! Forget about what happened with Alice, and let's just play some music! I think those are good songs," Donny retorted.

Cole heaved a sigh, picked up his guitar and started strumming a Hank Williams tune. "My heart's just not in those songs. I want to lay off the stuff that puts women down; that's all."

"Cole, you can't help it if Alice is unstable. You didn't make her do anything—it was up to her. She needs to take some responsibility for her actions. You can play whatever you damn well please, and I don't think there's anything wrong with these songs."

"We've already lost Ross over these songs. What's the big deal? Why do you want to play songs like that so badly?" asked Cole. "Is it really so important to you to sing those kinds of songs?"

"Hey, we can do whatever we like, sing whatever songs we want," Donny snapped back.

"Or whatever songs you want. I don't want to sing them; Ross didn't want to sing them. Shouldn't we all at least like the songs?" asked Cole. "'Cause, really, I don't like either one of them, to tell you the truth."

"It's about more than the songs. It's about our freedom to just be guys," Donny said, "and to have a bit of fun. They're just jokes, nothing serious. What harm can they do?"

"I just feel creepy singing them," said Cole. "There are lots of songs out there. Why don't we choose something fun and happy and summery that doesn't say mean things about women? I just can't see singing these in front of people after what happened with Alice."

"Well, this conversation's going nowhere. Why don't we just practise some of our regular tunes and leave these ones for a while. We're wasting time when we should be practising," said Donny. "I still don't see why it's such a big deal."

CHAPTER 120
Grand Send-Off

Jon was preparing to leave for his grandmother's within a few days, and the rest of the community was feeling sad about it. He'd be missed!

Maude, the owner of the Love Bite, decided to have a celebration in Jon's honour at her restaurant on a Saturday evening. Jon, his friends and the people he'd gotten to know through his SPIN farm came out to spend time with him and wish him well on his move. The nights were getting warmer, so the patrons were able to spill over to the outdoor patios.

The Sleeping Dragon sang a few farming songs, and many people got up and said a few words in Jon's honour. Food and drink flowed freely, and there was lots of laughter—an all-around good party.

George took off his bicycle helmet and sat at a table at the back waiting for his friend Rodney to arrive. He'd flown in from France the night before and would be staying at Rodney's place. He and Rodney would spend a day or two together before Rodney took off on a biking expedition. This arrangement would give Rodney someone to feed his cat, Beaner, and would give George a place to stay.

Being at the Love Bite was an affirmation of George's belief in the strength and goodness of raw humanity. He hadn't spent a lot of time in Silverdale but longed to connect and wasn't sure how.

He sipped on his smoothie and looked at the five-dollar bill on the table in front of him. It was the currency he'd seen on the website before his trip.

197

Earlier that day, he'd helped a young mother get her children, groceries and a stroller into her vehicle. She'd thanked him and handed the money to him before driving off.

Later, he'd checked the website, then gone around to some of the businesses that used the community currency. Here was another brilliant idea that blossomed from the ground up, enriching everyone who touched it, encouraging generosity, collaboration and local spending.

He looked up as Rodney walked briskly toward him with his bicycle helmet under his arm. "Hey, sorry I'm late," said Rodney, pulling up a chair. "I popped a tire on my way over and had to change it. Are you over your jet lag yet?"

"That's okay," George said good-naturedly. "The jet lag's wearing off, but I'm still a little bleary: all the better for people watching. And I'm enjoying a perfect smoothie."

"The place is really hopping tonight, eh?" laughed Rodney.

"It's a send-off for someone named Jon, as far as I can tell. Do you know him?" asked George.

"I've met him at the outdoor market once or twice over the years. He's a big part of the local food scene," Rodney said. "Seems like a great guy. It's too bad we're losing him."

George smiled across at Rodney. "I may be biased, but this community seems to have an abundance of great people." They both ordered veggie burgers and fruit crumble for dessert when their server came to their table.

Rodney laughed. "I think you're right. This valley seems to attract them."

Suddenly, the crowd broke into rhythmic clapping and chanted, "Speech!" Finally, Jon stood up and walked into the centre of the room. The crowd clapped and whooped. Jon looked at everyone and smiled until the clapping stopped and there was silence.

"Thanks, everyone!" he said, looking awkward. "I'm quite shy and don't really know what to say, but one thing I know is that what I did wasn't just about gardening. It was about the goodwill, shared vision and co-operation of all of you. We've all done our parts to care for the land and our community."

He paused and looked around. "And I'm so proud that the SPIN farming tradition will be continued by an amazing group of friends, who you've all gotten to know these past few months. You'll be in good hands, and I promise to keep in touch." There was more applause. "Let's invite my friends Dagmar, Ross, Leroy, Lydia, Tam, Cammie and baby Bella, otherwise known as The Sleeping Dragon, to sing us another song."

Amid more applause, the singing group got up. They whispered to each other, and then Lydia said to the crowd, "Thanks, everyone, and from our hearts, thanks, Jon. We promise to do our best to treat you as well as Jon has." When the clapping died down, she said, "We'd like you to sing along with this one. It's a validation of our connection and collective power. We'll start singing, and just join in when you feel like it, and we hope you'll find room to get up and dance too."

Dagmar started shaking a shaker in a quick, rhythmic beat, and the group quietly started to sing, "We are the dance of the moon and sun. We are the power that's in everyone. We are the turning of the tide. We are the hope that is deep inside. We are the flow, and we are the ebb. We are the weavers; we are the web."

As people started to sing along, the energy in the room grew. The two verses were sung on top of each other, and harmonies were added. Lydia and Leroy started dancing, and those who couldn't find a space to dance clapped and sang along. They continued their song for about five minutes and then slowly wound down as the energy in the room waned. The friends sat down after their performance to more applause. The end of their song found people starting to disperse for the evening.

George and Rodney finished up their veggie burgers and watched the restaurant begin to empty. This spontaneous show of appreciation and expression of community empowerment had touched George. Why was he able to see it while others in his circle wouldn't or saw it only as a threat to their power?

As the restaurant continued to vacate and the space mellowed, George began to feel sleepier. Jet lag was catching up with him. It intensified his longing for the kind of connection these people seemed to have with each other.

"So ready for the bike tournament?" George asked Rodney.

"As ready as I'll ever be," Rodney said. "How was your flight?"

"Long, uneventful," said George. "It's great to finally be here."

Their server returned with their crumble, George's tea and hot water to top up Rodney's. George took a bite and melted at the warm sweetness in his mouth. A piece of heaven! George said, "Say, this crumble's good, isn't it?"

"Yeah, sure is."

"I don't know how long it's been since I've felt so nourished," said George.

"Maybe since the last time you were in Silverdale?" Rodney joked.

"Maybe." George was glad to be sitting with his friend.

"Ready to go?"

"Yeah, I'm beat. And thanks for the loan of your bike," George said.

"No problem. I've got a few kicking around. C'mon; let's go home," said Rodney.

They paid their bills and left a couple of dollars as a tip on the table. George added his community currency.

As they rode back to Rodney's place, they sliced through a cool, refreshing breeze. The town was quiet, and the stars were shining.

Back at Rodney's, they put the bikes away in the shed in the backyard. Beaner, Rodney's grey tabby cat, greeted them both at the door. George and Rodney found their way to bed as quickly as possible. Beaner curled up at the foot of Rodney's bed, happy to have him home again.

CHAPTER 121

Checking In

"Dan, how's it going?" said Leroy into the phone. "Sorry it's been so long—I've been pretty busy lately."

"Not bad. Jim's finished his project and will be driving home in a couple of days," Dan said. His voice betrayed the brokenness of his spirit, as much as he tried to sound upbeat for the benefit of his stepson.

Leroy sighed. Then, on an impulse, he said, "Why don't you come out for a visit? Maybe you and Jim can drive out together. We're living in this incredible mansion, and we have lots of room."

There was silence at the end of the phone. "Sorry, I'm not very good at making decisions these days," Dan said. "Maybe I could use a change of scenery. I don't know … It would be great to see you and Lydia and the others and see where you're living."

"We'd love to have you, and I can't explain it, but it's like we're caught in this burst of great energy lately. I'd love to hear your take about what's going on," said Leroy. "I've never experienced anything quite like this before. It's surreal."

"Surreal?" asked Dan. "Actually everything's felt surreal since your mom …"

"I know exactly what you mean. For sure, it has. That's probably a big part of it for me. But there's something else going on, and it's surreal in a different way." Leroy hoped his explanation didn't sound too crazy. "It's helping me a lot. Maybe it would help you too. I'd love it if you'd come and stay for a while."

"Let me give it some thought, okay?" Dan said. "Honestly, I've never been so indecisive, but I'll talk to Jim about it and get back to you in the next couple of days, all right?"

"Sure, and please don't feel pressured," Leroy said. "Just know that we'd love to have you and there's plenty of room. We could go on some nice hikes and just hang out, go for a swim in the pool in the backyard. A change of scenery might do you some good."

"Thanks, Leroy," said Dan. "I really appreciate the offer, and I'll call you soon. Bye for now."

"Bye, Dan. Take care of yourself, eh?" said Leroy gently.

"I will. You too."

Leroy laughed, "I will, and I have a whole household that takes care of me too. Maybe that's part of the great energy I was telling you about. Anyway, bye, Dan. It was great talking with you."

"You too, Leroy. I'm so glad things are going well for you. I know Mel would be happy about that too."

CHAPTER 122

Deeper Green

Dagmar looked at the screen of her laptop. She was about to write the first instalment of her new column that would be published every month or so on the SPIN farm website, which they'd decided to rename the Sleeping Dragon so their farm and musical group would have the same name.

Dagmar had the idea of creating a column called "A Deeper Shade of Green" that would help people to live a greener lifestyle at a deeper level than just the three Rs. She and some of her friends as well as the people they'd moved in with had been living in a deeply green way for many years, and she wanted to share some of the things that were on their minds. It seemed to her that most people were ready for more depth in their commitment to environmental restoration.

She started typing.

> We've heard the terms *reduce, reuse, recycle* for years. But a lot of us are ready to go much deeper in our commitment to environmental restoration.
>
> A good starting place is where we reclaim our personal power.
>
> You know those advertisements that cost so much money? They're designed to affect our spending patterns. In other words, our spending patterns mean a lot to some

people. That's a sure sign that what we do with our money has a lot of power.

But our money is just one facet of our personal power. When we define ourselves as citizens and not just consumers, we embrace a whole other level of personal power. As citizens, governments are accountable to us. We have a vested interest in the state of the world because citizenship implies rights and responsibilities based on our personhood. As citizens, we engage in public debate and feel an obligation to others and to future generations. Citizenship is part of being a whole mature person, an engaged member of the global community and someone who pays attention to the state of the world.

Where we put our time, attention and money all have implications. In this column, I will explore some of these implications and would be interested in hearing what you've discovered on your journey into being more deeply green.

Dagmar stared out the window for a moment, then opened up a new document that she named "Topics" and put it into her "Deeper Green" folder.

On it she typed:

Topics

- The big picture
- Our spending power
- News sources
- Finding Balance
- Good news

She took a break and promised herself to come back later to expand on these.

CHAPTER 123

The Market

George woke up with a start, forgetting where he was for a moment. Then he remembered his flight and relaxed deeply when he realized that he now found himself in this lovely part of the world.

Rodney had left for his bike tournament earlier, and there was still some warm coffee in the Bodum. He drank it and reheated some leftover stir-fry he found in the fridge for breakfast.

After a quick shower, George left the house. He decided to walk the kilometre or so into town instead of biking. It was a beautiful day, and he felt like being on foot. The morning was a little cool, but the robin's egg blue sky promised increasing warmth. The trees lining the streets had fresh green leaves sprouting from their branches. A few shopkeepers were sweeping the sidewalks and taking out their sandwich boards.

There were more empty storefronts than the last time he'd been here, but the town still seemed fairly vibrant. The people walking the streets were an eclectic mix: businesspeople on their way to work; young people in casual, colourful clothing; elderly folks enjoying the spring weather. There were also a few panhandlers, silently sitting against the walls with signs describing their predicaments and hats they hoped people would toss a coin or two into. George threw a coin into the first one he saw.

It didn't take George long to reach the other end of town, and he headed toward the outdoor market. Vendors were setting up their booths and chatting with each other.

He recognized some of the people he'd seen in the restaurant the night before as they set up their stalls. In one stall, among the lettuce and spring greens, the Sleeping Dragon folks were rearranging late tulips and early lilacs, displaying them to their best advantage. There were also two wooden chairs painted sky blue with fabric seat cushions in a yellow-blue-and-turquoise floral design that looked beautiful in the mix.

There was a stand being set up with coffee and fresh baked goods, another with handmade soaps and one more with colourful fairly traded clothing.

He looked up and saw a large butterfly with a paper body and wire outlining where the wings should be. On the table below he saw a ceramic figure that looked like a fish or a woman's body diving into water. The tail had been shaped like a cup. The raku glaze shimmered in shades of turquoise and silver. A woman was arranging items and pamphlets on the table.

George walked over and looked at the ceramic figure. "What an intriguing sculpture!" he said, gently running his hand over it.

"Thanks," said the woman, smiling at him.

"Did you make it?" asked George.

"Yes, I did," replied the woman. She introduced herself as Mayzie as she continued to arrange things on her table.

"Can you tell me a little bit about it?" George asked.

"There's not much to tell, really," Mayzie said. "I just let my hands do whatever they wanted, and this is what came out."

"Neat!" said George.

"Really?" Mayzie said. "I thought that answer might be disappointing, since there's no deep symbolism or message."

"There might still be," George said, "but it's coming from a place that's uncontrived. I have a lot of respect for that place."

"Do you?" asked Mayzie. "I know what you mean. When we relax and trust, good things come out."

"I sometimes worry about that place becoming endangered, that we're losing touch with something primal," George said. "I mean, look at us. We think we're so smart, yet we've threatened all of life with our so-called brilliance. Maybe it's because many of us have abandoned a place inside ourselves that should be sacred."

Mayzie looked at him appraisingly, then asked, "Can I tell you about this butterfly? It's something you might also like. My friend Alice came up with it, and it's a tool for transforming things."

"Please do."

"Okay. Well, the way it works is if your inner critic is telling you something that's hurtful or disempowering, you listen to it, then write down what it's saying on a Post-it note, and you put it on the body of the butterfly. The body is like a cocoon. Then you think about those words and find the empowering thought inside of them that can transform them. When you hear those empowering words, you take the Post-it down, write them on the other side, embellish them with paint and put them on the wing of the butterfly."

"What a great idea!" George exclaimed. "So on a Post-it, I'd write down, 'We're losing touch with the primal voice inside,' and put it on the cocoon. May I?" Mayzie handed him a Post-it note and a marker, and he wrote down those words. "So now, I think about those words and what I can do to reframe them into something empowering, is that right?" he asked.

"Yes, that's exactly right."

George closed his eyes and thought for a moment. "I was attracted to your sculpture because it came from a very deep place," said George. "So you were paying attention to that primal intelligence that is often ignored. Therefore,

I'm witnessing someone paying attention. Maybe I should recognize this as an indication that we're starting to listen to this inner intelligence."

George reached for the Post-it and on the other side wrote, "We are starting to listen to our inner wisdom." Mayzie handed him a paintbrush and some watercolours, and he painted pink, gold and yellow dots and swirls around his words. Then he carefully put it onto one of the wings of the butterfly.

Just then another woman approached the booth and handed Mayzie a cup of coffee, saying, "Here you go. Sorry it took so long, but the coffee's just been made."

"Thanks, Alice," said Mayzie, taking the cup of coffee from her. "Look at your butterfly! This gentleman's been the first to use it."

"What a wonderful tool!" said George, smiling at Alice.

"It's exactly what I needed at the time, and it seems others did too," she replied, smiling back.

"Alice, Mayzie, I'm George," he said. "Really nice to meet you both. What's this organization you're with?" he asked.

"It's for people who tend to empathize too much and in the wrong places," said Alice. "It's been a lifesaver for me."

"And for me too," added Mayzie.

"Do you volunteer?" George asked.

Mayzie and Alice looked at each other; then Mayzie said, "Well, sort of. In return we stay at the facility and do what we can to help each other to heal."

"I see," said George, not quite sure if he did. "So you live in a facility where you try to help each other to heal from …?"

"From relationships where we've given too much, mostly," Alice said.

George picked up one of the pamphlets on the table and took a look. "Empathy is the most revolutionary emotion. - Gloria Steinem" was emblazoned on the front in an emerald green script.

"So your group involves empathy?" he asked, gazing into Mayzie's eyes.

"Sort of," she said. "Everyone who spends time at this facility has lots of empathy but tends to direct it in ways that don't serve them very well." She looked into the sky, contemplating her next words. "We seem to repeat destructive patterns developed in our childhood, and we're looking for ways to heal together." She paused again. "In other words, we have personal baggage, and we're trying to figure out how to carry it forward in the best way possible—maybe even leave some of it behind."

George put the pamphlet into his back pocket, intending to read it later.

"Empathy is a wonderful quality," George said. "I bet learning to channel it properly could do a lot to make the world a better place."

"The problem for many of us is that we are easily targeted by people who know how to exploit that quality, and it can hurt us deeply. Many empathetic people are vulnerable to exploitation. At the facility, we're figuring this out together and finding ways to create boundaries where we need to," said Alice.

George nodded his head up and down appreciatively. The term *collateral damage* popped into his mind, a term that to him implied that some people's lives were more important than others'—that some people were just *collateral*.

"Anyway, nice chatting with you," George said. "I'm going to get a cup of coffee and take a look around. Thanks for telling me about yourselves and your organization."

"Nice to meet you, George," said Mayzie.

"Bye, see you again," said Alice.

George walked over to the stall with coffee and got a cup. He was happy but not surprised to see a sign that said "fairly traded, organic" on the stand beside the coffee decanter. He handed the man a ten-dollar bill. "Sorry, it's the smallest bill I have," said George.

"That's okay; I've got change. Would you prefer it in regular money or our community currency?" he asked.

"The community currency, please," George said, glad for another chance to participate in this pleasant addition to the local economy.

"Here you go!" the man said, handing him his change in the bills George was becoming accustomed to.

George wandered around the market, taking in the setting. It was on the outskirts of Silverdale in a park with a waterfall and lots of big trees. He enjoyed the sound of the rushing water and the freshness of the air. The Sleeping Dragon folks had finished setting up their booth, and it caught George's eye. It was visually stunning. They'd arranged it beautifully: produce, flowers, the chairs and baked goods.

He walked over and asked for one of the rhubarb muffins, recognizing the woman who helped him. "I saw you singing and dancing at the Love Bite last night," he said. "A splendid evening, wasn't it?"

"Sure was," the woman said. "I think Jon enjoyed his send-off. We're going to miss him around here."

"I'm sure," said George. "He seemed to be a highly valued member of your community. Say, do you take the local currency?"

"We certainly do," the woman answered brightly. "We love the stuff!" Then she pointed to the sign that let him know the percentage their group accepted.

"Thank you!" said George, giving her an extra dollar of the local currency.

"Hey, thanks!" The woman smiled.

"A pleasure!" George replied.

As he walked around, he felt a kind of malaise and wasn't sure where it had come from. Maybe it was the lingering effect of having just met Mayzie and Alice, these human reminders that caring, vulnerable people are routinely targeted and taken advantage of. That fact had always saddened him.

He took a bite of his muffin; it was still warm. The taste of rhubarb and cinnamon made everything right with the world for a precious moment.

Coffee and muffin in hand, he returned to the booth with the butterfly and the unique clay sculpture. Mayzie was sitting quietly at the booth, and her face lit up as he approached.

"Hello again," she said.

"Hi," he said, "I thought I should come back here because there's something I can't put my finger on that's making me sad. I thought some butterfly therapy might help."

"Gee. When did it start?" asked Mayzie.

"Hmm, let's see … I think it was after talking with you and Alice earlier," George said slowly. "That conversation seems to have brought something up for me."

"Do you think you could condense whatever you're feeling into words that would fit on a Post-it note?" she asked him, passing him the pad of Post-it notes and a pen. "That way we can see if we can get it from the cocoon stage to the wing stage."

George stood there with his eyes closed for a long moment, and then he said, "It has something to do with knowing there's a whole institution full of people who are what I call *collateral damage*—people who are preyed upon because their empathy is apparent. I find that so sad."

"I see what you mean," Mayzie said. "The good thing about it is that we're supporting each other. We're finding healthy ways to direct our empathy and learning to protect ourselves from people who are predatory."

"I agree that that's a good thing," George said. "Still …" He was groping, trying to identify that feeling and what it was about: if he could only name it. "It was like a dull heaviness of my heart," he said, "like—I don't know—maybe my own empathy, feeling the betrayal so many have experienced." He stopped again. "But there's more. The guilt of my own privilege? My unintended complicity with a system that encourages people to take advantage of others?"

"What you're saying is bringing up stuff for me too," said Mayzie, "and mine's easier to identify. It's rage."

"Rage. That's understandable. I think there's lots of rage about that in me too but maybe in a different way. It's about what I've observed, not what I've experienced."

Mayzie took the Post-it notes and pen and wrote, "Rage," on one of them and attached it to the cocoon. Then she put them back in front of George.

"There's also exasperation and a sense of helplessness. What can I do?" asked George. "There's so much systemic violence and exploitation. It seems as though people are blind to the part they play. It's just business as usual, part of the game, the way things are, you know? Our economy, lots of movies, music videos, programs on TV—they all reinforce this notion that people degrade and take advantage of each other. Where do we begin?"

"Good question," said Mayzie. "Maybe we just have to start where we are and acknowledge the things we do to help things get better. I bet that coffee you're drinking is organic and fairly traded. Everything has a ripple effect. You're helping someone to get paid a fair wage and helping the planet to be a little healthier."

"It's great that the only coffee available here right now is organic and fairly traded," George laughed. "It makes it easy to do a small good thing."

"Yeah, it is great, isn't it?" Mayzie smiled.

"Okay, I think I've figured out what I'm going to put on my Post-it note," said George. He picked up the pen and wrote, "Exasperation, guilt, helplessness," and stuck it onto the cocoon. "There might be more, but I definitely feel those things."

They looked at their words on the cocoon. In the background, they could hear the rush of the waterfall, the whir of traffic and the voices of people talking and laughing at the market.

"One thing I like about rage," Mayzie said, "is that it contains a lot of energy. Something I've noticed about others and myself at this facility is that we often have no energy. It's like we experience a kind of emotional flatness. Feeling drained and lost seems to be part of the deal for most of us. We can tell when someone's starting to recover when they become more animated and lively—and angry."

"So rage is powerful. Can it be harnessed in a way that helps you?" he asked.

"I think so," Mayzie said. "Feeling rage is a big part of the healing process; it's the desire for justice and can be a very energizing step, especially when we're surrounded by people who fully understand what we're going through."

George said, "I bet rage in isolation could be dangerous, but when you're with a group who gets what you've been through, I imagine you'd be able to explore it honestly with them and feel supported in the process. And maybe help everyone get in touch with their own personal power."

"For sure," said Mayzie. "That support makes all the difference." She then picked up her Post-it with the word *rage* on it and on the other side wrote, "Embracing my power." Then she surrounded the words with red, purple and deep blue stars, hearts and squiggly lines and put it on one of the butterfly wings.

George was looking at the words on the Post-it he'd written on. "What do I do with 'guilt, exasperation and helplessness'?" he pondered aloud. "I've always detested unfairness and cruelty but have never really known what to do about it. Oh, I do small things, like using my money to support my values, and I don't exploit people in my personal life, but there's got to be more I can do."

"George, doing those things is a lot," Mayzie said. "To some people, those are non-issues. Some people don't care who they hurt or what they support."

"I suppose," George said, sounding unconvinced. "I still feel like there's more I could be doing, but I just haven't figured out what." He took down his Post-it note, turned it over and wrote, "Renewed commitment," then drew lines of brown, grey and red. "The colours are like brick and mortar. I want to recommit to my passion for a world that's kind and fair and figure out the best way of doing that." He stuck his note on the other wing of the butterfly.

Alice wandered up to the booth with a plate of food. "Hello again, George. Mayzie, sorry I took so long again, but there was a line for the falafels. Would you like to go and get something?" she asked. "I'm happy to watch the booth."

"Sure, I may as well take a stroll around the market and see if anything appeals to me. Thanks," Mayzie said.

"I enjoyed our conversation, Mayzie. Thanks for helping me work through that," said George.

"It was a pleasure. Thanks for helping me too, because you did, you know," Mayzie said.

"Glad we were mutually helpful. Anyway, I'm off. I hope to see you again," he said.

"I'll be in the same place next week." Mayzie smiled and waved goodbye.

CHAPTER 124

Commitment

As George walked home, he thought about what commitment meant to him. Maybe speaking up where before he'd remained silent. What about the privileged position he was born into? What could he do with it to help create a healthy and just world?

The sun was shining, and the buskers were out. He reached into his pocket prepared to throw money into a man's open guitar case. As he got closer, he heard the man sing, "A little bit of Sandra in the sun, a little bit of Mary all night long …" He put his money away. Part of commitment to a better world was to not support attitudes that encouraged objectifying others. The way women were viewed by many in society sickened him.

Walking down the street further, he saw a man with a ponytail playing a variation on a piece by Enya on the violin. George threw some bills, both regular and community currency, into the man's open violin case. The man nodded, smiled and continued playing.

George realized that a lot of his reaffirmed sense of commitment to healing and justice would be about remembering it in each moment and expressing it in large and small ways.

As he walked, his mind wandered to the few relationships he'd had with women over the years. They'd all been short-lived. Each of them had such different priorities and values from his that there wasn't enough common ground as a basis for continuation. There was speculation in his family that he was gay. Was he? He didn't think so. He was sexually attracted to women and not men. Why couldn't he meet someone who cared about making the world a better place the way he did?

He'd always been a bit lonely. He loved his family and friends but felt he was reading from a different page, marching to a different drummer. Privately, he sometimes suspected that his mother shared some of these feelings and wondered if he'd inherited them—and his ability to hide them—from her.

He walked down the path to Rodney's cabin and was greeted by Beaner. George bent down and scratched the top of the cat's head, which had Beaner purring.

Suddenly he realized that he was tired. Maybe he wasn't quite over his jet lag. He walked over to the sofa and had a nap.

CHAPTER 125

Delayed Reaction

Dagmar adjusted her sun hat and continued weeding. She was feeling a little blue these days and couldn't put her finger on why. Was everything just catching up with her? Her life was so different from what it had been six months earlier—she'd been through a lot of changes. Was it just that she now had the emotional safety to experience all the things she'd been up against back then? she wondered.

That night as she and Ross were lying in bed, she said, "I don't know why, but I've been feeling a little sad lately."

"Sad?" asked Ross. "I hope it's not something I've been doing."

"No, I don't think so. It might be a delayed reaction to the stuff I was going through before we moved into the abandoned house. It was really stressful, and I was so busy trying to cope that I don't think I allowed myself to feel just how scary it was. I love my life now with you here and doing the things we're doing. It's just a malaise that's hard to understand."

"Hmm," Ross said, "it must have been scary, especially for someone as responsible as you. If I can do anything to help, let me know, okay?"

Dagmar rolled over and kissed Ross's cheek. "Sometimes I think I'm so used to being stable that I block out the hard stuff. In a way, the fact that I'm feeling it is a good sign. It means I'm letting my guard down." She sighed. "Thanks for being here for me, Ross. It means so much to me."

Ross held her close and kissed her cheek. After lying there for a long moment, he said, "It's a privilege, Dagmar."

They lay there silently. Dagmar breathed in the subtle scent of Ross's body, which she'd grown accustomed to. It comforted her in this new sadness. Everything felt right in Dagmar's life: she felt valued and respected; she enjoyed the work and activities she was involved with; her relationship with Ross was deepening. What was lurking in her psyche that was bringing up this feeling?

She closed her eyes and let her mind wander and remembered the desperation she'd felt when she had been unable to pay her bills and her life had felt as if it was falling apart. She'd tried so hard to find ways to make money and—nothing. That fateful night when she and Ross had wandered the streets together, she had been so far beyond stressed that she'd been numb.

"Ross," she said.

"Yes?"

"I'm just realizing how scared and desperate and alone I felt before we found the abandoned house. I'd never been so afraid in my life, but at the time I just had to carry on."

"You tried everything back then. I remember running into you and you'd always tell me about something new you were doing."

"Yeah, and none of it panned out, or I made very little money at best," said Dagmar. "It was so hard." Tears welled up in her eyes.

"I bet," Ross said, stroking her hair. "And now it's better than it's ever been, at least for me."

"Yeah, me too," Dagmar said. "I guess these feelings just need to come out; they must have discovered that it's safe enough to show themselves." She stroked his chest and kissed him with feeling.

"You have no idea how crazy I felt when I first stayed with you and these people! You really helped me to regain my sanity," said Ross. "I'm honoured to be able to help you now, with whatever you're going through."

"Just talking about those fears is bringing up other fears for me, like the environmental stuff. Sometimes I'm scared it's too little too late. Do you think we're going to get through this?"

Ross sighed. "I want to say, yeah, it's going to be okay, but I have to be honest. No one knows, do they? One thing I do know is that we have better chances if we don't give up. All we can do is our best, and there are no promises that things are going to get better."

"Thanks for putting it into perspective," Dagmar laughed. "I appreciate your honesty. At least that's something I can count on."

"You bet you can," said Ross, kissing her. "Thanks for showing me the importance of honesty and trust. I might have said something different six months ago, before we got together."

"You're still a charmer but in a way I like much more," said Dagmar, snuggling closer to him.

They found themselves looking out the high window. The sky was a deep shade of cobalt blue, and the stars were especially bright and twinkly that night.

"Ross, do you get scared?" Dagmar asked.

"Yeah, sometimes. I guess I just make myself busy or think about other things, instead of really allowing myself to feel the fear," Ross said. Then he laughed. "I'm not sure if that's a good thing or a bad thing."

"Maybe it's a bit of both," Dagmar said. "Feeling it too much of the time can be paralyzing, but running from it doesn't seem very good either."

"Sometimes I think the trick is to have a clear vision of the future we want and then do all we can to make it a reality," Ross said as he stroked Dagmar's shoulder almost unconsciously.

"That makes sense to me too," said Dagmar. "Wouldn't it be amazing to live in a world that's unpolluted, in a society where everyone was able to live happy, productive, fulfilling lives?"

"Sure would," said Ross, "and that's the alternative we're working toward, isn't it? Why are power, money and control so attractive to some that they're willing to sacrifice the future of life on our planet? It's a kind of insanity, don't you think?"

"For sure," said Dagmar. "It's like a sickness. And the scary thing is we're all being persuaded that it's just the way things are, like that way of viewing the world is our only option." Then she added, "How do we create a new story? I wonder. How do we help people to see how beautiful life could be if we lived by a different narrative?"

"Good question," said Ross, leaning back against his pillow. "So many things are framed in a false way, like jobs and the environment. Don't people realize that restoring our planet will create lots of jobs? Or how about being spiritual or political? Why shouldn't we nurture our spiritual side and do the political work needed to make the world a better place? Isn't doing what we can politically a spiritual act? And don't we want to meditate so that we don't get burned out on the political stuff?"

Dagmar sighed. "What about the movies with the good guys and bad guys and lots of shooting? They can't be doing wonders for our collective psyches."

"That's for sure," Ross said. "I used to love those movies, but now the thought of them just depresses me. Funny how that happened. I haven't seen a movie like that in ages and don't miss them at all."

"Hey, I feel much better after our rant. Thank you." Dagmar leaned over and kissed him on the cheek.

He kissed her back. "Sweet dreams, Dagmar. I love you," he said.

"I love you too," Dagmar replied.

They both drifted off to sleep.

CHAPTER 126

Planning Session

It was Saturday morning, and Velvet's and Ronnie's environmental groups were having a daylong meeting at Tina's. They were downstairs in Tina's rec room planning their next environmental actions.

Jess was giving Tina a hand in the kitchen, helping to prepare snacks and a spaghetti lunch for them.

"Isn't it amazing how we've changed over the past few months?" asked Jess. "We're both different people from when we first met."

"Yes," Tina said. "Ellen is certainly intuitive. I think making friends with you has been the most therapeutic thing that has ever happened to me in all my years of therapy."

"Me too," said Jess. "Just having another person who really understands makes all the difference in the world, doesn't it?"

"Sure does," Tina said. "Feeling understood and accepted is beyond compare."

"Hey, why don't we bring Ellen some flowers next time we see her?" Jess suggested. "It'd be nice to say thank you in a way that's a bit more personal."

"Yeah, that's a great idea!"

"It's gotta be a tough job," said Jess.

"I used to feel embarrassed about being so stuck in such a destructive pattern, but I just couldn't figure out how to get out. Know what I mean?" Tina's eyes watered as she cut up the onions.

"Oh, yeah," Jess said. "How do we get so trapped?"

"I don't know. All I know is that it feels great to be unstuck. Thanks, Jess. You've really helped me."

"You too, Tina, thank you," Jess said as she sliced the mushrooms.

When the vegetables were all cut up, Tina reached into the cupboard and brought out two large jars of tomato sauce. She divided the vegetables equally between the frying pans and browned them in tamari, then added one jar of the sauce to each of the frying pans. She added a few herbs, turned down the heat and covered them both.

"There," Tina said. "They can just simmer away until it's time to put on the pasta."

"I wonder what kinds of ideas they're coming up with down there," said Jess.

"Me too. Hopefully nothing too radical," Tina said.

CHAPTER 127

Faith

Mayzie looked up at the sky for a moment after having pinned her Post-it to the cocoon of the butterfly. She was at the outdoor market, the sky was blue and there was a gentle breeze. The lovely morning invited faith in the goodness of the world, but she was having a hard time conjuring up faith in humanity and in herself at the moment. The Post-it note had the word *doubt* written on it.

It was a slow morning, and she and Alice stood lazily behind their booth. On a day like this, a lot of people would be enjoying the great outdoors doing things like hiking, canoeing or kayaking.

Mayzie sighed, then blurted out, "Alice, remember George, the guy I was chatting with last week? He came by again this morning, and I'm going to meet him for tea after the market closes."

"He seems very nice," said Alice.

"But don't people all seem nice at first?" asked Mayzie. "It's not so much him but me. After what happened to me last time, I don't trust my own judgement. Do you know what I mean?"

"Yes, I do. The kinds of experiences we've gone through make it hard to trust. Having second thoughts about people seems pretty normal after the kind of pain we've endured."

"I feel shaken over having a cup of tea with someone I've just met. It feels like I'm completely overreacting, but I'm so emotionally vulnerable right now," Mayzie confided. She showed Alice the Post-it she'd put on the cocoon. "I feel so much doubt and anxiety, and I don't know how to deal with it."

"I really get how you feel. On the one hand we don't want to cut ourselves off from getting to know people, but on the other it's so hard to trust after being betrayed. I don't have any answers. All you can do is your best to read people carefully and take your time getting to know them."

Mayzie nodded in agreement. "Yeah, you've summarized my dilemma. Maybe I need to take a more exploratory approach. I'm getting to know George better and can keep an emotional distance. There are no guarantees in life, and all we can do is take things one step at a time and keep our eyes open." She reached for the doubt Post-it and turned it over. She closed her eyes and thought for a moment.

Suddenly Alice called out, "Ross!"

Mayzie looked up, and a man around her age with a woman on his arm walked over. "Alice!" he said, and they gave each other a warm hug.

"Have you met Dagmar?" Ross asked Alice.

Alice said to Dagmar, "You look awfully familiar, but I don't know that we've ever met."

"You look familiar to me too. Nice to meet you," said Dagmar.

"How've you been?" Ross asked Alice. "You're looking good."

"Thanks," Alice said. "I'm still feeling pretty fragile but am getting better every day."

"So glad to hear it," Ross said.

"How've you been?" Alice asked.

"Never been better," said Ross. "I've been through a lot of changes these past few months, and everything's great. Dagmar and I share a house with some amazing people, and we've taken over Jon's SPIN farm. Do you know Jon?"

"Yeah. What's he up to?" asked Alice.

"He's moved back east to be with his grandmother, who needs a hand with her farm," he said.

"He'll be missed," said Alice. Then she asked, "Are you still playing music?"

"Just on Sundays at the Love Bite," Ross said. "Anyway, I feel like a new man. The biggest change is inside of me, and much of that is thanks to Dagmar."

Dagmar chuckled. "As they say, you can lead a horse to water ... but you're the one who chose to drink. I couldn't do that for you." She squeezed his hand. "I'm so proud of the changes you've made."

Mayzie was observing the friends chatting, and Alice turned to her. "Ross and Dagmar, this is Mayzie."

"Nice to meet you both," she said. She had a good sense about them. They both seemed authentic and caring.

They chatted for a while, and then Ross and Dagmar wandered off.

Alice smiled. "I've never seen Ross look so happy. I get the sense that they really value and trust each other, don't you?" she asked Mayzie.

"Yes, I picked up on that right away. Wouldn't that be wonderful to have?" she asked.

"It sure would."

"Maybe that's part of my answer. When I think about the guy who landed me in this place, in my heart of hearts I know I couldn't have had a trusting, loving relationship with him. It takes two. If someone just wants to take advantage of you, it's important to see and acknowledge that. Maybe what we need to do is be aware of what we want in a relationship and then carefully evaluate the people we're getting to know—see if they share our vision and are capable of having the kind of relationship we want."

"Yeah, maybe that's part of the problem people like us have. We're so focused on caring for others that we don't pay enough attention to what we need," Alice said.

"Just talking with you and meeting your friends has me feeling more at ease about having tea with George," said Mayzie, running her hand through her curls. "What do I want? I'll keep that in mind as I get to know him." Mayzie picked up a felt pen and wrote the words *faith* and *discernment* on the other side of the doubt Post-it. She painted pale blue and white dots on it and stuck the note to one of the wings of the butterfly.

CHAPTER 128

Tea for Two

G eorge walked over promptly at three o'clock and helped Mayzie and Alice pack up the booth and put things away. When everything was done, he and Mayzie walked over to the Love Bite and got a table by the window.

"How was your time at the market?" asked George.

"Pretty quiet," Mayzie said. "When the weather's beautiful like this, people tend to spend their time enjoying the great outdoors."

"Is that something you enjoy?" George said.

"Yes, and I'd like to do more of it."

"I enjoy that sort of thing too," George said. "Maybe we can go for a hike sometime."

"That sounds like fun." Mayzie smiled at him, and he smiled back.

"How's that butterfly at your booth doing?" George asked.

Mayzie paused for a moment. A server came by and asked them what they wanted. They each ordered a cup of tea and decided to share a piece of peach pie.

"The butterfly …" Mayzie said and sighed. "To tell you truth, I added to the butterfly today. First I put the word *doubt* on the cocoon and really struggled with it."

"What exactly were you struggling with?"

"Well, you know the organization I'm with is for people who've been taken advantage of. I'm part of it because I'm still trying to cope with feelings of betrayal, and when I get to know someone new, I feel panicky and afraid to trust." *There, I said it,* Mayzie thought.

"That's understandable," George said. "Is getting to know me bringing up some panic in you?"

"Yes," said Mayzie. "I really like you, but I don't trust my own judgement."

"I get that, Mayzie, and I'm so sorry about whatever happened to you that makes it difficult for you to trust," George said softly. He paused. "I want to reach over and touch you, but I don't know what to do. I don't want to frighten you."

"Thanks for being so understanding," Mayzie said. "I'm sorry I'm such a wreck right now. Really, I'm feeling quite fragile."

"Thanks for opening up to me. It takes a lot of courage to be so authentic when you're in such a vulnerable place," George said. "Can I tell you something personal too?"

"Okay," Mayzie said, looking at him with interest.

"I'm from a family that, well, that you'd have every reason not to trust," George confessed.

"Do you have a criminal background?" Mayzie asked.

"No, far from it, but maybe it should be considered criminal," said George. "I'm from what's being referred to these days as the one percent:

you know, the very wealthy. But I have never agreed with the world view I grew up with."

"Really?" asked Mayzie. "You must be very strong."

"I don't know. I was just born this way. There's such a view of entitlement and having a blind spot the size of—well, look at all the harm and misery in the world that's caused by our economy. I'm from the people who benefit from all of that. I've spent my life seeing what my family and peers seem blind to, and I don't know what to do about it."

"George, thanks for sharing that with me. It sounds like such a burden."

"I tell very few people, but when you brought up trust issues, I felt I owed it to you to tell you. I wouldn't blame you at all for not trusting someone with my background," George said.

Their server brought them their pie and tea and said, "Sorry I took so long. I warmed the pie up—it's much nicer that way." She gave them an additional plate, two forks and a knife.

"Thank you," said George. "That was very thoughtful of you."

"Yes, thanks," said Mayzie.

"My pleasure." Their server smiled. "Enjoy!" She walked away briskly, and Mayzie and George smiled as they noticed her brightly striped stockings and purple hair.

"I love this place!" said George. "It's a microcosm of the world I'd like to see: quality, uniqueness, caring, healing, accepting. It's so different from the values I grew up with."

"I love it too." Mayzie grinned. "And for the same reasons. It's so fresh and innovative and comforting at the same time."

George picked up the knife and cut the piece of pie in half, put one of the pieces on the extra plate and gave the bigger piece to Mayzie. Then he looked at her and said, "Some things are just so ingrained," he said. "It's so automatic for me to take the 'manly role' and cut the pie."

"Well, if that's the least of it, you're forgiven," Mayzie laughed.

They both took a bite.

"Mmm. This is delicious!" said Mayzie.

"Isn't it, though!" George said. They happily ate their pie and drank their tea.

"So, George, you've gotten me curious," said Mayzie. "What kinds of things have you done to counter your upbringing?"

"Well, I've developed an almost insatiable interest in different ways of viewing the world and am particularly fascinated with systems of thought that honour intuitive knowing. Intuitively, we understand basic fairness. Empathy is very intuitive and so is appreciating nature. At an early age, I understood that I had to behave as though I shared the beliefs of the culture I was born into. But deep down I never did. And the part of me that I had to keep hidden was the biggest part of me. I hid it and guarded it like a treasure, even though everything about my upbringing seemed geared toward dismantling that part of me—that part of all of us. Most of the people I grew up around had that part slowly cultivated out of them. I've always wondered how they could not care about future generations, how they could promote things that poison the earth and rob the poor. I discreetly do what I can to change all that by what I do with my money and my time."

"You really are very brave and strong to have resisted those things," said Mayzie.

"Mayzie, you're also very brave and strong to have admitted how vulnerable you're feeling."

"It was all I could think of—no, that's not right. I could have pretended, but I didn't want to. Honesty felt like the only sensible thing," said Mayzie. She chose her words carefully but wasn't sure that she was able to convey what had been going on for her.

They looked at each other and felt very close after having revealed so much about themselves.

"Hey, I'm surprised at how much we've shared, and I want to know you better," said George. "I realize you're feeling very vulnerable right now, and I want to make sure that nothing bad happens to you. Do you think you could trust me enough to come with me on a hike?"

"You know, I'd like that. I want to get to know you better too. I'd love to go for a hike," Mayzie said, feeling exhilarated.

"Would you like to go exploring tomorrow?"

"Sure. I can't reveal the address where I'm staying, but I could meet you somewhere."

"Have you been here on a Sunday morning? I've always wanted to hear the music. Why don't we have breakfast here and then go for a hike?" he asked.

"Sounds like fun!" She smiled. "I'll pack us a lunch."

"Shall we meet here at, I don't know, nine o'clock tomorrow morning?"

"Okay," said Mayzie, feeling good about the situation, "I'll see you then!"

CHAPTER 129

Arrival

Leroy led Dan and Jim into the bedroom where they'd be staying. There was a double bed and a large sofa bed that had been pulled out. The sheer curtains moved gently from the slight breeze coming in through an open window, and there were fresh flowers on the dresser.

"Five stars!" laughed Jim, putting his luggage in a corner.

"And you haven't even tried the food yet!" Leroy laughed. "Are you hungry?"

"A bit," said Jim, "but my stomach's kind of unsettled after all that driving. I could go for a little something, though."

"How about you, Dan?" Leroy asked.

"Yeah, I could go for some supper," Dan said, then reached down and dug through one of the smaller bags. "We knew you'd have plenty of veggies, since you're gardening for a living, so I brought dessert." He pulled out a box that contained 12 small mason jars. "It's organic, vegan lemon pudding cakes. You just bake them at 350 for 15 minutes or so, and there's no waste. You just reuse the jars. Cool, eh?"

"Sure is!" Leroy said. "Mom would have loved it!"

"Yeah, she would have," said Dan. "We can think of her as we eat our dessert tonight."

"Thanks for including her. I'm sure she'll be with us in spirit." Leroy made eye contact with Dan and then looked down. He hadn't told Dan about the dreams he'd been having about her yet.

The three of them walked into the dining room where Lydia and the rest of the household were setting the table. Cammie walked out holding baby Bella. "Hi, Dan. Great to see you!" she said. Then turning Bella to face him, she said, "Dan, this is Bella."

Bella smiled at him, and he smiled back, charmed. "Hello, Bella. Nice to meet you," he said. Then, looking at Cammie, he said, "Congratulations! She's such a beautiful baby! Is she always this happy?"

"She's very good-natured," Cammie said.

Tam walked in. "Hi, Dan. So nice to see you! I'm so sorry about Mel," he said, putting his arm around Dan's back.

"I appreciate that," Dan said. "To tell you the truth, I'm still reeling." He sighed. "One day at a time, I guess, eh?"

"I hope you enjoy your stay with us. This is such a beautiful part of the world. Hopefully some of its healing magic will rub off," said Tam.

"I'm open to healing magic!" said Dan. "Meeting Bella is already healing. What a wonderful little girl you have."

"Thanks. She's pretty special," he said proudly.

They gradually sat down together in front of bowls of soup. Cammie said, "We weren't sure how you'd be feeling after such a long drive, so we made vegetable soup: nice and easy on the stomach. There's homemade bread too." Cammie then introduced the two men to Dagmar and Ross, and they all dug in.

CHAPTER 130
Catching Up

The group of them quietly ate their meal of soup and bread until Jim said, "You really lucked out getting to stay in this enormous place."

"Yeah, we sure did," Leroy said. "The odd thing is how quickly we've become used to it. At least I have."

"I think part of it, at least for me," Lydia said, "is that right after we moved in we wound up with a whole new business venture, so we've been busy with that ever since." Then she added, "I was ready for a change after coming to see you and spending time in the city. Coming back to a dark, dreary house where we had to sneak in and out was getting really hard for me."

"I think we were all pretty happy to move into such a great space," said Cammie. "It's so much nicer for Bella too."

Leroy looked across at Jim and asked, "Jim, why don't you tell us about the movie you were making?"

"Sure," said Jim. "I've been working on it on and off for a few years now so just had to wrap things up. Basically, it's the story of two good friends who have different political and spiritual ideologies and how they deal with that. Hopefully it'll help people to recognize and embrace some of their own complex situations. I think many of us have these kinds of dilemmas, and they can contribute a lot to our growth as human beings if we can come to terms with them in constructive ways."

"That sounds intriguing," said Dagmar. "What kinds of ideologies are they torn between?"

"Well, one is raised in a deeply religious household. All goes well until she reaches her teen years and becomes concerned about environmental issues. She becomes good friends with another girl who is from a strong social justice background who is also concerned about the state of the environment. The two girls throw themselves into environmental action while experiencing family difficulties. Eventually, as they grow up, they learn to appreciate the good parts of everything they've been exposed to, including their upbringing. They do what they can to mend fences with their families while nurturing their own unique perspective and values. Through lots of shared experience and discussion, they develop worldviews that include spirituality, activism and authenticity and find peace in their own way. Their friendship becomes an anchor in each of their lives, and they enrich each other with the constructive aspects of each of their upbringings. They meditate together and include social justice issues in their environmental activities."

Jim looked around the table. "That's a drastically condensed version, but there you go: the story in a nutshell." He gave them all a broad grin. "And staying with Dan while we finished up was perfect."

Dan said, "Jim staying at the house with me was ..." He sighed. "I don't know what I would have done without him to help me through this time," he said, looking down.

"Hey, maybe you don't realize what an honour it was to be with you. If I wasn't there, I'd have been worrying about how you were doing all the time," Jim said. "I really want you to know that."

"I'm glad it worked out so well for both of you," Leroy said. "It was a comfort to me knowing that you'd have a good friend with you, Dan. Jim, can you stay an extra day with us?"

"I'd love to, but I also want to get home to Beth. We miss each other," Jim said. "It was a long haul for her, although she's gotten used to my erratic schedule over the years. I appreciate the offer, though. This region's beautiful! It would make a great setting for a movie."

"Will you come with us tomorrow morning for our performance at the Love Bite at least?" asked Ross. "It's an amazing restaurant, and I bet you'd enjoy our music."

"I could do that. It would be great to hear you, and if I leave right at noon, I can get to another friend's place along the way home by evening," he said, smiling at Ross. "How could I pass up a morning at a restaurant with a name like the Love Bite?"

CHAPTER 131

Sunshine

At the Love Bite the next morning, Jim sat across the table looking at Dan basking in the sunshine. Jim took pleasure in this simple joy that Dan was obviously experiencing.

Leroy and his housemates were setting up, and their server brought them each a cup of coffee or tea. They'd slept in and skipped breakfast so ordered the continental. To their delight, their server brought them each a large plate of tofu scramble with mushrooms, peppers and other veggies; a basket of warm fruit-filled croissants and a plate of melons cut up into bite-size chunks. They took turns cutting fresh parsley and rosemary from the pots on the table onto their tofu scramble.

Jim was glad he'd decided to stay for the morning. He loved the ambience of the place and looked forward to his friends' performance.

"Aren't you glad that you came out?" Jim asked Dan. "It looks like this change of scenery might be exactly what you needed."

"I felt pretty resistant but really am happy to have come. I can see Mel in some of Leroy's actions and manners of speaking, and that's comforting," said Dan. "And besides, they're all lovely people to spend time with, aren't they?"

"They sure are," Jim said. "And I can hardly wait to hear their music."

Jim and Dan looked up and saw a woman walk through the door and look around. She smiled as she saw a man at a back table waving.

"They're like a couple of rays of sunshine, don't you think?" asked Jim, watching the two of them settle in.

"Yes, they seem to be radiating joy," Dan said.

The sound of a guitar being tuned emanated from the floor as Ross finished turning the tuning pegs of his guitar. The members of the group were standing in formation, looking ready to sing. Leroy stepped forward and said, "Hello and welcome. We're the Sleeping Dragon, and we'd like to dedicate this song to Dan, who is in the audience right now." People clapped, and Dan gave an embarrassed wave.

There was a haunting guitar intro, and then, in beautiful harmony, the group sang, "Earth moves in a mysterious way, her wonders to unfold. She fashions beauty out of clay like straw spun into gold."

All were mesmerized by the harmonies and the message about the grandeur of the earth. Dan listened with his eyes closed and applauded loudly when they finished.

George and Mayzie sat motionless through the song. Afterwards, Mayzie said, "That was spell-binding." Then she whispered, "I met the older couple in the band at the market yesterday. He's a friend of Alice's."

"They're enchanting," George said. "I love those kinds of harmonies."

"So do I. Somehow, people singing together like that makes everything feel right with the world, don't you think?"

"Yes, I agree. It's so uplifting."

"Nice to experience something so soul-soothing on a Sunday morning," Mayzie said to George, smiling.

"What a wonderful prelude to a hike!" said George.

Dan and Jim ate their breakfasts and enjoyed the music and the sunshine. As always, the songs were about love and healing, and the music soothed its listeners like the gentle sunshine.

During their break the group joined Dan and Jim. Dan thanked them for the song, then said to Leroy, "Thanks for forwarding the cartoon Simon and Lester made with that song. I thought it was beautiful, and I emailed them to let them know."

"I loved watching it but found it a little painful at the time," Leroy confessed. "It was a very thoughtful acknowledgement of Mom."

"Yeah, that's pretty well how I experienced it too," Dan said.

"Your music's really special," Jim said to the group. "It delivers something we all yearn for, without even knowing we yearn for it. Does that make sense?"

"I know exactly what you mean," said Dan.

"We get a lot out of it. I think it heals us as much our listeners." Leroy got up with the others and said, "Anyway, time for our next set."

The next set was a little more lively, and a few of the songs involved Dagmar with a shaker and Lydia and Leroy dancing.

Sunshine caught the crystals hanging in the window and sent rainbows racing around the room. Dust particles danced in the air, and sunshine cast its lazy, languorous spell. For a little while all was right with the world for the people in the restaurant.

CHAPTER 132

Tree House

After their morning at the Love Bite, George and Mayzie hopped on a bus and got off a few miles out of town. They walked down the road a ways until they came to a trail in a wooded area on one side and a gravel road to a beach on the other.

"We have a choice. Would you prefer a hike in the woods or a stroll along the beach?" George asked Mayzie.

"I think I'd prefer a hike in the woods," Mayzie replied. "What about you?"

"I fancy a hike in the woods too," George said. "Shall we see where this trail leads?"

"By all means," Mayzie said with a smile, and they headed up the trail.

It was comforting to be in the woods, with its birdcalls and the sweet smell of wilderness. They trudged along the winding trail together enjoying the peaceful experience. They were walking through a deep old-growth forest, the trees gradually becoming larger beside a steep embankment. George and Mayzie gazed up into the trees' canopies, mesmerized by the dappled sunlight shifting with the gentle breeze.

"Hey, those vines around the trunk of that tree almost look like stairs," Mayzie said. The wooden, hardened vines wrapped around the tree like steps.

"Why don't we climb them and see where we find ourselves?" George suggested. "Do you want to go first?"

"Okay, sounds like an adventure!" said Mayzie enthusiastically, and she started climbing. "They're pretty easy to climb so far," she said, after going up four or five of them.

They climbed up the tree for a few minutes and found an elaborate tree house, high in the canopy, not visible from below. Mayzie pulled herself in first, and George came up shortly after.

"Wow! What a find!" said George. "This place is amazing!" They stood up on the floorboards and were able to stand straight, not hitting the domed ceiling in the sizable structure.

"Let's check it out," said Mayzie.

"I wonder if someone lives here. It doesn't show any recent signs of life, does it?" George said, noticing the coating of dust on the floor and countertops. There were no signs of activity. The room was neat, and the counters were empty.

"No, it doesn't," Mayzie said, "but maybe someone only stays here occasionally. It's hard to tell."

They found themselves in a kitchen, with a sink and a small electric stove against the trunk of the tree. There were cupboards along the outer wall and doorways into other rooms. Mayzie walked over to the cupboards, opened one of them and found dishes and plates. There were also cupboards and drawers beneath the countertop beside the sink. She opened one of the drawers and found cutlery. Dishes, plates and cutlery were all mismatched. Between the tree trunk and the far wall was a small table with cushions around it.

"This place has been built with care over time," said George. "I wonder if the way we got up is just one entrance. Maybe the place extends to the embankment beside the forest and there's another entrance there," he wondered aloud, peeking through one of the doorways. It led to another room under the canopy of the tree. He walked through, then called back, "Mayzie, look at this!"

Mayzie followed his voice and found herself in a living area with a doorway going toward the embankment. There were futons on the ground with small round tables beside and in front of them. George was bending over one of them to take a closer look. "These tables are made from tires," he said.

"It looks like a lot of the furnishings have been scavenged and repurposed. This area could be used for sitting or reading and could sleep people as well."

"Brilliant, isn't it?" said Mayzie. "Someone's created a home from almost nothing." They walked back to the kitchen and sat down at the table. "Do you feel like having a snack?" she asked, removing her backpack and opening it up. "I have all kinds of things to eat."

George sat down beside her, watching with interest as she took nectarines, strawberries, crackers and guacamole out of her backpack. She also had a container of salad and some coconut water and something that looked like truffles.

"What are those?" asked George, pointing to the round, chocolaty balls in a jar.

"They're peanut butter balls. Peanut butter, rehydrated dried fruits and hemp seeds all rolled together and then rolled in cocoa. They taste like truffles but are very healthy. Wonderful for taking on a hike," Mayzie said.

"May I try one?"

"Please! Help yourself," Mayzie said, opening the jar and holding it out to George, who eagerly took one.

"These are divine!" he said. "Where did you get the recipe?"

"I just made it up," Mayzie said. "You can make them with any kind of nut butter or dried fruit."

"How wonderful it is to be sitting in this incredible dwelling eating a delicious peanut butter ball here with you," said George.

Mayzie reached into the jar and got out a peanut butter ball for herself. "Would you like some coconut water? I don't get it often, but once in a while I really enjoy it."

"Yes, thanks. Shall I get us a couple of cups?" he offered, getting up.

"All right. I'd love to feel more connected to this place by using cups from here."

"Me too." George got the cups.

They sat in the kitchen sipping on coconut water, sharing food and taking in their new surroundings.

"Everything in here looks to be at least 60 years old. These cups, for instance, look like they could have come out of my grandparents' house," Mayzie said. "I wonder if this place has been empty for a long time or if whoever it belongs to just likes old stuff."

"Good question," George said as he stared at the ceiling. "Did you notice that there are a bunch of pulleys near the ceiling? I wonder what they're for."

Mayzie looked up too. "So do I," she said as she examined them. "What a place! Someone's put a lot of time, innovation and energy into it." She took a sip of her coconut water, then looked at George. "Shall we do some more exploring after we finish our snack? I want to know everything about this place."

"So do I."

They finished up and washed the cups they'd used. They ran them under taps in the sink where they were surprised to find running water and dried them with a tea towel hanging on the knob of one of the cupboards. Then they put them away.

George found a small stepladder leaning against a wall. He took it to the centre of the room, unfolded it, climbed up a few rungs and reached up so he could pull on one of the pulleys. As he did, the outer wall, which was made of heavy layers of fabric, lifted with the pulley to reveal mosquito netting that surrounded the enclosure. "Wow!" he said. "Great way to get a cross breeze or to keep the place insulated. The fabric must be waterproof on the outside." He let the pulley and thus the fabric come down.

"Let's see what's in the other rooms!" exclaimed Mayzie as she peeked through another doorway that appeared to go to an area that was dug into the embankment. The boarded floor sloped down toward the entrance.

George walked with her and said, "I guess as the tree grows, this section becomes higher, so the flooring that connects them is a walkway that adjusts—neat!"

It was darker inside, although there was a window at the far end. There was a small desk with a few drawers and an office chair in front of the window that looked into the canopies of the trees. Further back, there was a nook with a double bed and a small table beside it. A candle was perched on the table.

"Isn't this cozy?" Mayzie said. She sat down at the desk and looked out at the trees. "I can't imagine a nicer work area. Although I doubt there's Wi-Fi."

"It feels like it's out of another time, doesn't it? The small rooms, this old-fashioned wooden desk and the way the spaces are divided up," George said. "I wonder what's through that door." He pointed to a door that was adjacent to the one they'd come through.

They walked through the door, which was a little stiff to open, and found themselves in a sunny living room with wicker chairs and stools. There was a skylight and ferns growing out of the walls. They were very large and seemed to be connected to a watering system within the walls themselves.

"This room is so inviting!" said Mayzie. "Do you feel like sitting here for a while?" Mayzie pointed to a doorway further down. "And there's another door. I wonder where it leads."

George walked over to it and opened it up. "It goes outside to a little overgrown pathway," he said. "What an amazing structure!" He came back in, sat down in one of the wicker chairs and put his feet up on an ottoman, which was made from a tire with rope wrapped around it. "This is so comfortable."

"So's this one," said Mayzie, who suddenly felt tired and lazy.

George was getting more relaxed with the help of the chair and the sunshine. He closed his eyes.

CHAPTER 133
Sharing Stories

They sat quietly for a while soaking in the ambience of the space. Mayzie looked over at George and said, "I barely know you, but I feel so at ease with you."

"I feel the same way with you," said George. "Yet we hardly know each other." Then as an afterthought, he said, "This is an ideal place to tell each other our stories, don't you think?"

"The perfect setting if you ask me," laughed Mayzie. "I'll just get a couple of cups from the kitchen so we can drink coconut water while we chat." Mayzie disappeared into the kitchen and reappeared with the cups. "Want some?" she asked George.

"Yes, please," he said. "Thanks for bringing it and for getting the cups."

"You looked so comfortable; I didn't want to disturb you," Mayzie said. She brought him a cup of coconut water, then poured a cup for herself and settled back into her chair.

"Okay," she said, "who wants to go first?"

"I want to know all about you," said George. "Why don't you start?"

Mayzie heaved a sigh. "Well, I'm from a pretty ordinary background. The granddaughter of immigrants from Wales."

"Ah, Wales—a magical country!" George exclaimed.

"I've only been back once a long time ago, but I remember that it was beautiful," said Mayzie. "Anyway, I'm still trying to figure out what I'm going to be when I grow up," she laughed. "I've had lots of different kinds of jobs and am one of three staff members at the centre where I'm working and love that. I also do some volunteering, mostly for different social and environmental groups."

"What would you say motivates you the most?" asked George.

"Right now what motivates me is doing what I can to help humanity and our planet to heal," she said. "As a species, we have so much, but we're losing it, and I think it's because we've forgotten how to appreciate what we have: in nature, culture, art, we have boundless treasures. Our vision seems so narrow and petty. How do we broaden it so we can see what we have? If we could just see it, maybe we'd want to protect it so we can pass it along to future generations. How are we able to miss the big picture and what's truly important?" Mayzie paused, shook her head and took a sip of her coconut water.

"I hear you loud and clear," George said. "How do we change our understanding enough to make a difference? It's something I contemplate often."

"Working at the centre, I sometimes wonder if most of humanity isn't so deeply wounded that we can't see beyond our pain. I mean, hearing some of the people's stories there …"

"What kinds of stories?"

"Well, the people there are all very compassionate," Mayzie said, heaving a sigh and looking up through the skylight. Although light came through, it was hard to see through its haziness. "They—we— have all gone through some kind of trauma in an intimate relationship, and that's what brought us there. Sharing our stories, we've discovered that we're almost like opposite sides of the coin of the people who took advantage of us. It's like we learned in childhood to ignore certain things that should be warnings and to allow ourselves to trust people we shouldn't."

"What kinds of warning signs?"

"Let's see … Emotional rescue comes to mind. People who take advantage often tell stories, which may be true, but these people tell them to engage our compassion. This gets people like me hooked, and we make excuses for why abusive behaviour is acceptable. I've seen a couple of emotional patterns, including increasing one-sidedness. So basically one person does all he or she can to meet the other's needs, while the other doesn't reciprocate. That's a really common one."

"It's great that the centre gives people a chance to compare notes in situations that sound isolating and degrading," George said. "What are some of the other commonalities?"

"Well, often secrecy is involved. We've had people who thought they were getting into relationships, but then the other person later said that all they wanted was a secret sexual relationship, that the empathetic people had misread the emotional signals. There might be secrecy around money or substance abuse. Often, there's a kind of stiffness to people who are predatory. Since they have so many secrets, they find it hard to just relax and let things flow. They're more interested in presenting an image than genuinely caring or being transparent."

"So how does the centre help people to recognize and remedy their propensity to get involved with these types?" George asked, looking over his cup of coconut water at Mayzie.

"Mostly, we try to establish a respectful environment and share our own discoveries with each other. Often when people come to the centre, they're shadows of themselves. They're just used up and heartbroken. Something that both abuser and abused share is low self-esteem, so we try to support each other in a way that encourages self-love. Also, when we share our experiences, we find out that some very personal details are actually quite common. For instance, sexual predators tend to subtly cross personal boundaries and manipulate people into having sex. This should be a heads-up right away, but often people have become hooked by then, and these types have an uncanny ability to know exactly when to strike."

"I wonder how people learn to love themselves. That sounds like such a challenge," George said.

"It sure is!" Mayzie said. "So we try to create an environment where people value each other and themselves and find solutions together, like listening; respecting each other's needs; encouraging healing activities like writing, art, gardening—that sort of thing. Also, we reinforce the message that the desire to help is what the world needs the most right now. A caring nature is a thing of great value, so we try to learn to use it wisely."

"I agree," said George. "Our planet needs caring people so badly."

"You feel that way too?"

"Oh, yes!" George exclaimed.

"Anyway, enough about me. What about you?" asked Mayzie.

"What about me?" George repeated. "Well, I've lived a pretty spoiled life in most respects. I grew up in Britain on a lavish estate. My ancestors made a lot of money through armament sales, slavery and plundering other countries, not something I'm proud of."

Mayzie looked at him closely and said, "It sounds like a totally different world."

"Yes, you're right. And a totally different worldview too. I love my family and friends, but I've never been able to share their worldview, even though it's been drilled into me in every possible way from as early as I can remember. We're the chosen ones; we're worthy and special and above all the rest. At least that's the view of the people I'm surrounded by, bless them. Only I've never believed any of it."

"How come?"

"I don't know," George said, "no idea. Glory and wealth can be a kind of poison. Often, they destroy people's innate compassion, and I know compassion's innate. Even the wealthy can feel it intensely for people of their

230

class, but for others, not so much." George laughed. "Have you noticed that our global economic institutions favour privatization? Medical care, energy, transport and education: privatization drives costs up for ordinary people, but where do you think all those profits go? Who do you think benefits from wars, regardless of which country wins, because they've sold armaments to both sides? This has always sickened me, and I thank you for listening and for not running out the door as I tell you this."

"George, I've always felt that no one should be persecuted because of the situation they were born into. That goes for you too. You can't help it that you were born into the privileged class. It's what you do that's important, and I'm sure your background gives you an understanding of things that could really help to change the world for the better."

"These privileged people are scared right now. People everywhere are onto them, and people are revolting in every way imaginable. People are divesting and getting universities and other institutions to divest, and they're demonstrating. Some countries are even shunning the International Monetary Fund. The class I'm from is out of touch, and they know it, but they don't know what to do," said George with concern in his voice. "They give to charities that do some good, but many are like Band-Aids. Most of them don't look at the economic structure that causes social and environmental problems in the first place."

"What a complex bundle of emotions you must be feeling," Mayzie said. "These are the people you know and love, but they have fundamentally different values from you. I get the sense that you'd like things to change but are concerned about the welfare of the people you've grown up with too. Is that right?"

"Yes, in a nutshell," George said. "And I see what you mean about being compassionate and empathetic. You really picked up on the inner struggle I experience."

Mayzie smiled and shook her head. "Like you, I can't help myself. I know I'm empathetic and compassionate but want to make sure I channel these qualities in a way that's healthy. Listening to you, I'm not picking up any danger signals, and, believe me, I pay attention and look out for them." She took a sip of her coconut water and then asked, "With the state of the world being what it is, do your friends and family feel the concerns that many of the rest of us do? If the planet goes down, it takes down all of us, them included. No one knows what's going to happen with global warming, and there may be all kinds of unforeseen consequences that could affect everyone in unpredictable ways. There's nowhere to hide."

"Unfortunately, for the most part, their arrogance, single-mindedness and blindness are almost unfathomable," George said. "I've studied sociology and psychology trying to understand not just them but other cultures too, especially very old cultures that are more rooted in a different way of being in the world. I hate to say it, but the culture I'm from is one based on feeling superior and, therefore, quite ambivalent toward others. It's kind of like how we're able to exploit animals. Most people don't think about the terrible life of the cow whose flesh makes up the hamburger they're eating or the chicken when they're snacking on wings."

"I remember how traumatizing that realization was, and I've been vegan ever since," Mayzie said.

"Really? I'm vegan too!" said George, smiling.

"All right!" Mayzie exclaimed, smiling back at George. "How do we reach these people, George? How do we help them to experience the same kind of epiphany that we did that stopped us from eating meat?"

"That's a good question," George said. "It's one I've given a lot of thought to, and I just don't know."

"I can understand how they'd be afraid. In the past, when there've been revolutions, those at the top haven't fared well. But, you know, we're at such a unique point in history. Our challenge is to all learn how to work together. They could contribute so much toward our planet's healing. They could be heroes! I wonder what would convince them to use their power to help the world become magnificent for all of us."

"You know, people are making films, trying to reach the hearts and minds of everyone. You just never know what will work, do you? Sometimes it feels like we're living in an arid climate; everything is tinder-dry, and we're just waiting for a spark to ignite it all. What's it going to take to get us to see our predicament and persuade people to use their power to bring about a liveable world? I have a feeling it'll be something completely unexpected, something that will help everyone to see our situation with fresh eyes ..." George gazed up at the skylight, pondering his point.

Mayzie fidgeted for a moment; then she said, "I hate to break up our discussion, but I wonder if we should start finding our way back. I wouldn't mind seeing where the path leads on this side of the building. How about you?"

"I'm curious about it as well," George said. "Afterwards we can catch a bus back into town."

Mayzie got up from her chair and took their cups to the kitchen, and when she returned, she put on her backpack. She walked over to where George was still sitting and reached out her hand to him. "Are you ready to go?" she asked.

He took Mayzie's hand and let her pull him up. Their eyes and hands connected at the same time, and they shared an electric instant of connection. Both feeling a little awkward, they walked toward the door together. George opened it and found two overgrown paths. Looking up one of them, they could see what looked like an outhouse.

"Hey, great!" said Mayzie. "I know what that is, and it's just what I need right now. You don't happen to have a knife I can use, do you?"

"Sure," he said, handing her a Swiss Army knife and pulling out the blade. She cut her way through the undergrowth until she reached the outhouse. She opened the door that creaked a little and found a clean, odourless interior with a toilet seat and an old *Resurgence* magazine from 40 years earlier beside it. She took a seat and flipped through the magazine. It was beautiful, with essays about environmental issues, artwork and poetry all inspired by the magnificence of the earth. There was a roll of toilet paper hanging on one of the walls for which she was grateful.

Returning, she said to George, "Have you ever heard of a magazine called *Resurgence*? There was a 40-year-old copy in the outhouse, and it was so beautiful."

"Yes," said George. "It was the printed voice of the British environmental movement for a long time. It sounds as though you've found a collectible."

"I think I'll just leave it. The outhouse is so clean and lovely; I don't want to disturb a thing." She handed George his knife and thanked him.

They looked down the other trail. "It's going to be a bit of a bushwhack getting out of here, but I'll use my knife to get us through any spots that are overgrown. Are you up for it, or would you rather leave the way we came in?" George asked.

"Why don't we give it a try and see how far we get?" Mayzie suggested.

CHAPTER 134

Sacred Grove

George led the way along the overgrown trail with his Swiss Army knife in hand, cutting away at the undergrowth. They couldn't see where they were going but could feel the downhill grade. Late-afternoon sunshine filtered through the branches of the trees above them.

After hiking through heavy growth for about 20 minutes, they came to an oak grove.

"Look at these beautiful big trees, eh?" said Mayzie.

"Yes, aren't they something! This feels like a special place somehow," said George.

"Maybe it's a sacred grove," Mayzie said. "It feels that way to me."

"It does to me too."

The sweetness of the forest air enveloped them, and they sank into the soft, deep moss underfoot.

"Would you like to sit here for a while before we carry one, have a snack maybe?" asked Mayzie.

"I'd love another one of those peanut butter balls," George said.

They sat down in the centre, and Mayzie removed her backpack, got out her jar of peanut butter balls and offered it to George.

"Thanks," he said, grabbing a ball and then popping it in his mouth. Mayzie took one out too, and then as she sat on the ground, she said, "Ouch!" She got up and looked at what had caused the pain and found a beautiful rose-coloured crystal on the ground. "George, look!" she said, holding it out to him.

"Wow! That's beautiful!" he said, taking it from her and holding it up to the sunlight. In the light, the rounded triangular crystal was a pale pink with rose-coloured swirls and bits that glittered inside. After admiring it, he handed it back to her.

"This will be a reminder of the great day we've had and this magical place," she said.

"Perhaps it's a sacred token," said George. "Maybe it'll bring you luck."

"It already has." Mayzie smiled. "I feel very lucky to be here in this special place with you." She blushed.

"I'm so glad you feel that way," George said, touching her hand. "Because that's how I feel too."

She looked into his eyes, and he leaned over and kissed her.

CHAPTER 135

Under a Spell

Mayzie froze. She put her hand on George's arm and said, "Suddenly everything feels like it's moving so fast. I'm scared."

"I understand. So am I," he confessed. "Sorry if I frightened you. I don't know what to do now. How should I proceed? I want to be close to you, and it feels like you want to be close to me too."

"Why don't we just lie here under these giant trees for a little while and meditate on it?" She looked at him and said, "I want to be close to you too, but I need to get grounded. Do you know what I mean?"

"Yes, I understand," said George. "We haven't known each other long, but I feel like we have such a special affinity. This hasn't happened to me before. Where in the past there've been roadblocks, with you it's like everything you say and do is an opening door. Does that make sense? We seem to be so right for each other."

"I know what you mean," Mayzie said. "We seem to understand each other at such a deep level it's almost scary."

"And we're in a sacred grove. How did we even get here?" George mused. "Look at all the magic we've just experienced. It's like we're meant to be."

Mayzie sighed and looked at him. What was holding her back? She said, "You know, after the experience that landed me in the centre where I work, I find it hard to trust my own judgement. George, you seem like a wonderful guy, and I feel so close to you, but I …"

"It must be so scary," George said, looking into her eyes. "How do you know you can trust me? I promise that I have the best of intentions toward you, and I want us to be very close. I want us to be that special someone in each other's lives, because I feel like we already are."

She looked into his eyes, then slowly leaned over and kissed him. The smell of the moss, the trees and their dramatic forms against the blue sky became part of their closeness. Their kisses became passionate, and they held each other close. Lying down in the soft moss, they stroked each other's bodies: undoing buttons, removing clothing, their movements languid, rhythmic and sensual. The air, the trees, the sounds of the forest all became part of the eroticism of their movements. They became spellbound in this magical place and with each other. They and their setting merged into flesh, birdcalls and the sweet fragrance of the woods around them.

Afterwards, they lay spent in each other's arms. "That was the most profound experience I've ever had," said George. "It's as though suddenly everything came into clear focus." He looked at Mayzie, her cheeks red and lips full. She was beautiful, lying with her head against the moss.

"The depth of connection I felt with you felt like a connection with all of this too," Mayzie said, returning the warmth in his eyes. "It's as though we were drawn here, like we were making love for all of this."

"That's exactly what I'm feeling," said George. "Mayzie, I initially just came here for a visit, but I'm not leaving. I want to be here with you. Please trust me, okay? I promise that I have your very best interests at heart."

"I believe you," Mayzie said, "and believe me too when I say I have your best interests at heart, okay? I feel like we're being called, maybe by the earth herself."

"I do too," said George. "It's like we've communed with a kind of power that needs to be expressed. Something you and I have in common is our concern for our planet. We've just consummated something holy, and I feel that our commitment to the greater good is a big part of it."

CHAPTER 136

A Shift

Dagmar sat on the front porch, sipping tea and looking out at the yard filled with indigenous plants. Something felt distinctly different that day, but she couldn't put her finger on it. It was as though something diffuse had gelled or as though something that had been just under the surface had appeared and become powerful. What was it exactly?

It was Sunday, and they had all gone back to the house after their gig at the Love Bite and had said goodbye to Dan's friend Jim.

Afterwards, Leroy had taken the car out to show Dan around the different yards where they were farming. The gardens were all growing well, the operations were running smoothly and relations with the family who owned the mansion were harmonious: something different and powerful was emerging, and they were part of it.

Phoebe had her hands full with all the green renovations that were starting to happen, and she and Liam had organized training sessions for various tradespeople so they'd be able to keep up with the demand. This was part of the change too.

There was even a different atmosphere at the food bank. The few times Dagmar had been there she'd noticed a big change in Mary. Mary had always walked with a limp but was now moving effortlessly. The community currency enabled people to help each other more and find creative solutions to their food and housing needs. The feeling of apathy that had so often permeated the building had been replaced with optimism and excitement.

It almost felt as though the earth herself was nourishing those who cared for her. Together people were finding the power to create solutions and support each other.

Dagmar hadn't felt this kind of optimism for a long time. Suddenly there was hope for the future. There was a sense that their children's children's children would experience a better way of living than they could ever imagine and that they were at the beginning of the big change that was going to turn things around.

Just then Ross sat down beside her. "There you are!" he said. "You're in a great spot to be enjoying this beautiful Sunday afternoon." He leaned over and kissed her on the cheek.

She patted him on the knee and asked, "Have you noticed a change in the air?"

"Things have gotten better for us, certainly," Ross replied. "But, yeah, now that you mention it, it's as though the whole atmosphere around us is becoming—I don't know—more optimistic, more upbeat. Is that what you mean?"

"Yeah. Lately things feel different," Dagmar said. "It's like a lot of small changes are suddenly having a cumulative effect."

"I know what you mean: it's subtle but really powerful," said Ross, "like the things we've all been plugging away at for years are coming to fruition."

"It's wonderful, isn't it?" said Dagmar, looking into his eyes. "For a while, I didn't think I'd ever feel hopeful again. It's like everyone's finding solutions, and they seem to be working out, and their collective impact is huge."

"And it feels like the very beginning of something much, much bigger, don't you think?" said Ross. "I wonder where things will go from here."

They sat sipping their tea in the sun for a while, enjoying their day of downtime.

"You know, I used to privately wonder why we're here at this time in history," said Dagmar. "I'd wonder if we're here to bear witness to the end of our species or to finally turn things around. For me, the jury was out, but now it feels like we're building momentum to finally change things for the better."

"Yeah, something has really tipped, and it's hard to describe," Ross said. "I'm excited to be alive and to stay attuned so I'll know what to do next. It's so different from the way I felt even six months ago. Somehow I've been saturated with love and concern, when before I was going through the motions, feeling numb and out of touch with the core of my being. Now everything's aligned in some way it wasn't before, and it feels great.

"Even our Green Team meetings have changed—no more power struggles and instead collaboration between other groups, huge victories, lots of happy people. And we're learning to work with and support First Nations, who hold the key to resolving this." Ross counted on his fingers as he spoke. "It's as though we've all just woken up to our real priorities." Then he asked, "Say, do you feel like walking the labyrinth? We haven't done that in a while."

"I'd love to!" Dagmar replied. "Walk by the old place on the way, maybe? Sounds like a lovely thing to do on a Sunday afternoon."

They got up and wandered slowly toward the labyrinth, enjoying the sunshine, birdcalls and fresh greenery all around them.

"I never cease to be moved by the beauty of this place," Dagmar said with a sigh, taking in the spectacular scenery all around her: the mountains, the lake, the big trees and lush and varied plant life.

"Magic's everywhere when we have the eyes to see it, eh?" said Ross, taking it all in.

As they walked through the empty lot by the abandoned house, Dagmar spontaneously put her hands together and gave it a little bow. Ross saw her, laughed and did the same. "I know what you mean!" he said. "Who knows what good is being hatched in this place. Look what happened to us. Look what happened to Glenda and her friends. And the people there now were already helping to create homes for people. I can only imagine how much good they're doing."

"It almost looks like it has a kind of glow around it," said Dagmar, "like an aura of helpfulness or something."

"Yeah, I think I see it," said Ross.

They walked further down, both feeling exalted by their encounter with the first home they'd had together and all the good things it had brought into their lives.

The warm afternoon sun shone lazily down on the town, its dappled light shimmering through the leaves of the trees as the breeze gently stirred them. They could see the bricks of the labyrinth under the large oak trees in the park. As they approached, it seemed to invite them with its circular pattern leading to the centre. Ross got there first. He bowed before the entrance and started his walk. Dagmar waited about 10 seconds before bowing at the entrance and beginning her walk.

When Ross reached the centre, he stood quietly, then bowed to each of the four directions. He clapped his hands three times, creating a sharp, clear sound. He bowed to the north one last time before leaving the centre for his return walk. He smiled at Dagmar, who was just approaching the centre. She stood silently for a moment and clapped her hands. The sound was distinct and metallic. She stood silently before beginning her return walk.

When she left the labyrinth, she found Ross waiting for her. He reached out his hand, and she held it, and they strolled along the side of the lake together, enjoying the afternoon.

CHAPTER 137
Dan's View

After their lunch at the Love Bite, Leroy took Dan on a tour of the gardens he and his friends were caring for. Dan had been born and raised in the city, so he found it interesting to see food growing so profusely.

"It's all organic? That's great!" said Dan.

"Yeah, even certified by a local certification body," Leroy said. "Jon arranged it when he had the SPIN farm." Leroy picked some spinach and some other greens and put them in a cloth bag. "This'll go toward dinner tonight."

As they got back in the car, Leroy looked at Dan and asked, "So how are you doing? I'm so glad Jim was able to spend time with you. Are you going to be okay on your own?"

Dan thought about it for a moment. "Yeah, I think I'm ready for a bit of space now." He nodded. "It still really hurts not having your mother around, but I have friends and interests and have been slowly reconnecting."

Leroy drove on for a while without saying anything. Then he asked, "Do you ever dream about Mom?"

"Yeah, all the time. Do you?" asked Dan.

"Yeah, and it feels like she's trying to tell me something, but I can never figure out what."

"Maybe you're listening too hard."

"What do you mean?"

"Well, I don't know what happens after we die, but if Mel's still around in any way, I know she misses us," said Dan. "She'll be using her creativity wherever she is."

"I'm sure," said Leroy.

"At least we have each other," said Dan. "We can share insights to help us through this."

They picked a few more greens from the gardens and then drove back home.

CHAPTER 138

Superhero

When Leroy and Dan came home, the other housemates were preparing dinner. After getting Dan comfortable checking his email in the living room, Leroy brought the fresh greens into the kitchen, rinsed them off and made a large salad. Soon enough dinner was ready, and they all sat at the big dining room table and enjoyed their evening feast. This one involved new potatoes, an assortment of colourful vegetables and a tofu dish.

Baby Bella was sitting in her high chair between Cammie and Tam trying some of the food. She seemed amused but didn't seem to realize that food was for eating and not just playing with. Cammie wasn't in a rush to wean her but thought Bella might like to try some of the food the rest of them were eating.

Lydia announced to the group, "Simon and Lester sent their latest cartoon, and they say it's a jump back in time to the origins of this unique superhero! Feel like watching it after dinner?"

Lots of enthusiastic yeses came from around the table.

After their meal, they quickly cleaned up the dishes and put the kettle on. Lydia had her laptop hooked up to the TV screen and had the new cartoon ready to play. When all were comfortably seated with their cups of tea, Lydia started the show.

It started with Lav, the slender, balding man from previous episodes, meditating. There was quiet music playing in the background. Then it showed the same man in the garden, in his jeans and his red-and-white-plaid shirt, weeding with his friend Cat.

"I don't know how to describe it," Lav said, "but meditating's become really intense. It's like something is coming into focus that's really powerful, and I don't know what exactly will emerge."

"Is that so?" Cat said. "It sounds like it's really building up to something."

"I'm not sure what, but it's like I'm tuning into something bigger than me, something that wants my help. It's like I'm being asked to summon something deep within so I can make an important contribution to the world." Lav looked up into the sky. "I wish I could describe it better, but it's such a vivid feeling. I've been meditating longer and more often each day. After I do a bit of work in the garden, I'm going to go back to my meditation spot and try to tune in."

Lav returned to his outdoor meditation spot, a private corner of the garden. He quieted his mind and breathed rhythmically. "I can feel something building and surging," he said to himself. The shot zoomed in tightly on his face, which had a look of tranquil concentration. When the camera pulled back out to frame Lav again, his outline was slightly blurred. The colours around him were intensified and his meditation spot looked surreal. Everyone in the mansion knew they were supposed to be inside Lav's head. All of a sudden he felt himself shooting into the sky, connected and in tune with the mysterious force that animates the universe. Amid swirls of colour, stars and spirals, Lav's clothing turned into a lavender superhero outfit.

The people in the mansion cheered at the birth of a new superhero!

Suddenly he flew north to where there was fracking for natural gas and drilling for dirty oil in the tar sands. As he flew above, sinkholes appeared and buried giant bulldozers. The earth shook, and the wind blew, sending stacks of pipes for pipelines rolling all over the ground. Frightened workers got into their vehicles and drove away as the site ran amok.

An angry red-and-purple cloud gushed around the site like lava, and Lav flew in and embraced the cloud, soothing it. "Anima mundi, we will honour you. Please forgive us. We know you're alive and not just a lifeless resource to exploit." He flew around the raging cloud, tuning in, comforting, sending peace and love. "Please give us another chance." He hovered above the seemingly endless environmental destruction of the tar sands for a few minutes.

Lav flew back to his home, back to where he'd been meditating. As he landed, he sighed deeply. He looked down and saw that he was again wearing his jeans and plaid shirt.

Shaken, he walked into the garden where Cat was still pulling weeds and asked, "Hey, did you notice anything in the last few minutes?"

"Like what?" she asked, standing up and arching her back.

"I just had a really odd experience while meditating and am trying to figure out what just happened," he said. Then he explained his experience as best he could. "It feels like I actually flew, but maybe it was an out-of-body experience or something. It felt so real. I wonder if anything actually happened at the tar sands."

Cat looked closely into Lav's face. Although he seemed shaken, he looked pretty normal.

That evening, Cat called Lav and said, "Turn on the news."

When he did, a reporter was talking about what had happened in the tar sands: a number of giant bulldozers had fallen into sinkholes, and a large stack of pipe intended for the pipeline had rolled down with the shaking and were strewn all over the ground.

Lav sat on his bed with his mouth open. *What just happened there?* he said in voiceover. The scene faded out.

Lydia turned it off.

"Well, that's certainly a different kind of superhero," said Dan.

"Pretty wild, isn't it?" said Leroy.

"I like the way it focuses on things that really matter these days," Dan said. "It makes you wonder what on earth we're thinking, doesn't it? I mean how long has the writing been on the wall, yet here we are watching the weather become more wild, the land and water becoming more polluted, and we're simply carrying on as usual."

"Maybe it's just hard for people to know where to begin," Lydia said. "So they don't do anything, because it feels too overwhelming."

"I'm sure that has something to do with it," Dan said, "and, of course, people with vested interests do their best to keep the money rolling in regardless of the consequences."

"But it feels like there's been an important shift recently," said Dagmar. "Even watching this cartoon feels like part of it. It's like there's a different awareness that isn't just being talked about but being lived in a way it hasn't in the past."

"This may seem strange, but I think I know what you mean," said Dan, "Since spending time with you and your household, I feel like there's a renewed energy that's doing something different."

"It's really neat that you tuned into that too, Dan," Ross said. "Maybe we are at an important turning point."

CHAPTER 139

Dining at Nimby's

"Good old Nimby's!" Donny said to Cole. "It's nice to go to a place where you know what to expect—no surprises, just good old ordinary food, eh? Especially after a hard day's work." He could hear some familiar tune from the seventies playing: the Doobie Brothers? Doo doo do-do do-do-do.

Their waitress put a double cheeseburger with fries and a strawberry milkshake in front of Donny and a plate of fish and chips and an orange pop in front of Cole.

"Yeah, there's something comforting about this place," Cole said, "a regular family restaurant." He saw a few seniors sitting together or with adult children and wondered why there weren't more people their age. Probably all at trendy places like the Love Bite, with their strange array of foods.

"Business seems slow," said Cole. "What gives? I wonder."

"Who knows? It's a changing economy, and lots of people seem to go in for those trendy places these days," Donny said, then added, "I could eat a horse! I've got a huge hunger on after working in the sun all day."

"Yeah, me too. That overtime pay's gonna be nice!"

They ate in silence, happy to go out for a bite to eat and not have to prepare something themselves.

"Are you going to go to one of those green-building training sessions?" asked Cole.

"You mean the ones where we learn the basics of installing solar panels, applying solar paint, installing heat pumps, that sort of thing?" asked Donny.

"Yeah, those ones."

"May as well," Donny said. "They're free, and it sounds like there'll be lots of work coming up."

"Yeah, I'm going to take one too," said Cole. "Doesn't hurt to stay current, does it?"

They paid their bill, left the waitress a tip and left. When they got home, they practised a few songs together. Then Donny said, "I don't feel too well—heartburn or something. I'm going to make it an early night."

Cole looked over at Donny and noticed that his colour looked off. "Good night," Cole said as Donny walked up the stairs to his bedroom.

"Night," Donny replied.

Cole fooled around on the guitar for a while, then walked into the kitchen and did some of the dishes that had piled up over the week. May as well get some of them done so he'd have a plate to eat his breakfast on in the morning. His stomach didn't feel too good either.

CHAPTER 140

Sirens Again

That night, Cole woke up to Donny calling him. He walked into Donny's room and said, "Hey, what's up?"

"I think I'm having a heart attack. I have this horrible pain in my chest," said Donny. "Call 911, okay?"

"Okay," said Cole, trying to remember where he'd put his cellphone. He found it beside his bed and punched in the numbers.

"Can I get an ambulance? I think my roommate's having a heart attack," he said into the phone. He gave his address and described Donny's symptoms to the woman on the other end of the line.

Soon they heard sirens, and two ambulance attendants were at the door. Cole led them up to Donny's room. Donny was holding his chest and looked blue around the lips. The ambulance attendants hurried back downstairs and out to the ambulance and then returned with a stretcher. They put Donny on it and carried him to the ambulance.

"Looks like a heart attack, all right," said one of the attendants to Cole. "Do you want to come along for the ride? You can answer some questions on the way to the hospital."

Cole got into the ambulance. One of the attendants put an oxygen mask over Donny's face. "You're going to be fine, but we're just giving you a little extra oxygen," the attendant said in a comforting voice. "Just relax, and try to breathe slowly, okay?"

Donny nodded.

The ambulance attendant turned to Cole. "Would you mind telling me what you were up to earlier in the day?" he asked.

"Well, we both had been working extra hours to try to get a job finished; then we had dinner at Nimby's. Afterwards, Donny said he wasn't feeling so good, so he went to bed early."

"What did Donny have for dinner?" the attendant asked, getting out his notebook.

"A double cheeseburger with fries and a strawberry milkshake," Cole said. As the attendant wrote down the words, he seemed to wince almost imperceptibly.

"Has Donny been under any stress lately?" the attendant asked, pen poised.

"He and his girlfriend split up a few months ago, and he moved in with me," said Cole. "Other than that, I don't think there's been too much stress in his life. Working quite a bit of overtime these days."

"What kind of work?"

"Construction."

"And can I get both of your full names?" he asked, and Cole gave him the information.

The ambulance attendant wrote down his answers, then looked up at him and smiled. "Thanks for your help," he said as they pulled up to the hospital. "We can handle things from here. Do you want us to call you a cab? You may as well get some sleep."

"No, that's okay. It's all downhill from here, so I'll walk home," said Cole. Looking at Donny, he said quietly, "Hang in there, buddy. I'll come and see you tomorrow," Donny looked as if he was sleeping.

There were more attendants at the hospital entrance, and they took Donny on his stretcher out of the ambulance.

As he started down the hill, Cole waved goodbye to the ambulance attendant and said, "I'll come around tomorrow to see Donny after work."

It was a short walk, and he was back home in minutes. Cole opened the front door, took off his shoes and climbed up the stairs to his room. He couldn't sleep, although he was tired. The tune from the seventies he'd heard at Nimby's earlier kept running through his head. Why couldn't he get to sleep? Was it all the commotion getting Donny to the hospital? Or was it the fish and chips he was struggling to digest? Maybe it was all the caffeine and sugar in the soft drink he'd had with his burger or maybe a combination of all those things.

He thought about Alice and the way she used to eat, probably the way she still ate. He always thought of her as being neurotically health-conscious. Her food was kind of boring compared to fish and chips, but he'd always felt pretty good after eating it.

Alice. How could she have done what she did? What kind of a stunt was that to pull? He wondered if she ever missed him.

Ross came to mind. He'd been one of the boys until he got in with Dagmar and the crowd that sang at the Love Bite. He seemed pretty happy these days but didn't want to play with them anymore. So much was changing, and Cole felt as if he was being left in the dust somehow. Things just weren't what they used to be.

Cole thought about simpler times: James Bond movies, hot dogs, guys playing guitar and singing any songs they felt like, flirting with the girls. Why was everyone so uptight about everything these days?

He fell into a fitful sleep.

CHAPTER 141

Processing

Alice had just come in from the garden and was washing up. After having a late-night snack, she felt compelled to go into the centre's art studio. She'd written *Cole* on a Post-it note, and it was sitting in the middle of her butterfly waiting to be transformed. That one was going to take some deep inner work, and she knew it.

How could she have allowed herself to be taken in by someone who really didn't care about her feelings? What was the lesson to be learned, and how could she learn it?

Since distancing herself from Cole and being in this healing space, she'd recovered much of her dignity and sanity but felt the need to explore what had happened. She was finally feeling strong enough to do it. There was something about rescue in her: he'd told her about the hard things that had happened to him earlier in his life, and they had immediately engaged her sympathy. She'd found herself doing things for him, looking for a smile—she'd wanted him to be well. How had this feeling evolved into her being used in every way possible by someone who really didn't care, and how could she protect herself while still being open to love, compassion and caring?

Since coming here, she'd learned that predatory people sought out those who were empathetic and caring. She'd seen that over and over again with the people at this place of healing. It was one thing to know this intellectually but another altogether to retrain herself at the depth of her being.

When she looked at his name there, she still felt compassion but pain, rage and betrayal as well. What would it be like to have those same feelings of love and compassion but also respect for the person she was feeling them for?

Watching the way Cole behaved in the world, it hadn't taken her long to lose respect for him. She'd seen firsthand his indifference to people's feelings, his willingness to use others and the inner rigidness that resulted from keeping secrets and not wanting to expose himself. The reality he presented to the world looked good, but there was a lack of spontaneity that betrayed that airbrushed version of himself.

And then there was the intense jealousy he'd shown in his body language and cross-examinations when she'd had any interactions with other men, an emotion he'd always denied having. "I got over jealousy years ago," Alice remembered Cole saying, attempting to conceal the parts of himself he didn't like.

Little betrayals everywhere—a half truth here, an omission there, making others wrong in small ways so that he could look good. This was not a quality she could respect. *And let's face it,* she thought, *mutual respect is essential in a healthy relationship.* And that's what she wanted one day, a relationship based on trust, respect and deep caring, things that Cole was incapable of.

Something inside of her shifted, and she picked up the Post-it with Cole's name on it and on the other side wrote, "A relationship based on trust, respect and deep caring." Actually, many of her relationships with friends and family were based on those things. How did things go so awry with romantic relationships?

She left the room and went to bed.

Later that evening, Mayzie sat in the studio with her elbows propped on the desk, chin on her hands. It was comforting being in this space with works in progress scattered all around her. Like everyone else here, she was a work in progress, and this was a place where they allowed themselves to tune into themselves in a way that was visceral, visual and tactile. There were just a few pocket lights on around the perimeter of the room, so works in clay and paintbrushes in jars cast long shadows around the room.

Her hands wanted something malleable to work with, so she found a piece of clay and started working it. Its familiar damp coolness felt good on her skin, and she allowed her hands to roll, stretch and form it in any way that felt right.

She thought about what had happened with George that day and tried to make sense of it. She was very attracted to him and found him thoughtful, kind and decent. She also believed that the events of the day were as much a surprise to him as they were to her.

Once they'd found their way back to the road, they'd taken the bus back into town, and he'd treated her to sushi for dinner. Then he'd called a cab for her, paid the driver and asked when he could see her again. They'd agreed to talk on the phone the following day.

Mayzie looked down to see that her hands had formed two intertwined stems that gracefully tapered at the top and held a shallow dish. At the top the tapered endings held a crescent moon above the dish. It looked as though the dish could be giving or accepting an offering. What had she and George just been part of? She felt that it was the will of the grove that had brought them together as much as it was her will or George's. Was that possible? No matter what went on in her mind, in the depth of her being it felt right. If she allowed herself to go with something much bigger than her and George, everything seemed fine.

CHAPTER 142
Big Folding

Tina and Jess sat at Tina's kitchen table folding pamphlets and listening to reggae music. They'd promised their kids they'd help out with the campaign to stop the pipelines.

"Well, 350 down and 250 to go!" laughed Jess as she completed another pile of 10 folders. "I think when we get these done we'll have earned a little treat at the Phoenix, don't you?"

"Yup," Tina said, continuing with her folding.

"How did our kids manage to get us involved with their environmental activities?" asked Jess. "I've got to hand it to them both; they're pretty smooth."

"Yes, they sure are. I bet those persuasive abilities will come in handy when they're all grown up," Tina laughed.

"Could be worse," said Jess. "Our kids are saving the world, and we're helping them, all the while listening to music and looking forward to a visit to the Phoenix as a reward."

The phone rang, and Tina picked it up. "Hey, Velvet. What's up?" asked Tina, having recognized the number on the call display.

"Mom, you and Jess can stop folding!" Velvet shouted into the phone excitedly. It was hard to hear her over the cheering and laughter in the background.

"What? I thought you said this was really important to you," said Tina.

"It was, and I'm so grateful for your and Jess's help, but everything's changed, and we won't need those brochures anymore," Velvet laughed. "You won't believe it!"

"Believe what?" exclaimed Tina, her skin prickling.

"Turn on the radio, okay? It's all over the news," said Velvet in that self-assured voice teenagers sometimes use with their parents. Then she hung up.

Tina turned on the radio and heard people talking excitedly. The interviewer said, "So after crunching the numbers, your corporation realized that the costs of extracting dirty oil outweighed the benefits, and now you're switching to producing clean technologies instead. Have I gotten that right?"

"Yes, that's right, Maria," said a man. "After all, our company already owns the largest solar-panel-production factory in the world and the second-largest wind-power-generation factory. But we're actually going a step further. We're lobbying governments around the world to stop subsidizing oil, gas, coal and nuclear energy—in other words, energy that has caused a lot of environmental harm—and are urging them to subsidize clean energy instead.

"It's not just the numbers, either. All of us have families, and we're personally invested in our communities and the health of our planet too. In our company lunchroom on Friday, I overheard some of our employees talking about their conversations with their teenagers at home—what their kids thought of the way their parents were making a living and the consequences to the environment, that sort of thing. My daughter had just had a similar conversation with me the night before. At some point, we have to really hear and respond to a different point of view, and I feel we've reached that time.

"Later that afternoon, we had an executive meeting and were brainstorming what to do about some of the tough issues we're facing: First Nations are exercising their legal rights to stop the project; affected communities are rejecting our proposals for pipelines and tankers outright; a number of environmental organizations are taking us to court; protesters are getting arrested; universities are divesting. There's even a group organizing a referendum to vote on whether or not to allow pipelines and tankers on the coast. On top of that we've had a couple of unexpected capital costs. Cleaning up damage from spills is not only costly but also causes irreparable damage to the environment."

"It sounds like that project has a lot of strikes against it, Al," Maria said.

"So true, and our traditional approach has been to keep on fighting. Anyway, as we were brainstorming, I thought, *Why not?* and threw out the suggestion that we take a whole new direction with solar and wind power instead. At first there was a stunned silence—what I'd said was, well, unthinkable. Then our chief financial officer spoke up and said that he'd, in fact, crunched the numbers for exactly what I was saying but had been reticent to share them. He also added that each year the numbers for oil would get worse, not better. There's an incrementally increasing carbon tax here in this province where the pipelines were supposed to be built, and greener technologies are being adopted at an unprecedented rate. Anyway, he gave us an overview, and the numbers were compelling."

"So he'd been thinking along the same lines but was afraid to go against the dominant culture," Maria paraphrased.

"Yes, exactly. As it turned out, once the ice was broken, there was so much enthusiasm in the room; it was breathtaking. I'm so glad that I went ahead and put the idea out there. You know, if I hadn't, we would have had key people—our best and brightest—with this idea in the back of their minds feeling like they had no other choice but to keep ramming this thing through. Now we've got their wholehearted commitment to a new direction that will truly produce wins for everyone: it'll create employment; shareholders will maximize earnings while minimizing risks; we'll be able to employ people in local communities, including First Nations communities; and most importantly, we'll be restoring our environment, on which we all depend, as my daughter, Jewel, keeps reminding me."

"And she really sounds like a jewel, Al. I'm sure millions of people are incredibly grateful that she spoke up and influenced you as she did," Maria said.

"She certainly is a jewel," Al said. "And to make the most of our commitment, we're starting by restoring the tar sands."

"I can just hear our listeners' cheers in response to that statement. What a profoundly practical and symbolic gesture!"

"As I'm sure you and your listeners know, the tar sands is the biggest energy project in the world and, sadly, has been dubbed the most destructive project on earth." Al sighed and stopped for a moment. "Sorry, Maria. Just last week, I was doing all I could to push this through, and I feel pretty emotional still about this change in direction."

"What are you feeling?" asked Maria.

"Remorse. Guilt. Like, what took us so long to see the elephant in the room, you know?" Al said. "Sometimes we become so entrenched in the way we see things, we can't see other possibilities or concerns. I'm a different person from the person I was last week."

"What's that like?"

"It feels wild and wonderful! And at the same time, what we're doing is completely responsible and a good business decision, good for our corporation and for the whole world," Al said. "What's most exciting is the precedent we're setting, because other large energy producers are probably going through the same things. And governments as well: they use their citizens' tax dollars to subsidize a lot of things that harm our environment. The vehicles for doing this are international trade deals, and, like us, the parties involved have just been doing things the same way for a long, long time. I know there are individuals who participate at this level who have the same kinds of reservations I had, and I truly hope our actions give them the inspiration, courage and leverage they need to make the big changes that will serve our planet and everyone on it."

"Al, thanks for coming into the studio today and sharing this, I have to say, revolutionary news," said Maria. "We have just a few moments left. Is there anything you want to say before you go?"

"Yes, thanks for having me, Maria," said Al. "I just want to invite everyone who can make it to the ceremony we'll be having at the tar sands. We'll be celebrating our change in direction and the beginning of the restoration of that region. We're inviting people to come and plant a tree and to learn more about what steps we'll be taking to clean up the land, water and air in our transition to clean energy. And there'll be food, music and much merriment."

Tina turned off the radio. "Can you believe it? No tar sands means no pipelines."

The two women looked at each other, both with tears in their eyes. "That's incredible! And I had no idea that I'd have such a strong emotional reaction," said Jess. "I guess the tar sands has been one of those things that's been around for so long that this news is more than we even allowed ourselves to dream of."

"This is a real turning point for humanity," said Tina. She threw a handful of brochures up in the air and said, "Let's find that party!"

She phoned Velvet back. "Hi, hon," said Tina. "Where's the party? We're coming over!" She could hear whoops and laughter in the background as Velvet gave her directions to the house party.

"Let's stop at the Phoenix on the way and pick up some treats!" said Jess.

CHAPTER 143

Reconnecting

George called Mayzie and asked, "Did you hear the incredible news on the radio?"

"About the tar sands? Yes! Isn't that amazing?!" she said. "Never in my wildest dreams would I have imagined seeing the company shut them down, restore them and switch to clean energy."

"And this is just the beginning! Imagine what else is going to happen! I can picture the end of fracking, of GMOs—I can even imagine a change in the way international business is conducted. I know these people, and they're highly competitive. They'll be trying to outdo each other to see who can score the most points."

"It's the beginning of the end and the beginning of the beginning too!" Mayzie laughed. "Anyway, I should get back to work. See you at four at the Love Bite?"

"Okay, see you then. Have a wonderful day in the meantime."

"You too!" she said smiling.

She felt as if she was in a dream as she floated through the rest of her day. George, the news about the tar sands, the amazing people she was working with. It was almost as though she wasn't working at all, just spending time with friends taking care of each other.

Later that morning, she sat down with Alice.

"I started to resolve some deeply personal issues in the art room last night with the help of my butterfly and was able to sleep well," Alice said. "I understand some things I need in a relationship that I'll be sure to look for next time around."

"I'd love to hear them, if you're comfortable sharing," said Mayzie.

"Well, I think, like lots of us here, I'm quick to rescue people when I know they're suffering, and sometimes that blinds me to other things. Anyway, I thought about the relationship that landed me here and realized that I would never have been able to have a healthy relationship with that man. There were some essential qualities missing, namely respect, trust and deep caring," said Alice. "Those three things will be the criteria for any future relationship I have. Oddly enough, those qualities abound in my friendships and with family members I'm close to."

They looked up and saw a butterfly flutter past their window, as if to bring the point home. They both laughed at the coincidence.

"Thanks for those timely words of wisdom," said Mayzie. "I just got involved with George—remember the guy who came to the booth at the market a couple of weekends ago and was working with the butterfly?"

"Yes," said Alice, "the one with the British accent. He seemed like a lovely guy."

"I'm glad you think so," said Mayzie. "Everything happened so quickly, and it surprised both of us. Anyway, he's taking me out for dinner tonight."

"Mayzie, that's wonderful!" said Alice, putting her hand over Mayzie's. "I'm really happy for you, and I get a good feeling about him."

"That's great to hear," sighed Mayzie. "I'm sure you can understand how easy it is to second-guess our own judgement when we've been through the kinds of experiences that got us into this place. Anyway, I feel like getting at some of those weeds in the garden. Want to join me?"

They went outside to the garden where the sun was shining and there was a gentle breeze.

Four rolled around quickly. Mayzie walked down to the Love Bite and saw George pull up in a yellow car. She walked over to him.

George got out of the car, walked over to Mayzie, held her hand and gazed into her eyes. "So good to see you again!" he said.

She couldn't help but smile. "Good to see you again too," she said. Then she strolled toward the car, and he opened the passenger seat door for her.

Inside the car, it looked and smelled brand new. "Is this a new car?" she asked.

"Yes, I just bought it. It's a Tesla," he answered proudly.

"A Tesla," Mayzie repeated. "Isn't that an electric car?"

"It is, in fact," said George. "I don't understand what happened yesterday, but I'm feeling this incredible pull to be part of the solution the world needs. This car represents part of my commitment." He pulled away from the curb and got onto the main highway.

"That's wonderful!" said Mayzie. "Taking those kinds of concrete actions is so important. This is the quietest car I've ever ridden in."

"It's almost eerie, isn't?" said George.

"A little, but I love it!"

They sat back enjoying the experience for a while as the yellow car wove along the highway in the sunshine through the tall trees.

"I heard there's a new restaurant out by where we went hiking called the Phoenix. Have you heard of it?" George broke the silence.

"I've heard good things about it but haven't tried it yet," Mayzie said.

"Do you feel like giving it a try?"

"Sure, I'd love to!" Mayzie smiled, feeling relaxed and content and exhilarated.

They quickly passed through town and found themselves on the bus route they'd been on the day before and went down the scenic road that wove its way along the shore of the lake.

"No matter how many times I take this drive, the scenery always takes my breath away," said Mayzie.

An hour later, they found themselves turning into Amaranth. As they drove along the main street, a small lavender building caught their eye.

"I see what they mean when people say it stands out," laughed Mayzie.

"It certainly does," George said. "It comes highly recommended." George found a parking spot, and the two of them got out.

CHAPTER 144

An Enchanted Evening

As they entered the restaurant, a server with an infectious smile said, "Welcome to the Phoenix," and, looking at each of them, asked, "Table for two?"

"Yes, please," said George, smiling back.

Their server led them through a restaurant that was about three-quarters full to a private table. On the side of the table against the wall was a flowering geranium, and in the centre of the table was a candle. The server pulled out the chair for Mayzie, and George took a seat across from her.

Mayzie ordered the special, which was locally picked mushrooms on a bed of quinoa with locally grown greens. George decided on a stir-fry with pecans. For dessert they ordered strawberry shortcake and a banana split to share. They each ordered a glass of red wine and had a leisurely dinner enjoying the fine meal. They chatted easily over their dinner.

"So I did a bit of snooping on the Internet to see if I could find anything out about the tree house we discovered and found nothing at all," said George. "Do you have any ideas?"

Mayzie thought for a moment and then said, "This region has an interesting history. A lot of draft dodgers from the United States found their way here in the sixties, so one of them could have built it as a place to hide out."

"That sounds like a possibility," said George.

"Doukhobors settled here in the early 1900s, and there was a Japanese internment camp in the area during the Second World War, so maybe someone from one of those groups built it."

"That's quite the history for a sleepy little region," said George. "From the looks of it, the 1960s seems like the most likely timeframe out of those three, but remind me who the Doukhobors were again."

"They're a Christian sect from Russia who came to Canada to escape persecution."

"Are they still around?"

"Oh, yeah, lots of them. Every third or fourth person you meet here. I have lots of Doukhobor friends," said Mayzie. "The people who've been here the longest are the Aboriginal people. The Department of Indian and Northern Affairs have declared them extinct, but they still live here."

"How can they be extinct if they still live here?"

"Good question," said Mayzie, "but a question the federal government didn't bother to ask."

"You've been a much better source of information than the Internet," George laughed.

Their server came by to ask how everything was, and both George and Mayzie nodded and smiled enthusiastically. "Everything is perfect!" said Mayzie.

On their way out, they thanked their server again and went back to George's car. It was still fairly light out. When they got into the car, Mayzie leaned over and kissed George on the cheek. "Thanks so much for a lovely dinner. That was really special."

"It was my pleasure. We sure lucked out with that place, didn't we? I'd heard it was good but had no idea it was that good," George said, and then he added, "Would you mind exploring with me a little bit? I'd like to see if there are some roads near the tree house we found yesterday. I'm still fascinated by the area and would love to know more about it."

"It was fascinating, wasn't it? I'm intrigued too," said Mayzie. "I'd be happy to scout around a little bit."

CHAPTER 145

Driving Home

They drove slowly down the highway back toward town, looking along the side of the road for the trail they'd taken.

As they sailed down the highway in the silence of George's new car, Mayzie said, "George, with your background, I'd love to hear your perspective on what will probably happen next after this turn of events with the tar sands."

George guffawed. "Well, right now the people I know will be in shock, and they'll be hopping mad," he said. "Then probably by tomorrow they'll be scrambling, trying to figure out what to do."

"What do you think they'll do in the next couple of days?"

"Lots of talking, for one thing," George said. "For them, it'll be as though the sky is falling. They'll avoid the press at all costs for a couple of days, until they've thought up a strategy. Who knows what that might be." George sounded a little worried. "Then again, they just might come around. What's just happened is hard to ignore, and they may see the sense of it. It's hard to say." George chuckled. "Anyway, I'm glad to be here and not there right now."

The sun was slowly fading, and as they got closer to town, they realized they'd missed the trail they'd taken at the side of the road.

"Doing a bit of sleuthing might make a fun project for another day," said George. "Would you like to stop somewhere and listen to some music?"

"I think I can hear some music coming from the park. I bet there's a celebration over the news of the tar sands. Want to check it out?" asked Mayzie.

"Yes, let's," George replied and drove toward the park. They could hear some funky music and cheering. When they were within walking distance, George parked the car. As they approached the park, they could see a bandstand with musicians playing, lots of people dancing with abandon and children running around giving spontaneous whoops of joy.

They were infected by the celebratory mood and joined in, dancing until the band took a break.

"How are you feeling?" George asked. "Would you like to stay awhile, or do you need to get back?"

"Well, I'd love to stay, but I'm getting a little tired. And I have to work in the morning," said Mayzie.

"Okay, I'll call you a cab," said George, getting his cellphone out of his pocket. "Thanks so much for coming out with me, Mayzie. I'm so happy to be getting to know you. For me, the time we spend together is magical."

"I know what you mean. It is for me too. You're so kind and understanding," Mayzie said. "Thanks for a wonderful evening."

"Let's keep in touch over the week, and maybe we can plan something for the weekend," George suggested.

"I have the market again from ten until three on Saturday, but other than that I'm free."

"Okay, let's see if we can think of something fun to do. Maybe we can find that trail again and see if there's a road nearby."

Mayzie's cab pulled up, and George opened the door for her. She turned to George and kissed him. "Thanks so much, George. I look forward to seeing you again soon."

George kissed her lightly on the lips. "An absolute pleasure, Mayzie. I'll call you soon."

Mayzie sat down in the cab and waved at George before closing her door.

CHAPTER 146

Hearts

Ross was sitting in a chair in the waiting room. Cole came out of Donny's room and into the waiting area. "How's he doing?" Ross asked, getting up and walking over to Cole.

"Not so good," Cole replied.

Ross winced. "Ooh, that's rough. How are you doing?"

"I didn't sleep very well last night and had a long day at work," said Cole. "Pretty tired, actually. How about you?"

"Doing well. Life is good," said Ross, walking toward Donny's hospital room. "I hope you get a good sleep tonight. Anyway, I'm going to go in and say hi to Donny. See you."

"Yeah, see you," said Cole, walking toward the exit.

"Hey, Donny. How're you doing?" Ross asked as he stood beside Donny's hospital bed.

"Been better, Ross. Thanks for coming by to see me," said Donny. Ross was disturbed to see Donny looking so pale and weak. Donny continued, "They have me on a waiting list to get double bypass surgery."

"Ooh," said Ross, not knowing what else to say. "Is that your only option? What about dietary changes to bring down your cholesterol?"

"I don't know. Do you think that really works?" asked Donny. "Bad hearts run in my family. I don't know if diet would change anything."

"Well, if you decide you want to try, I might be able to help. Just let me know, okay?"

"Okay, I'll keep it in mind," Donny said. "How're you these days?"

"Same old. Still with Dagmar, doing the SPIN farm thing, enjoying life," said Ross.

"You're looking good," said Donny, looking closely at his friend.

"Thanks," said Ross, wishing he could return the compliment. "Anyway, I'll let you get some rest. Nice to see you. Take care of yourself, eh?"

"Thanks," answered Donny in a weak voice. "I'll try."

Ross left the room with a heavy heart. It was hard seeing his friend this way.

CHAPTER 147

A Glass of Wine

Leroy and Dan had come home early from the celebrations at the park, leaving the rest of the group to sing and dance the night away. They both still had limited tolerance for crowds after Mel's passing. It felt good to be sitting in the quiet of the living room.

"Glass of wine?" Leroy asked Dan.

"Sure, that would be nice," Dan said, heaving a sigh.

"I know how you feel," Leroy said as he opened the bottle of red wine and poured a glass for each of them.

"It's tough, isn't it?" said Dan in a conspiratorial tone. "Sometimes the pain is just ... overwhelming." His voice choked.

"Sure is." Leroy raised his glass to Dan and said, "To Mom, wherever you are."

"To Mel, and I'm sure you're not so far away," said Dan, clinking his glass against Leroy's. "I often feel like she's in the house with me or that she'll be walking through the door any moment. A part of me just can't believe she's not here anymore. I want to share what just happened with her. She'd be so excited about restoring the tar sands."

"I know what you mean," said Leroy. "At some level it just makes no sense at all, does it? I keep dreaming about her and feeling like I'm missing what she wants to say to me ..."

"She loved you so much," said Dan. "Wherever she is, I bet she misses you like crazy. Maybe it's her only way of being with you."

"Maybe I'm not looking for the right thing," said Leroy, excited to share the revelation he was having. "Lydia said something about that one morning too. Maybe instead of listening for a message, I need to just be grateful that I'm getting to be with Mom again in my dreams."

"Yeah, sometimes the way we look at things makes all the difference in the world, doesn't it?" Dan said. He took another sip of wine. "This is nice wine. I'm so glad we came back and are here now, talking about Mel. It feels good to be with you, since we share a similar depth of grief."

"I know she'd be happy that we're helping each other through this," said Leroy. "She'd want that for both of us. Mom was so grateful to have you in her life, and I was really glad for her. Thanks for being so good to her."

"It was a joy and a privilege," Dan said. "I felt like I was living in an enchanted world with your mom. She was always making something beautiful or doing something nice for someone. Her being in the world made it a better place, and I'm grateful to have been a part of all that."

"I feel so lucky she was my mother," said Leroy, taking a sip of his wine. "Would you like a little more wine?"

"Sure, I'd love some," Dan said. Leroy filled Dan's glass. Dan was momentarily absorbed in the wine's beautiful burgundy colour and then said, "I see so much of her in you. Just the way you are is such a reflection of her influence."

"Thanks, Dan. I appreciate hearing that," said Leroy, going into the kitchen. "I'll be right back. I'm just going to get us a few snacks." A few minutes later he came back with a plate of crackers, guacamole, olives and sliced veggies.

"This is lovely," said Dan. "Thanks for taking such good care of me."

"I am my mother's son, after all," Leroy quipped, dipping a piece of cauliflower into the guacamole.

"She'd be proud!" Dan smiled. "And she'd be so happy that life is going well for you. She'd love the SPIN farm and the people you're sharing this place with and the whole life that you've created. Of course, she always adored Lydia. They're very similar: both so creative and caring. You've done well, Leroy, and I appreciate how you've shared your life with me."

"Anytime you want to spend time with us, you know you're welcome to. I feel like I've just been coasting on everyone else's great energy these past few months, but I know the people I share this house with would be happy to have you around," Leroy said.

Dan paused for a moment, then said, "I think I'm ready for some alone time in the house where we lived. Jim really cushioned the most difficult time, but sometimes I feel overwhelmed and can't seem to absorb what other people are saying. I just can't seem to respond. Know what I mean?"

"Yeah, I know. Sometimes pain takes up my whole field of awareness, and I'm not able to respond properly either."

Dan said, "Being here with you is great. But I think I need to just let everything sink in, come to terms with life. I don't know … I appreciate knowing that I can always come and stay with you, and I know I'll take you up on it sometime. Thanks. I hope you and your friends know you always have a place to stay in Vancouver."

"Thanks. It's nice to be keeping Mom alive by helping each other," said Leroy. "We're doing what she did for each of us."

"Yeah, that's true," Dan laughed, finishing his wine. "Anyway, I need to hit the hay," he said, getting up. "Good night, Leroy. Thanks for a great evening. It was just what I needed." He walked over to Leroy, who had also gotten up, and gave him a big hug, which Leroy returned warmly.

"Good night," Leroy said. "Get a good sleep."

"Thanks. You too," said Dan as he wandered off to bed.

There was a small amount of wine left in the bottle, so Leroy poured it into his glass, then finished the plate of food in front of him. The dancing and his conversation with Dan earlier that evening had left him hungry.

He sat staring at the ceiling for a while, sipping his wine and taking in what they'd just talked about. He was moved that Dan had shared the intensity of his emotional pain and felt somehow nourished by the experience. He wondered if his mom was with them in some way he didn't understand.

Leroy cleaned up the few dishes and got ready for bed. As soon as his head hit the pillow, he fell into a deep sleep.

CHAPTER 148

New Growth

Liam put on the kettle and made a pot of tea. He walked over to Phoebe and gave her a kiss on the cheek. She turned around on her chair and smiled at him. "You always surprise me," she said and snuggled her head against his arm. He stroked her hair.

"Phoebe, I know we're going to be as busy as all hell, but I'm so happy to be working with you, to just be with you," he said.

"I'm really glad," she said. "I bless my lucky stars for you all the time. You're so sweet."

"Little did I know that when I had my bedroom refurbished, I'd get much more than what I'd bargained for." Liam smirked, bringing them each a cup of tea.

"Is that right?" Phoebe giggled, raising her eyebrows. "You didn't have anything up your sleeve?"

Liam blushed. "Well, maybe just a little." They both laughed.

Sipping on their cups of tea, Phoebe said, "Just think of everyone else who's been doing what we do for so many years, struggling to get by, feeling like we're working within a tiny niche. That's all going to change. We, and everyone else working to create environmentally friendly homes, are going to be run off our feet. We're going to have to train a lot of people. Our suppliers are going to be producing full throttle. It's so great that reducing greenhouse gases this way will be such a strong driver for our economy."

"A week ago I wouldn't have dreamt this was possible," Liam said. "It's amazing how quickly things can change, isn't it?"

"It sure is," Phoebe said. "How many years have we been plugging away? Now suddenly we're going to be in high demand. First the credit union's granting policy for these kinds of upgrades, now the restoration of the tar sands. It's like someone just flipped a switch, and we're moving in a new direction."

"It took a while, but look at the bright side: it's a good thing we've had all this time to develop relationships with contractors, find reliable sources of materials and establish some protocols," said Liam. "All that time we were plugging away, we were getting things ready for what's to come. There's something to be said about the timing."

"You're right," Phoebe said. "We've been laying the foundation, and it's a good thing we've had the time to get it right."

They finished their tea and rinsed out their cups. "Let's go settle into that beautiful bedroom of yours, shall we?" said Phoebe. They walked into the sitting room that adjoined the sleeping area.

"You know, this is such a pleasant space with the wicker furniture and the plants; it would be nice to use it more," Phoebe said.

"Actually, why don't we sit here for a few minutes before bed? There's something I'd like to run by you," Liam said, taking a seat in one of the wicker chairs.

Phoebe sat across from him. "What's on your mind?" she asked.

"I've been thinking about that local currency that Dagmar and her friends use and toying with the idea of accepting it for the work I do," he said. "And I'd like to get your thoughts."

"Funny, I've been mulling over the same thing," said Phoebe. "From my understanding, it helps to keep money in the community so stimulates the local economy. Transport generates a lot of greenhouse gas emissions, so it would be great to have that extra economic incentive to source locally."

"That's my feeling about it too. It's such a concrete commitment to our values," said Liam.

"Thanks for bringing it up. I'd like to participate as well. It makes so much sense." She smiled at Liam. "This is the perfect spot for these kinds of conversations—those issues we just need to bounce off each other, to see if they hold water. Slightly more intimate than sitting around the kitchen table."

"And there's no one I'd rather share it with," said Liam. "Anyway, I'm ready for bed. How about you?"

"Yup, me too," Phoebe said, getting up and walking toward the bed. Liam stood up and surveyed his sitting room appreciatively before joining her.

CHAPTER 149

The Search

After an early dinner at the Love Bite, George and Mayzie drove down the road the bus had taken to see if they could find the path to the tree house.

"Look!" said Mayzie. "There's the way to the beach on the other side of the road. Wasn't it just past here?"

George slowed down and found the spot where the trail began. "Let's see if there's a road close by and scope out the area around it, shall we?" he said.

They drove slowly for a while; then, when they didn't see a road, they turned around to see if they could find one in the other direction before the spot where the trail began. About a mile ahead, they saw a road that went up the hill and took it. The road was quite narrow and winding, and it was hard to tell if they were getting closer to the tree house or not. Eventually, they came to a small house with a large garden at the side of the road. George stopped the car.

"Maybe we should knock on the door and ask whoever lives here if they know how to get to the tree house," said Mayzie.

"I'd rather keep it a secret," said George. "I wonder what we should ask. Maybe if there are any roads going in its direction?"

"That sounds reasonable to me," Mayzie said. They got up and walked over to the house. George knocked on the door.

A few minutes later, an elderly bearded man answered. "Hello," he said. "Is there something I can help you with?"

"Yes, as a matter of fact," George said. "We're wondering if there are any roads that will take us in that direction." He pointed in the general direction of the tree house.

"Well, if you follow the road you're on, it makes a wide arc away from that area. The only way to get into that area is by hiking," he said. "It's worth the hike, though. You'll come across a beautiful old-growth forest, and it's rumoured that there's a sacred oak grove in there somewhere, although no one I know has ever seen it. Who knows where these stories come from?"

"Well, thanks very much for letting us know," said Mayzie. "It's a beautiful area."

"Oh, yes," he said, "it's worth exploring, and I'm sure you'll find it worth your time to take a good look."

"Thanks again for your help. Bye now," said George, heading back to the car.

"Goodbye," said the man, shutting the door.

"A sacred oak grove," Mayzie said as they got in the car. "Isn't it something that no one he knows has actually seen it?"

"It sure is," said George. "We seem to have stumbled upon a very special spot."

"Stumbled upon—or were drawn to …"

"Yes, maybe we were meant to be there," George said. "The further we drive along this road the more distant the place feels. Shall we turn around and go back to the highway?"

"You know, that might be the best thing to do," said Mayzie. "It's getting a little late in the day. Maybe we should come back in the morning so we'll have more time to explore. What do you think?"

As he turned the car around, George sighed. "You're probably right. Can I pick you up tomorrow morning bright and early?"

"Sure," said Mayzie, "I'll pack us a lunch, and hopefully we'll find the tree house so we can eat it there."

They wound their way down the narrow road until they got to the highway and then drove into town.

CHAPTER 150

Coming Back to Life

Leroy put his arm around Lydia and lay there in bed contentedly. It was early, and the first light of dawn peeked through the top of the draperies.

Dan had gone home a few days earlier, and Leroy thought about the time they'd spent together. He kept coming back to the conversation they'd had over glasses of wine and the thoughts they'd shared about his mother.

This time his dream had been different and had left him feeling happy and at peace. He soaked the feeling in, grateful for everything he was experiencing.

When Lydia woke up, she gave him a kiss on the cheek and asked softly, "Did you sleep well?"

"Yes, I did," Leroy said. "And I dreamt about Mom."

"Really?" said Lydia. "What happened?"

"Well, we were sitting in her kitchen, talking and laughing. She was in a good mood and looking great," said Leroy. "And as she was talking, I realized that I was dreaming and felt so lucky to be with her again."

"Wow! What a change!" Lydia said, stroking his chest. "You sound better than you have for a long time. I'm so glad things seem to be shifting."

"Me too. Thanks for sticking it out with me," Leroy said, stroking her hair. "I think the visit with Dan really helped me. I'll give him a call later today and see how he's doing."

"Welcome back, sweetie," Lydia whispered, stroking his cheek. "It feels like you're slowly coming back to life."

"I know there'll be ups and downs still, but I'm starting to feel better. Just the way Mom would want me to," he said.

"She always cared deeply about your happiness, and I'm sure it would mean so much to her to know you're starting to feel better," Lydia said.

Leroy let out a grateful sigh as he lay in this delicious place that was his life.

CHAPTER 151

Revved Up

T am carried a couple of bags of produce into the kitchen of the food bank and noticed that the place felt revved up. Mary was moving easily as she prepared things on the stove—no sign of the sciatica that had been slowing her down. "Hey, Mary. How're you doing?" asked Tam.

"Great!" Mary answered. "There's less of a demand for food and more food itself. This place is humming!"

"I noticed that as soon as I came in," he said, putting the bags of produce on the counter. "The gardens are just bursting, so I'm happy to pass some of this along to you."

"And thanks so much for that," Mary said.

"So what do you think's brought on this turn of events?" Tam asked with interest.

"Well, a number of things," said Mary thoughtfully. "First of all, the community currency's really picked things up. Here's some for you, for the produce." She handed him a twenty-dollar community-currency bill. "Then with the green initiatives the credit union started, there's more work, so a lot of the people who were here now have jobs. And it feels like the economy's changing somehow; with these shifts, there's a new feeling of optimism. We now have a reason to be hopeful—a feeling I thought we'd lost sight of. Suddenly it feels like anything's possible."

"It's great, isn't?" Tam said. "We need hope and the promise of a better future. No matter who we are, I think the need to leave our children a better world is primal. Losing sight of that has been a sickness, and maybe we're starting to recover. We're becoming rich in these beautiful feelings that were all but lost not so long ago."

"I know what you mean," said Mary. "I once heard someone say that they thought the human race was suffering from a kind of collective post-traumatic stress disorder. Maybe that's true. How else could we be capable of putting profit before absolutely everything else, like the well-being of others and the condition of our planet?"

"Thanks for the local currency, by the way," said Tam.

Mary smiled. "Amazing how altruism and generosity can be built into something so seemingly inert, isn't it?"

"Sure is," Tam said. "It makes you look at everything differently: the way money works, the way all kinds of things work. What do they serve? Who do they benefit?"

"Questions worth asking; that's for sure," said Mary.

"Anyway, I'm glad things are going well for you. See you again soon," Tam said as he headed for the door.

"Bye, Tam. Always good to see you," Mary called after him.

CHAPTER 152

Heart Health

Ross walked through the door of Donny and Cole's place with a couple of bags of groceries, which he put on the kitchen table. His two friends were seated at either side of the table. "Hey, how's it going?" he asked.

"Pretty good," said Cole. "Thanks for bringing this stuff over. Sheesh! It's feast or famine lately. First the road was closed, and we couldn't get a lot food from the store; now we're back to normal, and you're bringing more food."

"Yeah, thanks for coming over to give a demo," said Donny. "I'm still a little weak, but I'm interested in looking at dietary alternatives to getting a double bypass."

"Hey, my pleasure," Ross said, taking things out of the grocery bags. "Here's a really basic vegan cookbook. It has some simple recipes for good, wholesome foods that will help to unclog those arteries of yours. I've got to tell you though that all that gunk—toxins and everything—gets released from your system when you first start eating like this, and it makes you feel kind of crappy for a few weeks. But then afterwards you'll begin to feel much, much better. So don't give up at the beginning, okay?"

"Okay," said Donny, "I'll keep that in mind. Do you ever get cravings for meat?"

"Nope," Ross said. "There's so much delicious vegan food, and I feel great after eating it. The surprising one is the dairy. It's so congesting. Just the thought of it grosses me out now, whereas before I thought it was absolutely necessary."

"You mean it's not?" asked Cole. "How do you get your calcium?"

"Leafy greens, sesame seeds, almonds—there's even calcium in oranges. And our bodies absorb calcium from plant-based sources more easily," Ross said.

Ross reached into another bag. "I brought you some greens from my garden: spinach, kale, arugula, and this is lamb's quarters, which is actually a weed, but it's more nutritious than spinach. So if you see it growing in a clean place, please pick it and bring it home! You'll be doing some weeding and getting a great food source. That goes for dandelion leaves too, although it's best to pick them when they're young and tender; otherwise they are quite bitter. They're loaded with calcium."

Ross then pulled out bags of rice, lentils, barley and some small, red beans. "These are all really filling and super easy to cook," he said. "You cook most grains, like rice and barley, two parts water to one part grain. I like to toast them a little first to bring out the flavour. You toast 'em, put 'em on low heat for about half an hour or 45 minutes and presto! You've got your cooked rice or barley."

"That sounds nice and simple," said Cole, "but kind of boring."

"That's what herbs, spices, miso and veggies are for," Ross said. "But let's get back to the lentils and beans. I like to toast them a little first too and then add boiling water as needed to just cover them. It might be a little more than two to one for the water. I just have a kettle of boiling water on the stove and add it as needed until they're cooked. Then you cook some veggies, add them to the soup with some spices, make a soup base out of miso and presto! You've got soup."

"What's miso?" asked Donny.

"It's a soup base made from fermented grains, so it's really good for you," Ross said.

"Sounds gross," said Cole.

"We drink beer, and that's fermented. Miso's a kind of salty paste you mix with water, tamari and herbs to make into a soup base, but you add it at the very end to keep the beneficial bacteria and enzymes in it alive," Ross explained.

"Beneficial enzymes?" Cole repeated. "What do they do exactly?"

265

"They're a digestive aid, and they strengthen our immune system and add vitamins to our diet," said Ross. "Would you like to make a simple lentil soup right now? I have all the ingredients."

"Sure," said Donny.

Ross showed them how to make a basic lentil soup, toasting the lentils first, then continually adding water just to cover the other ingredients. He added root vegetables like potatoes and carrots, so they could soften up with the lentils. Once they'd cooked for a while, he quickly fried some onions, mushrooms and celery in balsamic vinegar, tamari and herbs. He then added frozen peas and made up a paste of miso, tamari and herbs and added it to the soup. He took the pot off the burner and put the lid on.

He went over to the bags on the table and said, "Oatmeal's nice for breakfast." He pulled out a bag of oatmeal and a bag of raisins. "You just add boiling water to the oatmeal and raisins, let it cook, add a sliced banana and sprinkle some cinnamon on it. That's it."

"I used to have it that way when I was growing up sometimes," said Donny. "I got out of the habit but remember that it was a nice way to start the morning."

"Speaking of breakfast, what about my morning coffee? Is that still okay?" asked Donny, looking concerned.

"From what I understand the coffee itself is fine, just no cream or refined sugar, but you should check with a health professional," Ross said. He added, "Another note on foods: it's really important to get organically grown foods and foods that don't contain genetically modified organisms. They're just so much better for your health! We put in bulk food orders so we can get them wholesale, and you're welcome to join us any time you want."

"We'll keep that in mind," said Cole. "Isn't it expensive to eat that way?"

"It's actually a lot less expensive when you consider that you're no longer buying meat or dairy products or over packaged, highly processed foods. Those things are all super expensive and hard on our bodies," said Ross.

Donny was making a sour face. "Coffee without cream? That's going to take some getting used to," he said.

"For sure, it will," Ross said, "but give it a week or so, and you might not miss dairy at all. That's what happened to me. When you realize that it's not good for you and just bungs everything up, you physically feel better not having it, and then you lose your taste for it altogether. Why not give it up for a week and see if you miss it?"

"A week's not that long," Donny conceded.

Ross reached into the bag and pulled out a square package of firm-looking stuff that seemed to be made of compressed beans. "This is tempeh and is a really healthy source of protein. It's fermented so gives you the added health benefits of fermented foods. Nuts and nut butters like peanut butters are also great sources of protein. But if you get peanut butter, please make sure it's organically grown. If it's not, it's just loaded with pesticides and herbicides. It's the only crop that can be rotated with cotton, which is grown with more chemicals than any other plant," Ross cautioned.

"Where did you learn all this stuff?" asked Cole.

"Friends, the market, the Internet—I don't know. Since I've been eating this way, it's just interesting to me; it's almost like osmosis. I seem to pick it up from lots of different places," Ross said.

Cole looked closely at Ross and realized that he looked pretty good compared to him and Donny. "That diet of yours seems to have helped you," Cole said.

"Oh, yeah, I can't imagine eating any differently now," Ross said. "Anyway, the soup's done. Do you feel like having a bowl?"

"Sure," said Donny.

"Yeah, I'd love to give it a try," said Cole. He went over to the pot and ladled out a bowl for each of them.

Donny took a tentative taste. "Hey, this is pretty good," he said. "Needs a bit of salt, though."

Ross handed him the tamari. "Just add some of this," he said.

Donny added the tamari and then said, "That's better."

Cole took a taste, added some tamari and said, "Hey, this is quite nice."

"I'm glad you like it," said Ross between mouthfuls of soup. "This is one of my favourites."

When they'd finished, Ross said, "Okay, I'm leaving the cookbook and these ingredients here for you. If you have any questions or want to order some food with us, just give me a call, okay?"

"Okay, thanks for coming by and giving us a lesson in heart-healthy cooking," said Donny. "If it can help me avoid getting a double bypass, I'm happy to give this a try."

"Worth a shot, eh?" Ross said.

"Hey, thanks, Ross," said Cole. "That was nice of you to bring all this food and the cookbook and show us how to prepare it. I look forward to experimenting a bit."

"My pleasure, you guys," Ross said, getting up from the table. "Stick with it, and I bet you'll feel way better. Bye for now."

They waved goodbye as Ross left the house.

CHAPTER 153

Back Again

The next morning, George and Mayzie had an early, quick breakfast at the Love Bite and then went to see if they could find the tree house. Mayzie saw the group who sang on Sunday mornings trickle in and was sorry she'd be missing their performance.

"Okay, I think this is the bus stop where we got off last time we were here," said Mayzie as they drove down the highway. George slowed the car down and found a place to park at the side of the road. They got out and started to walk toward the trail.

"There's the beginning of the trail," said George, and they headed down the trail quickly, retracing their steps to the tree house. They found the big tree with the hardened vines made into steps and climbed up. When they got there, everything was exactly the way they'd left it.

"Looking at it again, my sense is that this place has been abandoned," Mayzie said.

"I get that sense as well," George said. "Even looking at the amount of dust and cobwebs in the corners, it seems like it's been empty for a while. It reaffirms our earlier assessment."

They looked around for a while and revisited all the rooms.

"Do you feel like having a little something to eat and a drink in this lovely sitting room?" Mayzie asked George. "I adore this room! It's such a great place to relax."

"I'm ready for a snack," said George as they strolled together to the sitting room.

Mayzie had a jar of coconut water with fresh berries blended into it; it was a beautiful shade of pink. She got it out, and George went to the kitchen and brought back some cups. After making themselves comfortable, Mayzie poured them each a cup of the mixture.

"This is delightful!" George exclaimed.

"Thanks," said Mayzie. "Fresh raspberries and strawberries blended with coconut water. It's pretty hard to go wrong with those ingredients." She smiled. Then she said, "George, I'm still curious about what the people you grew up with will do now that things are moving in such a different direction."

George smiled and put his head back. "Well, it's hard to say, but, you know, they're human beings just like us. They have kids just like the guy from the tar sands, and they've been going through their own personal healing journeys too." He paused. "I almost wonder if in the back of their minds they've hoped that something like this would happen. I have a cousin who's talked about exchanging his oil stock for renewables but has never gotten to it. This might just push him to do it. And there are others like him too."

"Really?" asked Mayzie, sipping on her drink.

"Yes. Historically, our global economic system has been destroying the planet and concentrating wealth into a few hands. Where I'm from, the people believe in the system because, of course, they're the main beneficiaries of it, and it's drilled into us in every way imaginable," he said. "But in the back of all our minds, we know it can't continue for all kinds of reasons. Periods when wealth has concentrated this way have generally ended badly for everyone, including the people at the top. The grace with which this change has occurred may inspire them to transition gracefully themselves. I mean, their kids are screaming bloody murder too. They want a healthy planet. They don't want people after their heads. They look at the Internet just like everyone else."

"Yeah, we tend to forget that all these systems in place were put there and are maintained by people who, no matter how wealthy and powerful, still have all the things in their lives that everyone else has to deal with," said Mayzie, rifling through her backpack and bringing out fruit, trail mix, peanut butter balls, crackers and guacamole.

"Oh, look what else I found!" she said. "It's the crystal from the oak grove. Now that we've heard that it's a sacred grove, it feels all the more special!" She held it up to the sunlight and admired its pale pink translucence. "Here, do you want to take another look?" she asked George, handing it to him.

"It's a beaut!" he said. He turned it around in the sunlight for about a minute, then handed it back to Mayzie. He took a peanut butter ball she offered. "These are so good!" he said.

Mayzie said, "So what can we ordinary people do to convince the people you grew up with to change course?" she asked, picking up a peanut butter ball and putting it in her mouth.

"Well, money really talks," George said, "so being conscious of what you're supporting when you spend is very effective. More people are catching onto that, I think. Advertising is becoming less effective—maybe there's just too much of it—and more people seem to be paying attention to the consequences of their spending. I find it a more interesting way to buy anyway. What's the story behind the food you're eating or the garment you're wearing? Was the environment harmed in the way it was produced? Were people paid fairly who were involved in growing or creating the product? The whole fair-trade movement took off because it captured people's imaginations and got them thinking along those lines."

"Some of my friends and I have it down to a fine art," said Mayzie. "It has us consuming a lot less. When we run our purchases through that kind of a filter, it makes it hard to impulse buy."

"That's a bonus! I guess on a bigger scale, getting institutions to divest from dirty technologies and arms manufacturing and investing in clean, peaceful technologies has even more of an impact. Banking at credit unions and community banks also helps," said George.

"Check," Mayzie said, pretending to check it off an invisible list. "I've banked at a credit union forever."

George smiled. "Me too! Another thing to do is turn off the TV, be very selective about movies we watch and find trustworthy news sources—I use the Internet. We should consciously write our own narratives to live by and find others who live by similar narratives. I like the ones that value community and co-operation, but often the ones we hear about via mainstream media are individualistic and competitive. They can be fine to a certain degree, but in excess, they don't help to create a caring culture."

"I'm so with you on that one," Mayzie said, "and it often seems like the ones who have the least are the most caring and generous. Funny, isn't it?"

"It is odd. You'd think it would be the other way around. Almost all Aboriginal people have a strong sense of community and care about the welfare of everyone. If the people I know were like that, no one would have a care in the world. We'd have clean, peaceful places to live, lots of great food, a healthy planet and, best of all, the many and varied gifts of people who are just struggling to survive. I sometimes wonder what kinds of music, art and literature we're missing because people haven't had a chance to explore their gifts. We could all be so much richer in that way."

"That's true, isn't it?" said Mayzie. "When we can barely survive or, worse, if we starve to death, no one's ever going to hear the music inside of us or see our uncreated masterpiece. We could all have so much more!"

"Things are changing," said George. "We're really at a point where we have to grow up or die as a species. Literally, the pressure's on. Hopefully our innate desire to survive wins out over the habitual greed that's been drilled into us."

"What about you?" Mayzie looked at him. "You have a perspective that most of us don't. Is there some way you're able to use it to make the world a better place?"

"That's the trillion-dollar question," he laughed. "I think about that constantly and wish I knew what to do." He sighed.

"One thing I'm going to do is spend time here. When I first came to this valley, it was just going to be a short holiday. But I feel like there's so much for me to learn here, like I'm supposed to be in this place. You're a huge part of that and so is the local currency and this tree house and that amazing oak grove … I've never felt more alive, and being here feels so right. If this isn't public land, I'd like to buy this property if I can and make sure it's protected forever, but that's not the end of it. It's like there's something profound I need to learn. Maybe when I learn it, I'll know what I can do to help to change things for the better."

"George, that's wonderful!" Mayzie exclaimed. "I'm honoured to be part of this grand epiphany you're experiencing. It feels magical to me too."

They finished their drinks and decided to head to the sacred grove. George cleaned and put away the cups they'd used, and Mayzie packed up the food and put the crystal in her backpack. Together they left through the door and found their way easily to the grove. When they got there, the sun was shining gently through the swaying branches of the oak trees.

"A totally different feel to the space today, don't you think?" Mayzie said.

"Yes. I feel like it wants something very different from us," said George.

"I'm feeling called to meditate. How about you?"

"Yes, I do too," he said.

They found spots on the mossy ground and sat down. Mayzie dug the crystal out of her backpack and put it in front of them. They closed their eyes and relaxed into a deep meditative state. Whatever they were being called to do, they both knew it would come to them here.

CHAPTER 154

Inspired Gig

The Love Bite was packed that morning, and the singers were still feeling inspired by the news of the tar sands and the change in direction that was taking place. A mood of elation permeated the room.

Ross stood up and said, "How's everyone doing?" and was greeted with cheers. When the cheering had died down a little, he said, "We're feeling the same way. It's not every day that the world takes a whole new direction." There was more cheering.

Lydia stood up and said, "These things don't just happen. People all over the planet are making things like this happen. I know; sometimes it's day in, day out, year in, year out—signing petitions, sharing information, doing what we can and wondering if it has an effect. Thanks to all our hard work, we're finally seeing some change for the better. Thanks to our vision, the future we want is coming about. And if anyone calls you a dreamer, just say thank you; we need great big dreams now more than ever before. Thanks, everyone, for sharing a dream of a peaceful, healthy, happy planet for all of us now and for generations to come! Here's a song we learned for the occasion. It's an old song from Dagmar's music collection that we liked. Some of you might recognize it. This band was popular in this neck of the woods many years ago."

Ross slowly started playing his guitar. Dagmar shook out a gentle rhythm on her shaker. Leroy sang:

> I can make the mountains ring, hear those birdies sing;
> Wind can set the trees to dancing.
> We can sing the sun to shine.

The others joined in.

> Set your mind to glowing.
> Laugh away your troubles; bring out the moonshine.
> Sittin' in a tree, sheltered from the cold of an evening breeze.

A few others in the restaurant joined in.

> You can change the world; set your mind to it, put your heart through it.
> Reach out to what you can find.
> You know where we all belong, so keep on dreamin'. Get yourself strong.

The verses were repeated, and the crowd sang along, swaying to the gentle rhythm.

The group had chosen the happiest, most love-filled songs in their repertoire to celebrate this new time that was upon them. Change was afoot, and they welcomed it. They knew it would benefit everyone, absolutely everyone—no exceptions. Sure, oil companies would lose money on oil, but most of them had also been investing in clean technologies.

As this new momentum of healing took hold, producers of armaments, pesticides and plastics would lose some profits, but they all had research-and-development departments, and the writing had been on the wall for a long time. They'd have to find something more constructive to offer the world.

It was a sunny, jubilant Sunday for all of them. Maude, the owner of the restaurant, was sitting near the back enjoying the performance. They smiled at her, remembering when they'd first sung on the street and she'd invited them to perform here.

In another section of the restaurant they saw Jared, and he was sitting with … Maya! Tam gave her a little wave, and she waved back. He hoped she could see the gratitude in his eyes. The time she'd spent at the mansion had done so much to benefit his household.

They ate their lunches quietly, basking in the great energy that filled the restaurant.

CHAPTER 155

Shooting Star

Dagmar and Ross lay in bed, looking through the high window of their bedroom. After their gig at the Love Bite, they'd had a relaxing day. They'd walked the labyrinth, done some laundry and a bit of housework and meditated in the meditation room. They'd splashed around in the pool in the backyard with Tam and Cammie, who were helping Bella enjoy the water. At the end of their quiet day Ross and Dagmar were feeling mellow.

"It's funny how much has changed in the past few months, isn't it?" said Dagmar, resting her head on Ross's shoulder. "Not in my wildest dreams would I have imagined being here with you, SPIN farming and now working with Phoebe a couple of times a week. And you'll be giving Liam a hand once in awhile. So much has changed and not just for us but for the world. We all seem to be moving in a completely different direction now."

"Yeah, I feel completely different from the way I did then. I don't fake things anymore. It's so freeing to just be myself and see where that leads," Ross said. "Thanks for setting me free, Dagmar, for helping me to be myself."

She kissed him on the cheek. "You're welcome, Ross. Thank you for being here with me, for sharing this grand and wonderful adventure."

"Some pretty amazing alchemy began when we moved into that abandoned house, didn't it?" he reminisced.

"Yeah, it sure did," Dagmar said. "Was it cause and effect, or did things just fall into place the way they were supposed to? Everything just kept on getting better for us, for everyone around us and even for the world. I wonder what that was all about."

"Sometimes things just work. Life is mysterious," Ross said with a smile. "But it did feel like we turned some kind of corner, like healing started going viral or something. It was as though our innate desire to heal and grow came into focus and our consciousness slid from our heads into our hearts where it belongs. Lots of small, personal choices kind of morphed into something big and strong. And good."

"And our hearts were aligned. We all just wanted the best for each other, and something about that goodwill created a really special space. It makes you wonder what animates the cosmos, doesn't it? Whatever it is, it feels like we plugged into it …"

"Maybe we're all learning to listen to anima mundi. Before all this happened, I don't know if I ever really listened or was listened to, for that matter. I felt deeply heard for the first time in my life and wanted to learn how to really hear. Remember how the others used to watch us to see how we were doing when we first moved in?" he reflected. "I could tell that they simply wanted to know that we were doing alright. Nothing more."

"It's touching, isn't it?" Dagmar agreed, "We were both lost and desperate, and wound up with a group of people who just wanted us to be all right. They showed us the power of deep listening: to ourselves, to each other, to anima mundi. And, really, they're all the same thing; just different facets of each other. When we get into the habit of listening closely to others, we start to pay close attention to everything. Maybe when we do that, we can hear the children of the future calling to us for help."

"Yeah, I think so. And I think the more we hear, the more it opens our hearts and makes us want to do everything in our power to help. I think it's a longing deep within all of us, but there's so much noise that we drown it out and fill it with things that don't satisfy," Ross said.

Dagmar leaned over and kissed him on the cheek again. "Thanks again, Ross. There's no one I'd rather be sharing this journey with; it's my true calling, and I'm finally hearing it."

Ross held her close and smiled. "The way seems simple, doesn't it? Just heal everything we can as we go. It's how we fill that deep longing."

Dagmar laughed quietly. "Well put."

As they slowly drifted off to sleep, Ross and Dagmar took one last look out the high window into the clear, sparkling night, just in time to see a shooting star. In that instant, they knew that the world had begun to heal.

CPSIA information can be obtained at www.ICGtesting.com
Printed in the USA
LVOW12*2026130315

430498LV00001B/1/P